THE THEORY AND MANAGEMENT OF SYSTEMS

McGRAW-HILL SERIES IN MANAGEMENT
Keith Davis, *Consulting Editor*

RICHARD A. JOHNSON

FREMONT E. KAST

JAMES E. ROSENZWEIG

THE THEORY AND
MANAGEMENT
OF SYSTEMS

McGRAW-HILL BOOK COMPANY, INC.

New York   San Francisco   Toronto   London

THE THEORY AND MANAGEMENT OF SYSTEMS

32631

TO
BLONDIE, DOLLY, and ZELDA

PREFACE

The achievements of the past become the challenge of the future. We have the wheel of Archimedes, the control of power in different forms, and the knowledge of many sciences and arts. These tools and knowledge have changed the way of life for people. For example, we are producing goods and services at record rates, while providing more leisure time for the workers than ever before. However, the possibility of satisfying the increasing needs of a growing population depends on how effectively the business firm of the future can be operated.

Most business managers are aware of their responsibility to increase operating efficiency, but the task of organizing human and material resources to meet this challenge is not simple—it taxes the resourcefulness of the most imaginative person. The large corporation has become a "sleeping giant" beyond most managers' ability to comprehend or analyze in total. The science of operating the business firm effectively, therefore, would be a significant achievement of this generation.

During the past few years there have been several new approaches to improving management, e.g., organization theory, decision theory, planning theory, and the behavioral theory of the firm. Each of these philosophies has helped to sharpen management; however, there is still a pressing need for an *operative* theory of management. It is our purpose to describe such a philosophy, the *concept of managing by system.*

A system may be defined as an array of components designed to achieve an objective according to plan. There are all kinds and types of systems. For example, there is the steering system in an automobile—the mechanical linkage and the driver who controls the direction the car will go; the heating system in a home—the furnace, heating units, and controls used to maintain the prescribed temperature; the billing system in a department store—the people, office machines, and paper forms required to bill the customer for his purchases; the control system of a missile—the sensory devices and the actuating and directional units which maintain the missile on course; the production system in a factory—the elements to provide materials, energy, and information in the proper ratio to yield a product; and the business system—all the activity involved in producing and distributing goods and services.

These examples illustrate the broad scope and infinite variety of systems. On the one hand, there is a system to accomplish a single task, and on the other, an economic system, a network of countless systems and subsystems. They may be structured or loosely defined; manual or automatic; information or producing systems. *The same principles apply in every instance.*

The theory of systems is not new; much of it has been developed and used in the natural sciences for many years. Further, it is being used to some degree in business. The need exists, however, to relate systems theory to business and industry within a general framework which will facilitate the *study, analysis,* and *operation* of business units.

This book is written for the student and for the manager. The systems concept will enable the student to understand the functional operations of a business as an integrated whole and will provide an analytical approach to help him succeed in his future business activities. Further, the concept will help the manager to analyze his business operation and provide a basis for reorganizing a business in terms of manageable systems.

There are four parts to the book. In the first part, we outline a theoretical framework for systems management. The concepts of planning, organization, control, and communication are described in developing the philosophy of management by system. The systems concept is illustrated in Part Two. Specific examples were selected which are of current interest and, in addition, illustrate the concepts developed in Part One. In Part Three the design and implementation of systems is discussed. This section includes a review of applicable techniques, e.g., mathematical programming, simulation, and network analysis. The final part of the book contains our appraisal of the impact the systems concept will have on the business firm in the future.

Richard A. Johnson
Fremont E. Kast
James E. Rosenzweig

CONTENTS

Observe how system into system runs,
What other planets circle other suns.

Alexander Pope, *An Essay on Man*

All philosophers find
Some favorite system to their mind
In every point to make it fit
Will force all nature to submit.

T. L. Peacock, *Headlong Hall*

Part One
SYSTEMS CONCEPTS AND MANAGEMENT

Introduction

The vast growth in size, complexity, and diversity of operations of the modern business organization has made the managerial functions exceedingly difficult, but more essential to the success of the enterprise. It is our contention that today's large-scale business enterprise should apply the *systems concept* to meet the growing complexities and proliferation of operations. It provides a framework within which the manager can integrate his operations more effectively.

1

In Part One we develop the theoretical framework for the systems concept and set the stage for a more detailed and practical discussion of systems application later in the book. Chapter 1 sets forth a general systems theory and shows how this broad theory has applicability as a framework for scientific investigation and understanding in a wide variety of fields or disciplines. It then traces the transition from a general systems theory to a systems theory for business.

In the next four chapters we discuss the relationship between systems concepts and the primary managerial functions. Chapter 2 covers the *planning* function; Chapter 3 looks at *organization;* Chapter 4 reviews the *control* function; and Chapter 5 discusses *information* and *communication* processes. It will be shown that systems concepts are important in the effective performance of these functions.

The last chapter in this part, Chapter 6, is one of the most vital sections of the book. The ideas on the utilization of a systems approach in the four management functions are drawn together to form an *integrated systems concept for business*. It is in this chapter that we merge the general theory with practical business operations. Over all, Part One provides the intellectual steppingstone to transcend from a broad, general theory of systems to the practical applications of the systems concept in the business firm.

Chapter One

SYSTEMS THEORY
AND MANAGEMENT

The systems concept is primarily a way of thinking about the job of managing. It provides a framework for visualizing internal and external environmental factors as an integrated whole. It allows recognition of the proper place and function of subsystems. The systems within which businessmen must operate are necessarily complex. However, management via systems concepts fosters a way of thinking which, on the one hand, helps to dissolve some of the complexity and, on the other hand, helps the manager recognize the nature of the complex problems and thereby operate within the perceived environment. It is important to recognize the integrated nature of specific systems, including the fact that each system has both inputs and outputs and can be viewed as a self-contained unit. But it is also important to recognize that business systems are a part of larger systems—possibly industry-wide, or including several, maybe many, companies and/or industries, or even society as a whole.

What does the concept of systems offer to students of management and/or to practicing executives? Is it a panacea for business problems which will replace scientific management, human relations, management by objective, operations research, and many other approaches to, or techniques of, management? Perhaps a word of caution is applicable initially. Anyone looking for "cookbook" techniques will be disappointed. In this book we do not evolve "ten easy steps" to success in management. Such approaches, while seemingly applicable and easy to grasp, usually are shortsighted and superficial. More fundamental ideas, such as the systems concept, are more difficult to comprehend, and yet they present an opportunity for a large-scale payoff.

In this book we shall develop the foundation for management by system. Before turning to aspects concerned primarily with business, it will be necessary to set the stage with certain introductory materials relative to systems in general and concerning an evolving body of knowledge called general systems theory. This background material will provide a basis for relating systems theory to business and for the integration of systems concepts and management. Those readers who are not particularly interested in general systems theory might find it desirable to skip directly to the Prologue, the last few pages of this chapter.

The discussion in this chapter is centered around the following topics:

Systems Defined
General Systems Theory
Systems Theory for Business
Systems Concepts and Management
Prologue
    Pervasiveness of Systems Concepts
    Plan of the Book

SYSTEMS DEFINED

A system is "an organized or complex whole; an assemblage or combination of things or parts forming a complex or unitary whole." The term system covers an extremely broad spectrum of concepts. For example, we have mountain systems, river systems, and the solar system as part of our physical surroundings. The body itself is a complex organism including the skeletal system, the circulatory system, and the nervous system. We come into daily contact with such phenomena as transportation systems, communciation systems (telephone, telegraph, etc.), and economic systems.

A science often is described as a systematic body of knowledge; a complete array of essential principles or facts, arranged in a rational dependence or connection; a complex of ideas, principles, laws, forming a coherent whole. Scientists endeavor to develop, organize, and classify material into an interconnected discipline. Sir Isaac Newton set forth what he called the "system of the world." Other examples are "system of politics" and "system of theology." Two relatively well known works which represent attempts to integrate a large amount of material are Darwin's *Origin of the Species* and Keynes's *General Theory of Employment, Interest, and Money.* Darwin, in his theory of evolution, integrated all life into a "system of nature" and indicated how the myriad of living subsystems were inter-related. Keynes, in his general theory of employment, interest, and money, connected many complicated natural and man-made forces which make up an entire economy. Both men had a major impact on man's thinking because they were able to conceptualize interrelationships among complex phenomena and integrate them into a systematic whole. The word system connotes plan, method, order, and arrangement. Hence it is no wonder that scientists and researchers have made the term so pervasive.

The antonym of systematic is chaotic. A chaotic situation might be de-scribed as one where "everything depends on everything else." Since two major goals of science and research in any subject area are explanation and prediction, such a condition cannot be tolerated. Therefore there is con-siderable incentive to develop bodies of knowledge that can be organized into a complex whole, within which subparts or subsystems can be inter-related.

There is an obvious hierarchy of systems that can be created; that is, systems, systems of systems, and systems of systems of systems. For ex-ample, the universe is a system of heavenly bodies which includes many subsystems of stars called galaxies. Within one such galaxy, the Milky Way, there is the solar system, one of many planetary systems. Similarly, an organism is a system of mutually dependent parts each of which might include many subsystems. Human life is comprised of microorgan-isms which form larger systems that are subsystems of the organism as a whole.

While much research has been focused on the analysis of minute seg-ments of knowledge, there has been increasing interest in developing larger frames of reference for synthesizing the results of such research. Thus attention has been focused more and more on over-all systems as frames of reference for analytical work in various areas. It is our contention that a similar process can be useful for managers. Whereas managers often have been focusing attention on particular functions in specialized areas, they may lose sight of the over-all objectives of the business and the role of their particular business in even larger systems. These individuals can do a better job of carrying out their own responsibilities if they are aware of the "big picture." It is the familiar problem of not being able to see the forest for the trees.

This disregard of the total system may be deliberate in the sense that functional or departmental managers are inclined to enhance their own performance at the expense of the total operation. However, it is more likely that such disregard is unintentional, resulting from the inability of decision makers in isolated segments to comprehend the interaction of their decisions with other segments of the business. The focus of systems management is on providing a better picture of the network of subsystems and interrelated parts which go together to form a complex whole.

Before proceeding to a discussion of systems theory for business, it will be beneficial to explore recent attempts to establish a general systems theory covering all disciplines or scientific areas.

GENERAL SYSTEMS THEORY [1]

General systems theory is concerned with developing a systematic, theoretical framework for describing general relationships of the empirical world. A broad spectrum of potential achievements for such a framework is evident. Existing similarities in the theoretical construction of various disciplines can be pointed out. Models can be developed which have applicability to many fields of study. An ultimate but distant goal will be a framework (or system of systems of systems) which could tie all disciplines together in a meaningful relationship.

One of the most important reasons pointing to the need for a general systems theory is the problem of communication between the various disciplines. Although there is similarity between general methods of approach— the scientific method—the results of research efforts are not often communicated across discipline boundaries. Hence conceptualizing and hypothesizing that is done in one area seldom carries over into other areas where it conceivably could point the way toward a significant breakthrough. Specialists do not seem to communicate with one another. For example:

> Hence physicists only talk to physicists, economists to economists—worse still, nuclear physicists talk only to nuclear physicists and econometricians to econometricians. One wonders sometimes if science will not grind to a stop in an assemblage of walled-in hermits, each mumbling to himself words in a private language that only he can understand. [2]

Of course, the conflict of ideas and difficulties of communication are even greater between the various cultures—the scientific, the social sciences, and the humanistic. This conflict has been intensified during the twentieth century. [3]

---

[1] Two articles provide the basis for this section. The name first appeared in an article by Ludwig von Bertalanffy, "General System Theory: A New Approach to Unity of Science," *Human Biology,* December, 1951, pp. 303–361. A more recent discussion, and one more pertinent to the specific task at hand, was that of Kenneth Boulding, "General Systems Theory: The Skeleton of Science," *Management Science,* April, 1956, pp. 197–208.

[2] Boulding, *op. cit.,* p. 198.

[3] C. P. Snow, *The Two Cultures and the Scientific Revolution,* Cambridge University Press, London, 1959.

brain symbolized top-level management, or the executive committee. In this sense an organization was represented as a self-maintaining structure, one which could reproduce. Such an analysis hints at the type of framework which would be useful as a systems theory for business—one which is developed as a system of systems and that can focus attention at the proper points in the organization for rational decision making, both from the standpoint of the individual and the organization.

The scientific-management movement utilized the concept of a man-machine system but concentrated primarily at the shop level. The so-called "efficiency experts" attempted to establish procedures covering the work situation and providing an opportunity for all those involved to bene-fit—employees, managers, and owners. The human relationists, the move-ment stemming from the Hawthorne–Western Electric studies, shifted some of the focus away from the man-machine system per se to interrelationships among individuals in the organization. Recognition of the effect of inter-personal relationships, human behavior, and small groups resulted in a relatively widespread reevaluation of managerial approaches and tech-niques.

The concept of the business enterprise as a social system also has received considerable attention in recent years. The social-system school looks upon management as a system of cultural interrelationships. The con-cept of a social system draws heavily on sociology and involves recognition of such elements as formal and informal organization within a total inte-grated system. Moreover, the organization or enterprise is recognized as subject to external pressure from the cultural environment. In effect, the enterprise system is recognized as a part of a larger environmental system.

Over the years, mathematics has been applied to a variety of business problems, primarily internal. Since World War II, operations-research techniques have been applied to large, complex systems of variables. They have been helpful in shop scheduling, in freight-yard operations, cargo handling, airline scheduling, and other similar problems. Queuing models have been developed for a wide variety of traffic- and service-type situ-ations where it is necessary to program the optimum number of "servers" for the expected "customer" flow. Management-science techniques have undertaken the solution of many complex problems involving a large num-ber of variables. However, by their very nature, these techniques must structure the system for analysis by quantifying system elements. This proc-ess of abstraction often simplifies the problem and takes it out of the real world. Hence the solution of the problem may not be applicable in the actual situation.

Simple models of maximizing behavior no longer suffice in analyzing business organizations. The relatively mechanical models apparent in the "scientific management" era gave way to theories represented by the "human relations" movement. Current emphasis is developing around "decision making" as a primary focus of attention, relating communication systems, organization structure, questions of growth (entropy and/or homeostasis), and questions of uncertainty. This approach recognizes the more complex models of administrative behavior and should lead to more encompassing systems that provide the framework within which to fit the results of specialized investigations of management scientists.

The aim of systems theory for business is to develop an objective, understandable environment for decision making; that is, if the system within which managers make the decisions can be provided as an explicit framework, then such decision making should be easier to handle. But what are the elements of this systems theory which can be used as a framework for integrated decision making? Will it require wholesale change on the part of organization structure and administrative behavior? Or can it be fit into existing situations? In general, the new concepts can be applied to existing situations. Organizations will remain recognizable. Simon makes this point when he says:

> 1. Organizations will still be constructed in three layers; an underlying *system* of physical production and distribution processes, a layer of programmed (and probably largely automated) decision processes for governing the routine day-to-day operation of the physical *system,* and a layer of nonprogrammed decision processes (carried out in a man-machine system) for monitoring the first-level processes, redesigning them, and changing parameter values.
>
> 2. Organizations will still be hierarchical in form. The organization will be divided into major subparts, each of these into parts, and so on, in familiar forms of departmentalization. The exact basis for drawing departmental lines may change somewhat. Product divisions may become even more important than they are today, while the sharp lines of demarcation among purchasing, manufacturing, engineering, and sales are likely to fade.[7]

We agree essentially with this picture of the future. However, we want to emphasize the notion of systems as set forth in several layers. This connotes basic horizontal organization cutting across typical departmental lines. Thus the systems that are likely to be emphasized in the future will develop from projects or programs, and authority will be vested in managers whose influence will cut across traditional departmental lines. This concept will be developed more fully throughout this book.

[7] Herbert A. Simon, *The New Science of Management Decision,* Harper & Brothers, New York, 1960, pp. 49–50. (Italics by authors.)

Just as a general framework for integrating research activity and conceptualizing in various scientific disciplines would be helpful, a systems theory for business would be helpful as a framework for integrating managerial decisions. Organizations of the future will be developed with distinct layers of activity and with physical processes of production and distribution providing the base. Semiautomated and automated decision making will take place at a second level, which is geared to the basic activity of the organization. Decisions of a nonprogrammed nature will be carried on at higher levels in the organization.

However, the focus of attention in the future is likely to turn more and more to patterns of flow throughout the organizations. For example, material flow could be the focal point for decision making, rather than particular activities which take place with regard to the material; that is, the flow of material through the organization would be the primary concern, with secondary concern given to the functionally specialized departmental activities which are established to adjust or transform that material during the flow process. Similarly, flows of other resources such as men and capital could be so considered, thus changing the emphasis from vertical-hierarchical to the material-flow process. Similarly, if organizations could be defined in terms of information-decision systems, a new look in organization structure might be fostered.

SYSTEMS CONCEPTS AND MANAGEMENT

Management is the primary force within organizations which coordinates the activities of the subsystems and relates them to the environment. Management as an institution is relatively new in our society, stemming primarily from the growth in size and complexity of businesses since the industrial revolution. As Drucker says:

> The emergence of management as an essential, a distinct and a leading institution is a pivotal event in social history. Rarely, if ever, has a new basic institution, a new leading group, emerged as fast as has management since the turn of this century. Rarely in human history has a new institution proven indispensable so quickly; and even less often has a new institution arrived with so little opposition, so little disturbance, so little controversy. . . . Management, which is the organ of society specifically charged with making resources productive, that is, with the responsibility for organized economic advance, therefore reflects the basic spirit of the modern age. It is in fact indispensable—and this explains why, once begotten, it grew so fast and with so little opposition.[8]

[8] Peter F. Drucker, *The Practice of Management*, Harper & Brothers, New York, 1954, pp. 3–4.

Managers are needed to convert the disorganized resources of men, machines, and money into a useful and effective enterprise. Essentially, management is the process whereby these unrelated resources are integrated into a total *system for objective accomplishment.* A manager gets things done by working with people and physical resources in order to accomplish the objectives of the system. He coordinates and integrates the activities and work of others rather than perform operations himself.

A general theory of management which has evolved in recent years focuses attention on the fundamental administrative processes which are essential if an organization is to meet its primary goals and objectives.[9] These basic managerial processes are required for any type of organization —business, government, educational, social, and other activities where human and physical resources are combined to meet certain objectives. Furthermore, these processes are necessary regardless of the specialized area of management—production, distribution, finance, and facilitating activities. Although the management process has been described in numerous ways, four basic functions have received general acceptance—planning, organizing, controlling, and communicating. They can be defined in terms of systems concepts as follows:

Planning. The managerial function of planning is one of selecting the organizational objectives and the policies, programs, procedures, and methods for achieving them. The planning function is essentially one of providing a framework for integrated decision making and is vital to every man-machine system.

Organizing. The organizing function helps to coordinate people and resources into a system so that the activities they perform lead to the accomplishment of system goals. This managerial function involves the determination of the activities required to achieve the objectives of the enterprise, the departmentation of these activities, and the assignment of authority and responsibility for their performance. Thus the organizing function provides the interconnection, or intertie, between the various subsystems and the total organizational system.

Control. The managerial function of control is essentially that of assuring that the various organizational subsystems are performing in conformance to the plans. Control is essentially the measurement and correction of activity of the subsystems to assure the accomplishment of the over-all plan.

Communication. The communication function is primarily one of the transfer of information among decision centers in the various sub-

[9] See, for example, Harold F. Smiddy and Lionel Naum, "Evolution of a 'Science of Managing' in America," *Management Science,* October, 1954, pp. 1–31.

systems throughout the organization. The communication function also includes the interchange of information with the environmental forces.

Although these four managerial functions are listed and described separately, they should not be considered as independent activities, nor is any exact time sequence implied. Adequate performance of these functions is dependent upon the performance of the other three. For example, effective communication and control depends to a major extent upon the adequacy of the organizational structure and the planning process. Thus the total management process involves coordinating all four of these activities in order to meet the over-all objectives of the system.

PROLOGUE

Let us return now to our original question, "What does the concept of systems offer to students of management and/or practicing executives?" We have cited examples of systems in our physical environment. We have noted how scientists are striving to develop a framework to integrate knowledge from various disciplines. Also, emphasis on systems is understandable in terms of the adjective systematic, which means planned, ordered, or arranged. Since both scientists and businessmen are interested in predicting the outcome of various decisions, the notion of systems is particularly important. Making decisions in an atmosphere of *no* system whatsoever would be hazardous; such situations could be described as chaotic.

Pervasiveness of Systems Concepts

Many of the most recent developments in the environment of businessmen and managers have involved systems concepts. For example, the trend toward automation involves implementation of these ideas. Automation suggests a self-contained system with inputs, outputs, and a mechanism of control. Yet the concept also recognizes the need to consider the environment within which the automatic system must perform. Thus the automated system is recognized as a subpart of a larger system.

The kinds of automation prevalent today range in a spectrum from sophisticated mechanization to completely automatic, large-scale production processes. Individual machines can be programmed to operate automatically. Large groups of machines also can be programmed to perform a series of operations, with automatic materials-handling devices providing connecting links among components of the system. In such a system, each individual operation could be described as a system and could be related to a larger system covering an entire processing operation. That particular processing operation could also be part of the total enterprise system, which in turn can be visualized as a part of an environmental system.

Completely automated processing systems such as oil refineries are also commonplace today. In such cases the entire process from input of raw material to output of finished products is automated with preprogrammed controls used to adjust the process as necessary, according to information feedback from the operation itself.

The systems concept is also apparent in other aspects of automation. The above examples deal with physical processing; another phase which has been automated is information flow. With the introduction of large-scale, electronic-data-processing equipment, data-processing systems have been developed for many applications. Systems concepts are prevalent, with most applications built around the model of input-processor-output and with feedback control established within the instructions developed to guide the processing of data. Here again, there is an entire spectrum of sophistication leading from simple, straightforward data-reduction problems to elaborate, real-time data-processing systems.

Physical distribution systems have received increasing attention on the part of manufacturers and shippers. The concepts of logistics, or materials management, have been used to emphasize the flow of materials through distribution channels. The term *rhochrematics* has been coined to connote the flow process from raw-material source to final consumer.[10] In essence, these ideas embrace systems concepts because emphasis is placed on the total system of material flow rather than on functions, departments, or institutions which may be involved in the processing.

In recent years increasing attention has been focused upon massive engineering projects. In particular, military and space programs are becoming increasingly complex, thus indicating the need for integrating various elements of the total system. Manufacturing the product itself (a vehicle or other hardware) is quite complex, often involving problems of producibility with requirements of extremely high reliability. This is difficult to ensure for individual components or subsystems. In addition, each subsystem also must be reliable in its interrelationship with all other subsystems. Successful integration of subcomponents, and hence successful performance of a particular product, must also be integrated with other elements of the total system. For example, the functioning of the Nike-Zeus antimissile missile must be coordinated with the early warning system,

---

[10] Rhochrematics comes from two Greek roots, *rhoe,* which means a flow as of a river or a stream, and *chrema,* which stands for products, materials, or things (including information). The abstract ending *-ics* has been added, as for any of the sciences.

ground facilities, and operating personnel. All elements must function as an operating, integrated whole.

These examples could be augmented with many more to indicate the pervasiveness of systems concepts and the need for integrative management. In many cases the significance of systems is recognized explicitly and utilized in the managerial processes. In other cases, however, recognition is not explicit; rather the concept of systems is implicit in managerial activity. The primary purpose of this book is to develop an operating theory of management based on the systems concept. We propose to develop a workable framework within which management can function in order to do a more effective job of operating subsystems and of integrating subsystems into a total enterprise effort. It is important to recognize that, because of the pervasiveness of systems, the systems concept is not necessarily new. As indicated above, it has been used explicitly in some instances, implicitly in others. Our purpose is to make it more meaningful and to show how it can be utilized effectively.

Plan of the Book

In order to help the reader decide which parts of the book might be most appropriate for his attention, we shall outline, in the remaining pages of this chapter, the over-all plan of the book. Some readers may want to cover all the material. Others may want to pick and choose according to their particular interests.

In Part One we relate the systems concept to the primary activities of the managerial process. Readers who are completely familiar with the concepts of planning, organizing, control, and communication may find that this section covers familiar ground. However, in this part we show in detail how each of the primary managerial functions can be related to systems concepts. Moreover, we show how, in each instance, there has been an evolution within each of these activities toward systems concepts. In other words, they are being carried out in terms of systems concepts more and more explicitly.

Another reason for developing the relationship between systems concepts and the primary managerial functions in Part One is to emphasize that the managerial process will be essentially the same in the future, even with complete cognizance of systems concepts. As indicated earlier, management via systems concepts is primarily a way of thinking. It provides a framework within which these basic managerial functions can be carried out more effectively.

After these functions are discussed separately, they will be integrated in terms of a composite systems concept. The material in Chapter 6 represents a summary of Part One and sets forth a definite framework within which the managerial functions can be applied and to which later sections of the book will be referred.

Once the theoretical concepts have been developed and an integrated systems concept set forth, we turn, in Part Two, to examples of application. These examples are designed to show the pervasiveness of systems concepts already in operation. The weapon-system management concept will be explored in some detail. Rhochrematics, the study of material flow from raw-material sources to final consumer, will also be developed. Automation in general and numerical control in particular will be described in terms of systems concepts and physical production. Data-processing systems will be discussed in terms of their relationship to producing systems and to information flow in general. These examples should give the reader a better "feel" for the systems concept as established in Chapter 6.

In Part Three we proceed to show how the systems concept can be implemented in day-to-day activity. The usefulness of management-science techniques will be evaluated. Network analysis in general and PERT/PEP techniques of critical-path scheduling are discussed as methods of integrating large-scale, complex project systems. Special emphasis is placed on system design as a way of maintaining organizational viability with reference to systems concepts. The impact of change resulting from implementing the systems concepts will be discussed with particular reference to people involved in systems. An important aspect of Part Three is the evaluation of the appropriateness of various tools and techniques in implementing the systems concept. However, no ten-step cookbook technique is set forth. This section must be approached with the admonition that management via the systems concept is primarily an attitude or frame of mind.

Part Four contains a look to the future, indicating the role of systems concepts in coming decades. It summarizes to some extent the material throughout the book. Then, using this summary as a springboard, we conjecture about the future as it is related to systems concepts.

Chapter Two
PLANNING AND SYSTEMS CONCEPTS

Although all the managerial functions are interrelated and the manager undoubtedly performs each at one time or another, any given phase of organizational activity must start with planning. Planning is the process by which the system adapts its resources to changing environmental and internal forces. It is a most dynamic function and must be carried out effectively in order to provide a solid foundation for the remaining managerial activities. The purpose of the planning function in the business organization is to provide an integrated decision system which establishes the framework for the activities of the organization. The systems concept of planning considers the enterprise as an integration of numerous decision-making subsystems. It is the primary function of top-management planning to design an integrated system which will enhance organizational performance.

This chapter discusses the role of the planning function, introduces the concept of planning as the vehicle for systems change, and concludes with a discussion of the systems concept in planning. One of the primary purposes is to build the intellectual foundation necessary for the development of an integrated systems concept in Chapter 6. The following topics will be discussed:

The Role of Planning
Definition of the Planning Function

THE ROLE OF PLANNING

The systems concept of planning has evolved as the result of many important changes in both the environment in which the business organization must operate and in the internal operations of the firm. Planning for the future is becoming an increasingly important managerial activity. As the industrial, social, and political environments become more complex, greater emphasis is placed upon planning as a means of minimizing the uncertainty of the future.

The American business enterprise operates in an environment of change. It must be prepared to accept change as the inevitable consequence of operating in a dynamic world. The general political, economic, social, ethical, and moral philosophies in our country have promoted an atmosphere of freedom of change for the business enterprise. In fact, continued success generally has demanded adaptation and innovation. This is in direct contradiction to many societies—both past and contemporary—in which political, religious, cultural, and other institutions placed major impediments in the path of economic progress.

Rapidly advancing technology has also emphasized the need for planning. Companies not abreast of current technology are in trouble over the short run. Moreover, companies that are not cognizant of the technical changes likely to occur over the next five to fifty years will also be in a disadvantageous position.

On the other hand, the business organization faced with a changing environment has often found many obstacles which make planning for optimum adaptation difficult. Even technological advances, which themselves are purveyors of change, can create degrees of inflexibility. For example, automation, while requiring major changes for its establishment, results in some inherent inflexibilities and increased resistance to change. In a typical multiproduct business, for example, automated operations are predicated on expected variations in volume, product mix, quality, and demand. Since automation establishes a relatively inflexible over-all system, it is vitally important that the right decision be made at the offset, thus emphasizing the critical importance of effective long-term business planning.

Other factors, such as the tendency for labor costs to become fixed, have created additional impediments to flexibility. The restrictions of the labor contract, growing fringe benefits, and provisions for guaranteed annual wages have tended to make even so-called "direct labor costs" more fixed and less subject to unilateral management discretion. Without evaluating the rationale of these trends, one of the major implications is to create a stability of conditions—in many ways similar to those created by automation and greater mechanization. Nor is management itself free from practices which restrict change and make planning difficult. Current experience with the impact of automatic computers on integrated systems of information flow indicates reluctance on the part of white-collar workers and management personnel with vested interest to accept the required modifications in organization and status relationships. As business organizations have increased in size and complexity, they have had difficulty in ensuring that the innovations necessary to meet new conditions and evolving objectives will be accepted by each department as guidelines to action. These and many other forces tend to make it more difficult for the business organization to sustain adaptiveness in a dynamic environment.

With a stable environment and small, uncomplicated operations, the planning function can be carried out relatively easily with a short-range viewpoint. With a more dynamic environment and large, complex units operating in the face of many forces restricting flexibility, the planning function becomes critical and must be thought of on the total-systems basis. Since the consequence of any decision has such a broad and drastic impact, management, through its planning function, must try for the optimal course of action. Herein lies the primary contribution of the application of the systems concept to planning. Under this concept of planning, the organization is viewed as an entity, with the primary responsibility one of planning the integrated activities of all the subsystems.

Managers on all levels of the business organization are engaged in all four basic functions of the management process. As the manager moves up the organizational hierarchy, however, he is likely to spend relatively more of his time planning than carrying out other managerial functions. Moreover, at the top level there is also a gradation of the amount of time spent on planning for varying time periods in the future. Top management not only should devote most of its time to planning, but must be cognizant of the necessity for long-range planning. Under the systems concept, it is top management's function to define the desired role of the organization in the future, to relate the organization to its various environmental systems, and to perceive the need which the organization can fulfill. No one else in the company is equipped to define the desired role of the company. The character of the company must be established, and its objectives and goals set forth explicitly as guidelines to decision making throughout the entire organization. Clear-cut statements of expectations, along with both external and internal premises for planning, help focus the effort of all managerial levels toward common objectives. The role of planning is primarily to provide the organizational stimulus for effective decision making throughout the enterprise.

In brief, the systems concept of planning requires consideration of the enterprise as an integration of numerous decision-making subsystems. The primary function of top-management planning is one of systems design, which involves (1) the establishment of goals, objectives, policies, procedures, and organizational relationships on a systematic basis for guidance of decision making and planning at various organizational levels, and (2) the provision for the flow of information to and from these planning centers. With these ideas in mind, it is desirable to define more explicitly the planning function, briefly set forth a structure of plans, and then examine in more detail the systems concept in business planning.

DEFINITION OF THE PLANNING FUNCTION

Planning has been defined as "intelligent cooperation with the inevitable." This definition, although short, does emphasize the futurity of planning. For our purposes, however, the following definition is preferable:

> Business planning is an integrative activity which seeks to maximize the total effectiveness of a company as a system in accordance with the objectives of the enterprise.[1]

This defines the planning process in terms of its system relationship; but just what is a plan? Here a simple definition is best. *A plan is a predetermined course of action.* Essentially, a plan has three characteristics. First, it must involve the future. Second, it must involve action. Third, there is an element of personal or organizational identification or causation; that is, the future course of action will be taken by the planner or someone designated by or for him within the organization. Futurity, action, and personal or organizational causation are necessary elements in every plan.[2]

Decision making and planning are closely related. A decision is basically a resolution of alternative choices. A decision is not a plan in that it need not involve either action or the future. Decisions, of course, are necessary at every stage in the planning process and are therefore inextricably linked to planning.

[1] F. E. Kast and Jim Rosenzweig, "Planning: Framework for an Integrated Decision System," *Washington Business Review,* April, 1960, p. 39.

[2] Preston P. Le Breton and Dale A. Henning, *Planning Theory,* Prentice-Hall, Inc., Englewood Cliffs, N.J., 1961, p. 7.

PLANNING AS A VEHICLE FOR SYSTEMS CHANGE

In a dynamic society, it can be concluded that the major way in which the business organization, as a subsystem of the total economic system, adapts to changing requirements is through planning. *Under the systems concept the planning process can be considered as the vehicle for accomplishment of system change.* Without planning the system could not change and could not adapt to different environmental forces. This distinguishes the social organization from other open systems. In other types of open systems change in the system occurs when environmental forces demand that a new equilibrium be established. In the organization these changes are dependent upon the *rationality* of the human decision processes. This aspect of rationality of decision making differentiates the human social systems such as the business organization from the inanimate, physical open systems, where the equilibrium adjustments can be described as automatic adjustment to change. For the social system the only vehicle for change, innovation, and adaptability is the human decision-making and planning process.

PLANNING: THE FRAMEWORK FOR AN INTEGRATED DECISION SYSTEM

Business planning is not an entity in itself—its primary purpose is to provide the guidelines necessary for the vital decision-making processes throughout the organization. Planning, therefore, should be geared to obtaining, translating, understanding, and communicating information that will help to improve the rationality of current decisions which are based upon future expectations. Expectations are developed through the process of forecasting and predicting the future. A great deal of effort has been devoted to refining predictive techniques to enable companies to forecast their ideological, political, legislative, and economic environment. Companies are becoming much more interested in broad economic data such as national income and product accounts and are relating industry, company, and product data to the over-all economic outlook.

However, forecasting is *not* planning. While forecasting provides a basis for understanding and formulating expectations, management must go beyond this orientation stage and must develop programs of action designed to optimize the company's over-all performance. Since these programs themselves may alter the future—not only of the company but of the total environment—forecasts, no matter how rigorously developed, are seldom completely valid. If a company programs its future to fit the forecast conditions, its behavior will be characterized as adaptive and its future success is a function of the predicted environment. On the other hand, if a company plans for aggressive action in pursuit of predetermined goals and objectives, its behavior can be characterized as innovative, that is, shaping the environment.

Business planning is an *integrative* activity which should seek to maximize the total effectiveness of the system. Frequently, in a complex organization, a great deal of planning is carried on by specialized functional or staff groups without a system for the coordination of these efforts. Unless there is a clear-cut understanding of what over-all objectives and goals are paramount, some of the subgroup activities may be maximized at the expense of total organizational effectiveness. All elements in a company must be aware of the expectations and directions set forth by top management and must understand the various premises upon which a course of action is founded. The means of achieving such understanding requires reviewing the planning function on an integrated systems approach. A logical approach to planning would include the following steps:

1. Appraising the future political, economic, and competitive environment

2. Visualizing the desired role of the company in this environment

3. Perceiving needs and requirements of customers

4. Determining changes in the needs and requirements of other interested groups—stockholders, employees, suppliers, and others

5. Developing broad goals, objectives, and plans which will direct the efforts of the total organization

6. Translating this broad planning into functional efforts on a more detailed basis—research, design and development, production, distribution and service

7. Developing more detailed planning and control of resource utilization within each of these functional areas—always related to the over-all planning effort

This approach, developed and understood throughout the organization, will provide an integrated decision system. Such a framework or master plan will be used to focus the efforts of the entire organization toward a common set of goals. Furthermore, if the underlying expectations and planning premises are set forth explicitly, all departments can carry out their planning functions within the same guidelines. Major decisions can be evaluated in light of the master plan to determine whether a particular course of action would carry the company toward or away from its desired future position. In this way the total systems concept tends to facilitate the integration of all segments of the organization.

HIERARCHY OF PLANNING

Planning provides the framework for an integrated decision system. In this approach to planning it is necessary to recognize the concept of a hierarchy of plans. Under this hierarchy, broad plans are established for the enterprise primarily in the form of goals and objectives at a high organizational level. The top-management planning function, under systems concepts, is really one of systems design and should give consideration to the over-all goals of the enterprise and to the integration of the operation of subsystems toward those goals. These broad goals and objectives are then translated into more detailed and specific plans, which are further translated throughout the organization to even more detailed and more specific plans. In effect, the planning process is one of spreading out the planning functions throughout the entire organizational system.

A well-documented example of this hierarchical relationship of plans is illustrated by the Allied invasion of Europe during World War II. First the broad objective of the invasion was established, and this led to a whole series of secondary goals and objectives, for example, requirements for weather conditions, goals as to the number and types of military men needed, and determination of materials requirements. These were translated into more detailed plans which were further translated throughout the military hierarchy down to the most detailed planning which took place at the lowest operating level.[3] This entire planning process was made more complicated by the requirements for secrecy of the entire operation.

We can see the hierarchical relationship in planning for another major project of World War II, the production of the atomic bomb. Planning of this program required an integration of immense technical, physical, and human resources over a vast area and under the pressures of military urgency and secrecy. The program could be accomplished only by the establishment of broad goals and objectives at the top, and then translating these into more detailed plans at lower levels.

Of prime importance in the establishment of a hierarchy of plans is the setting forth and acceptance of organizational objectives. Clear-cut, well-defined organizational goals and objectives help provide the basis for systematic planning at lower operating levels. Some of the benefits of goals as guides for further planning are that they provide:

1. The basis for unified and integrated planning
2. The premises within which more specific planning should take place
3. The primary basis for the performance of the control function

[3] Dwight D. Eisenhower, *Crusade in Europe*, Doubleday & Company, Inc., New York, 1948.

4. A primary basis for human motivation—a sense of accomplishment in terms of known goals and objectives

5. A basis for well-defined delegation and decentralization of specific planning to lower operating levels

6. A basis for coordinating the activities between various, often diverse, functional operating units within the organization

This concept of the establishment of goals as a basis for the planning hierarchy is of crucial importance. Yet it is certainly one of the most difficult functions of top management. As our industrial enterprises become larger and more complex, the determination of the goals in the organization becomes more difficult. For example, should the organization have as its primary function that of profit maximization or of consumer service? Or is the major objective one of long-run perpetuation of the enterprise, or just perpetuation of the management, or of the investment of the stockholder? Or is it to provide long-term employment for the employees? Every business organization has a multiplicity of objectives and requirements. And these objectives are generally in a dynamic state; the requirements made on the organization by both internal participants and external forces will cause most organizations to vary their short-run goals and objectives to meet these pressures. Thus we should recognize that the goals and objectives of an organization are dynamic and are subject to degrees of evolution and change.

The abstract nature of the highest-level goals and their value-oriented determination makes it vitally necessary for the managerial planning function to translate these broad goals into more tangible operating objectives. To say that the goal of an organization is to satisfy customers and to make a profit may sound good as public relations or as a company motto, but it does not serve effectively as a guideline to organizational decision making at operating levels. These broad, general goals must be translated into specific operating goals if there is a systematic planning hierarchy. This translation and the establishment of meaningful objectives for each function, each organizational unit, each functional specialty, and each job is one of the most complex problems in planning.

Some guidelines for the establishment of systematic planning can be suggested by looking at the various types of plans and how they fit into this broad hierarchy.

TYPES OF PLANS

Planning is one of the key managerial functions and occurs at many places and levels throughout the organization. Because of the wide latitude of planning, there often are conflicting ideas regarding plans. To help clarify some of the confusion relating to the planning processes it is helpful to look at the many types of plans which exist in a business organization. Plans may be divided into three broad groups:

1. Goals and objectives
2. Standing plans
3. Single-use plans [4]

Within each of these broad groupings there are a wide variety of more detailed plans, ranging from the broadest type of long-range goals and objectives covering the operation of the entire organization to the detailed planning for the activities of every individual within the firm. In the systems concept of planning it is necessary to recognize the importance of the interrelationships of all the planning activities toward accomplishing the objectives and goals of the organization.

Goals and Objectives

The importance of establishing goals and objectives to provide a hierarchy of planning was discussed in the previous section. Basically, goals are plans which are expressed as results to be achieved. Used in this broad sense, goals include such things as objectives, purposes, missions, deadlines, standards, targets, and quotas. Goals represent not only the end point of planning, but the end toward which the other management functions of organizing, communicating, and controlling are aimed. Typically, in a business organized along the functional lines of selling, production, and finance, separate goals are established for the performance of each of these functions. These then are further translated into more specific objectives for lower organizational levels.

Standing Plans

Standing plans are those types of plans such as policies, standard methods, and standard operating procedures that are designed to cover a variety of repetitive situations which the organization frequently faces. Standing plans are of importance to any established organization. It can be argued that even informal organizational relationships such as social groups and bowling teams have established plans. For the more formal organization the standing plans are a primary cohesive force connecting the various facets of the organization. Standard plans become the habit pattern of the organization similar to the habit pattern of individuals.

Policies are the broadest of the standing plans and are general guides to organizational behavior. Policies generally set broad premises and

[4] William H. Newman, *Administrative Action,* Prentice-Hall, Inc., Englewood Cliffs, N.J., 1950, p. 18.

limitations within which further planning activities take place. A policy is a general plan of action that guides the members of the organization in the conduct of its operation. Every large organization has a wide variety of policies covering its most important functions. Frequently these policies are formalized and written in organization or policy manuals. Even in those situations where policies are not written, the organization must still have policies which are understood clearly and known even though informally established. Quite often these informal policies are established because of the habitual pattern of decisions which arises when the organization is confronted with a particular problem.

Methods and procedures, like policies, are also standing plans. Usually they are less general than policies and establish more definite procedures and methods for the performance of certain activities. The basic difference between a policy and standard methods and procedures is a matter of degree, both providing guidance as to how a particular decision should be made.

There are many organizational advantages to the use of standing plans. Through the use of standing plans and the concept of "management by exceptions" the higher executive's influence is extended to all organizational levels. Once a decision has been reached, the standing plan that is established serves as a guideline throughout the organization for decision making. A further advantage of the standing plan is that it creates a uniformity of operations throughout the organization. Once established, understood, and accepted, it provides similarity of action in meeting certain situations. This is of vital importance to large-scale, complex organizations such as businesses or government. With policies, a client of the business organization is assured of a uniform decision regardless of the location of the facilities or level in the organization.

The use of standing plans is typical of the bureaucratic organization regardless of whether it is government, business, labor, or any other type of large-scale, complex organization. Herein, perhaps, lies one of the problems. Standing plans are useful when they provide for a uniformity of decisions and when they meet the requirement of the situation. They are not useful when the situation changes so abruptly that the plan does not fit the new situation. Attempting to force new and dynamic situations under a particular standing plan often can lead to irrational and dysfunctional organizational consequences.

Nevertheless, the wise use of the standing plan is essential to systematic planning. Standing plans provide the basic means for interweaving the organizational processes throughout the entire system. Without standing plans a systems concept to planning would not be feasible.

Single-use Plans

Essentially, single-use plans set forth a course of action to fit a *specific* situation and are obsolete when a goal is reached. This is in contrast to standing plans which are designed to have a continuing usefulness. Just as there is a hierarchy of standing plans, there is also a hierarchy of single-use plans ranging from (1) major programs, (2) projects, (3) special programs, to (4) detailed plans.

There are innumerable examples of planning complex programs, such as the programming of design, development, and production of a new space system. Rapidly advancing technology demands long-range planning of large-scale programs. Success of a major program depends upon the establishment of more detailed single-use plans such as special programs and detailed plans. These single-use plans should all be integrated into an overall planning hierarchy. In Chapter 7 the planning function for a complex weapon system, the Polaris Fleet Ballistic Missile Weapon System, is discussed in more detail.

In addition to understanding and utilizing the proper type of plan, it is necessary for management to integrate the various plans. They should be set forth in a broad systems relationship and should be consistent with each other. It is useful to emphasize again the hierarchical relationships between plans in which the more specific are subordinated to the limits of broader, more encompassing plans. Table 1 presents a conceptual diagram relating the types of plans in a hierarchical relationship.

SYSTEMS CONCEPTS IN PLANNING

We suggested that growing complexities of administration and technological advances have forced the adoption of systems concepts in business planning. This point should be reemphasized. The systems concept in business planning should start with the awareness of the need to think of several levels and the integration of these into a hierarchy. One useful way is to consider the three major systems which are paramount for any business organization:

1. The environmental system—sets forth the broad social, cultural, political, and economic parameters in which the business must operate.

2. The competitive system—describes the industrial structure, competitive relationships, and producer-customer relationships for the particular industry in which the company competes.

3. The internal organizational system—indicates the organizational structure, objectives and policies, and functional relationships which make the business a unique system.

TABLE I   Types of Administrative Plans

Scope	Goals	Courses of action	
		Single-use plans	Standing plans
Broad plans	Objectives (missions)	General programs	Policies
↑	Budgets and deadlines	Projects	Organization structure
↓ Detailed plans	Performance standards for expense, quality, quantity, etc.	Personnel assignments Detailed schedules, specifications, methods, etc.	Standard procedures Standard methods

Source: William H. Newman, *Administrative Action,* Prentice-Hall, Inc., Englewood Cliffs, N.J.. 1950, p. 54.

Effective business planning should receive informational inputs from each of these three systems and translate them into plans of action. Increasingly, business firms are becoming aware of the growing importance of relating their plans to environmental systems. The majority of broad, long-range plans made by companies are prefaced by forecasts of such environmental factors as population, gross national product, national income and expenditures, governmental receipts and expenditures, and even international considerations. Growth of interest in appraising and forecasting the environmental system is seen by the rise in the number of economists and other social scientists employed by business organizations to provide special skills in these areas.[5]

Planning must also give consideration to the competitive system. This idea is not new; the free-enterprise system has been referred to as an example of the competitive model. Planning information from competitors frequently is not obtainable. Competitive information on volume of sales, profit levels, rate of return, share of market and pricing, and so forth, may be available, but companies frequently do not attempt to obtain this information in an orderly fashion. As Daniel says:

> Competitive information, like environmental data, is an infrequently formalized part of a company's total information system. And so there seldom is concerted effort to collect this kind of material, to process it, and to report it to management regularly.[6]

[5] Clark S. Teitsworth, "Growing Role of the Company Economist," *Harvard Business Review,* January–February, 1959, p. 97.

[6] D. Ronald Daniel, "Management Information Crisis," *Harvard Business Review,* September–October, 1961, p. 116.

The third level of systems, the internal organization, must be given major consideration in the planning process. The functioning organization has certain strengths, skills, and specializations that are important inputs for planning. Furthermore, the organization is the source of internal information which must be communicated to decision centers. This system will be discussed in detail in the next chapters on organization, control, and communication. In general, managerial planning should give recognition to the integration of information from all three systems and should recognize the interactions among them.

Within the business system there are other important aspects of the systems concept in planning. With the advent of further mechanization and automation it is no longer possible to think of planning on a functional basis—sales, finance, manufacturing, and so forth. Rather, it is necessary to integrate planning for all functional activities into a unified system. Automation, for example, does not facilitate variations in product quantity and design, the meeting of individual customer requirements, or a number of other variables. With automation these factors become inflexible and must be standardized for an extended period. Therefore, in planning for the automated operation, the total functional efforts in marketing, finance, and manufacturing must be integrated on a systematic basis.

One idea for the integration of decision making in various functional areas is the concept of flows of information, money, orders, materials, personnel, and capital equipment in the company. Planning does not concentrate on functional performance, but on these flows. This is the concept of industrial dynamics as set forth by Forrester:

> It treats the interaction between the flows of information, money, orders, materials, personnel, and capital equipment in a company, an industry, or a national economy.
>
> Industrial dynamics provides a single framework for integrating the functional areas of management—marketing, production, accounting, research and development, and capital investment.[7]

Under this concept of planning, the organization is not a collection of separate functional activities but a *system* in which the *flows* of information, materials, manpower, capital equipment, and money are the basic forces which determine the company's growth and prosperity. It stresses the dynamic nature of these flows and their constant interaction. Many of the modern techniques of communication and decision making have utilized the concepts of flows. These will be discussed in a later chapter.

[7] Jay W. Forrester, *Industrial Dynamics,* MIT Press, Cambridge, Mass., and John Wiley & Sons, Inc., New York, 1961, p. 13.

Who Does the Planning?

In the large-scale business organization, one of the problems is providing for application of systems concepts to planning. Theoretically, business planning is one of the major functions of line executives. However, with the growing complexities and the need for investigation, analysis, and evaluation, planning has frequently come to be a specialized function. In many cases a specialized staff is set up to aid in the planning function. All too frequently this staff assumes that its role is planning rather than facilitating the planning activities of line management. Left to its own discretion, this staff proceeds to set up objectives, goals, and plans according to its own conception and premises, often developing elaborate research reports to substantiate its position.

The "planning gap" is a divergence in the expectations, premises, objective, and basic concept which exist between various units within an organization and which prevent the establishment of an effective, well-defined framework for integrated decision making.[8]

In a large-scale organization with many-leveled departmentation, diverse subobjectives, and organizational and human limits on rationality, it is improbable that this planning gap can be completely eliminated. To do so would be to assume full knowledge, absolute predictability, perfect communication, complete rationality, and full agreement throughout the organization. However, the use of systems concepts in planning provides a basis for evaluating plans against broader policies, goals, and objectives.

Example of Planning

An example of how the systems concept of planning might be adapted to an important area of management planning and decision making is illustrated by diversification planning. In a dynamic economy, product-line determination is one of the major planning areas, because the successful company must adapt continually to changing product-mission requirements. Many examples of this need are seen in a variety of industries, such as the product planning of the automobile companies in bringing out their various product lines, or the product-line planning of an aircraft company that is determining whether or not to move into the fields of propulsion and electronics. A framework for integrated decision making in diversification planning might be set forth as follows:

1. Appraising environmental system to determine those economic, social, and political forces that will influence decision.

---

[8] For a more complete discussion of the problems involved in the planning gap, see F. E. Kast and Jim Rosenzweig, "Minimizing the Planning Gap," *Advanced Management,* October, 1960, pp. 20–23.

2. Evaluating competitive system to appraise competitors, industrial structure, and potential customers.

3. Clearly defining and stating broad company objectives to provide guidelines for further appraisals.

4. Continually reappraising whether the company can meet these long-term objectives with its present product line and distribution channels, or whether it will need to develop a program of diversification.

5. Coordinating the diversification program with company objectives. A clear understanding of company objectives will help determine the types of programs which the company should consider. This will provide a narrowing process and will eliminate from consideration a number of marginal possibilities.

6. Continually appraising the tangible and intangible company assets and limitations for diversification. Aside from guiding objectives, the company will have certain characteristics, such as managerial skills, technological know-how, distribution channels, and facilities, which will be prime determinants of a diversification program.

7. Setting forth specific criteria for measurement of new-product ideas as related to the first six steps. Here the primary purpose is to determine the characteristics of the type of products which would meet requirements of the first six steps.

8. Establishing an environment favorable to diversification. A program of diversification is doomed to failure unless management is convinced that there is a need for this diversification and that it meets company objectives. Furthermore, top management must provide the initiative in establishing a climate in which the organization will come up with useful ideas and will channel them in for a check against established criteria.

9. Providing an established and well-recognized procedure for the evaluation of suggestions for product diversification in terms of the criteria of measurement. This will usually take the form of specific organizational adjustment, such as the creation of a product-diversification committee or department. If left to the chance that the regular line organization will perform this function, it is likely that their other duties and the constant demands for immediate results will push the longer-range consideration of product development into the background; the question will see the light of day only when the situation becomes critical.

Techniques for Application of Systems Concepts to Planning

Within the past two decades several major developments have occurred which forecast the transformation of the managerial processes of planning and decision making. These innovations have been made possible through the development of computers, mathematical techniques, and systems concepts.

To understand the significance of this movement better, we might refer to a table by Herbert Simon which sets forth the traditional and modern decision-making methods. He breaks down all executive decisions and planning into two broad types—*programmed decisions* and *nonprogrammed decisions*—and defines them as follows:

> Decisions are programmed to the extent that they are repetitive and routine, to the extent that a definite procedure has been worked out for handling them so they won't have to be treated *de novo* each time they occur. . . .
>
> Decisions are nonprogrammed to the extent that they are novel, unstructured, and consequential. There is no cut-and-dried method for handling the problem because it hasn't arisen before, or because its precise nature and structure are elusive or complex, or because it is so important that it deserves a custom-tailored treatment.[9]

The traditional techniques for decision making for programmed decisions include organizational habits, clerical routines, and the organizational structure itself. As we have seen in our previous discussion, organizational habit and clerical routine are most frequently translated into the standing plans. Policies and procedures provide the major vehicles for dealing with programmed decisions in the traditional sense. These habitual patterns of organizational behavior usually evolved through organizational adaptations to the best decision under the given circumstances. The trial-and-error aspect of this kind of programming is obvious.

For nonprogrammed decisions, the traditional means was to rely upon the development of executive judgment cultivated by selection, education, and training. There are obviously many psychological and sociological processes involved in the complex problem of nonprogrammed decision making. This is the area of uncertainty where it has been difficult for successful executives even to explain exactly how they arrive at "decisions." (An even greater difficulty often is determining whether or not the right decision has been made.)

Newer techniques for both programmed and nonprogrammed decision making suggest major changes in these traditional methods of planning and decision making. The development of computers, mathematical techniques, operations research, and simulation will have important bearing upon the planning process. These areas will be covered in Chapter 11, Management Science.

[9] Herbert A. Simon, *The New Science of Management Decision,* Harper & Brothers, New York, 1960, pp. 5–6.

TABLE 2   Traditional and Modern Techniques of Decision Making

| Types of decisions | Decision-making techniques | |
	Traditional	Modern
Programmed: Routine, repetitive decisions Organization develops specific processes for handling them.	1. Habit 2. Clerical routine: Standard operating procedures 3. Organization structure: Common expectations A system of subgoals Well-defined informational channels	1. Operations Research: Mathematical analysis Models Computer simulation 2. Electronic data processing
Nonprogrammed: One-shot, ill-structured, novel policy decisions Handled by general problem-solving processes.	1. Judgment, intuition, and creativity 2. Rules of thumb 3. Selection and training of executives	Heuristic problem-solving techniques applied to: (a) Training human decision makers (b) Constructing heuristic computer programs

Source: Herbert A. Simon, *The New Science of Management Decision,* Harper & Brothers, New York, p. 8.

SUMMARY

One of the primary purposes of an integrated planning concept is to provide a hierarchy of goals and objectives based upon predetermined premises about the external environment and internal organizational resources. This approach ensures that the planning decisions made in one functional area are related to those in other areas. As the operational departments in our modern organizations become more specialized and the changing environment requires more complex planning, the need for this integrative concept becomes even more apparent.

With application of systems concepts to planning based upon a hierarchy of goals and objectives, alternative courses of action can be evaluated. Without integrative planning it is difficult to ensure that the proposed courses of action will aid the organization in moving toward its established goal. With an integrated decision system, proposals can be evaluated within the framework of objectives and plans. If the proposal is sound but does not contribute to the achievement of the established objectives, two alternatives are open to management. Either the proposal must be discarded or modified, or the existing objectives and plans must be evaluated and adjusted to meet the changing environment. With this approach, the organization's planning activity remains flexible and hence can cope with a dynamic environment.

Effective business planning must receive information from three systems—environmental, competitive, and internal—and must translate these inputs into plans of action. It is no longer possible to plan on a purely functional basis; the organization is a system in which the flows of information, materials, manpower, capital equipment, and money are the basic forces which determine the company's future.

With the development of the newer techniques of decision making—operations research, electronic data processing, and simulation—the ability of management to view their organization as an integrated decision system has been enhanced. Although these techniques are relatively new, they have major applicability for the future.

Chapter Three
ORGANIZATION AND SYSTEMS CONCEPTS

General systems theory implies an interconnected complex of functionally related components or parts. As indicated in Chapter 1, many types of purely mechanistic systems are of the structured, closed-sequence variety. However, the business organization and other institutions of human interrelationship are unstructured, open-sequence systems. The business organization is a social, or man-made, system. It is only through the process of *organization* that the vast complex of men, materials, machines, and other resources are combined into an efficient, effective, and viable business enterprise. The same thing is true of other man-made systems or organizations. The primary cohesiveness is applied by man himself to systematize his social organizations. Thus the organizing function is vital to the systems concept.

In recent years the study of organization theory has drawn heavily upon general systems concepts and has also contributed to a better understanding of systems theory. It is the purpose of this chapter to look at some of the more important ideas in organization theory, to relate these to systems concepts, to show how we have been forced to utilize systems concepts because of the growing complexities in organizational relationships, and to speculate on the evolution of modern business organizations under the influence of systems concepts. The following topics will be discussed:

37

WHAT IS AN ORGANIZATION?

Since the words organization and system have similar connotations, it is important that we understand more clearly what is meant by the term *organization*. People usually have a general feel for it; for example, frequently someone who is apparently moving in all directions, with little purpose or coordination, is described as "unorganized." In another frame of reference the term organized is used in a derogatory sense to indicate the use of pressure or power, the highly organized political machine, for example. Just what is the difference between being organized and unorganized? What makes an organization out of a group of human beings? Pfiffner and Sherwood define organization as follows:

> Organization is the pattern of ways in which large numbers of people, too many to have intimate face-to-face contact with all others, and engaged in a complexity of tasks, relate themselves to each other in the conscious, systematic establishment and accomplishment of mutually agreed purposes.[1]

This definition emphasizes the systematic interrelationship between people working together to accomplish certain purposes. The social psychologist E. Wight Bakke emphasizes even more strongly the importance of thinking of human organizations in their social context, with the following definition:

> A social organization is a continuing system of differentiated and coordinated human activities utilizing, transforming, and welding together a specific set of human, material, capital, ideational and natural resources into a unique, problem-solving whole whose function is to satisfy particular human needs in interaction with other systems of human activities and resources in its particular environment.[2]

[1] John M. Pfiffner and Frank P. Sherwood, *Administrative Organization*, Prentice-Hall, Inc., Englewood Cliffs, N.J., 1960, p. 30.
[2] E. Wight Bakke, in Mason Haire (ed.), *Modern Organization Theory*, John Wiley & Sons, Inc., New York, 1959, p. 50.

The similarity between this definition of the social, or human, organization and the definition of the unstructured, open system is quite evident. Organizational behavior in contrast to individual behavior is highly structured, more predictable, and stable. It is only by focusing individual behavior on the accomplishment of over-all goals that the organization is able to accomplish its objectives.

As there is a biological analogy for the systems concept, so there is a similar analogy between organization and biology. In many ways the individual organization in our society can be differentiated as a sociological unit comparable to the existence of individual organisms in biology. March and Simon have drawn this comparison as follows:

> Organizations are assemblages of interacting human beings and they are the largest assemblages in our society that have anything resembling a central coordinative system. Let us grant that these coordinative systems are not developed nearly to the extent of the central nervous system in higher biological organisms—that organizations are more earthworm than ape. Nevertheless, the high specificity of structure and coordination within organizations—as contrasted with the diffuse and variable relations *among* organizations and among unorganized individuals—marks off the individual organization as a sociological unit comparable in significance to the individual organism in biology.[3]

Pervasiveness of Organization

Human organizations take a wide variety of forms, from the strict military organization to the business organization, to the political organization, all the way to the more voluntary associations such as PTAs, Little League teams, and other forms of social activity. One of the characteristics of modern life is the extraordinary increase in size and complexity of human organizations. As man has evolved his more complex cultural, technological, and social institutions, so has he increased his organizational relationships. By way of contrast, look at the distinct differences between the informal, ill-structured, voluntary, and highly spontaneous sand-lot baseball of a generation ago and the highly organized, structured, and predictable relationships in Little League baseball today.

In Chapter 1, we discussed the hierarchy of systems; people similarly have a hierarchy of organizational relationships, often overlapping in activity. Take, for example, the relatively simple kinds of organizational relationships which exist in a familiar environment—university or college life. First, there is the organization or system represented by the total university. Within the university there are individual colleges or departments.

[3] James G. March and Herbert A. Simon, *Organization,* John Wiley & Sons, Inc., New York, 1958, p. 4.

Then there is another level of organization centered around the class and the subject matter being taught. In addition to these more formal aspects of college life, there are other organizations, such as fraternities, sororities, or other social groups. Furthermore, activities and service units are super-imposed upon these systems. In many universities intercollegiate athletics, particularly football, demand a major allocation of human and physical resources as separate organizations. Finally, there is a continuity of organizational relationships within the university system by means of alumni associations and other interest groups. Taken together, the university or college represents a complex system of subunits having a wide variety of goals, fulfilling a myriad of functions, and requiring some systematic direction in order to optimize the total university goals. This same hierarchical relationship would be true for most organizational systems—they are not isolated entities in themselves, but are generally a part of larger, more complex systems.

Interdisciplinary Nature of Organization Theory

Over the past several decades interest in the study of organizations and organizational behavior has become a focal point for interdisciplinary research. Increasingly, emphasis has been placed on the study of organization as a scientific field. Because this field is relatively new, there is no single well-defined community of scholars who are leaders in the field of organization theory. Scholars and researchers working in such diverse fields as biology, mathematics, animal psychology, logic, and philosophy have made indirect contributions to organizational theory. Other fields that have contributed more directly are sociology, anthropology, social psychology, psychology, political science, history, as well as fields related to business administration, such as general administrative theory, human relations, operations research and management science, and industrial sociology.[4]

[4] In an interesting book relating social-science research to business, Haire points out the various fields that are cooperating in developing or showing an interest in organization theory as follows: "In many ways, the interest in organization theory is a particularly apt example of the interdisciplinary focus of many of the social sciences. It broadens part of the economist's traditional theory of the firm. For the student of business, narrowly considered, there are customary problems of control and administration. The sociologist turns to status, roles, and the informal structure, as well as to the microcosmos itself. Political scientists join several other groups in the interest in power and authority in hierarchial structure, and in the institutional forms of governing structures. Social psychologists apply their concepts about group structures in communication nets." Mason Haire, "Psychology and the Study of Business: Joint Behavioral Sciences," in *Social Science Research on Business: Product and Potential,* Columbia University Press, New York, 1959, pp. 71–72.

EVOLUTION OF HUMAN SOCIAL ORGANIZATIONS

The cultural anthropologist often takes as his initial frame of reference the characteristics of family relationships within different cultures. Certainly the family represents man's earliest social organization. In every society the family is a basis for a cooperative system for the accomplishment of certain objectives. In all known societies, men are trained to perform certain skills and women others. The division of labor is so adjusted that the combination forms a largely self-sufficient unit for production and consumption. In the more primitive societies, the man was typically a provider and the woman a preparer of raw materials; together they were able to satisfy basic needs for food, shelter, and comfort. In this structured system, the children and other members of the family also had a definite relationship.[5]

From this earliest form of social organization, the family, evolved the tribe, village, larger political states, nations, and various other types of social integration. Each of these separate sociocultural systems has its own modes, behavioral norms, hierarchical relationships, and generally some differentiation or specialization of skills and labor.

Moving to more current consideration of social organizations, we find that a major distinction is made between the informal, small, face-to-face group and the more complex social institution, the large-scale business or political, labor, or other organization. Informal social groups have a dominant role in any culture. Moreover, they have an important bearing on the study of large business systems. The importance of these small, informal groups within the larger organizational system was indicated in the famous Hawthorne–Western Electric studies. These studies suggested that worker output and performance were as strongly influenced by the norms, standards, and rewards of the informal work groups as they were of the more highly structured formal organization. The large, complex organization is built upon the foundation of a number of more informal interrelated group activities. Here again, the over-all system—the business organization—is a composite resulting from the interaction of a number of subsystems.

Growth of Large, Complex Organizations

Through nearly all man's history, his social institutions were primarily on an informal face-to-face basis. Up through medieval times, the feudal

[5] For a discussion of the evolution of the family as a social institution, see Ralph Linton, "The Natural History of the Family," in Ruth Nanda Anshen (ed.), *The Family: Its Function and Destiny*, Harper & Brothers, New York, 1947, revised 1959, pp. 18–38.

system provided the primary large-scale social system to which the individual belonged. Within the past several centuries, the growing importance of large groups or organizations has been one of the most pervasive phenomena. The industrial revolution, with its demand for concentration of resources and greater scale, fostered large economic organizations. Modern governments are typically massive systems organized under the bureaucratic form. Man's social organizations have evolved toward larger-scale, complex, more diversified systems. This evolution is not restricted to Western culture. As other countries pass through the phases of industrialization, they also find it necessary to evolve large, more complex organizational systems. Witness the current evolution within India from a small, family-oriented society to one of more complex, centralized systems. The breakdown of the traditional family pattern and local social structure within China and the evolution of strongly centralized organizational systems under the Communists is even more dramatic. It would appear that this trend toward larger and more complex organization is basic in all human society, one which is moving in a massive wave through many cultures.

CHARACTERISTICS OF MODERN BUSINESS ORGANIZATIONS

The business organization with the primary objectives of production and distribution of physical products or services represents one of the most complex forms of man's social organization. Using the United States and Western culture as a frame of reference, we can look at some of the characteristics of these organizations.

Growing Size

The growth in size of business organizations is unparalleled. Even the small-to-medium-size business organizations of today would dwarf the largest firms of a century ago. The largest business organizations employ thousands of people and have annual sales volume well over one billion dollars. This growth in size has created many problems for the integration of the various segments or parts in the organization.

Complexity

In addition to growth, there has been a general increase in the complexity of the business organization. Whereas firms of fifty years ago concentrated on a limited line of products, most of the large corporations today have diverse operations. There has been a transition in the way business firms achieve growth. In the latter part of the nineteenth century and early twentieth century, most firms grew through vertical integration—by moving further back in the productive process or further forward in the distributive process for their given line of product. This was typical of the growth of U.S. Steel, Standard Oil, American Tobacco, and other large firms of the era. During the 1920s and 1930s the pattern of growth tended in the direction of horizontal integration—a movement toward the expansion of similar-type activities throughout a wide geographical area. This type of integration was typified by the chain-store movement. More recently, and particularly in the post-World War II period, the pattern of growth for most enterprises has been through heterogeneous growth and diversification into new and varied fields. This approach has increased greatly the complexities of the business organization. Witness the diverse activities of many giant corporations—General Motors, General Electric, Du Pont, General Dynamics, and many others. They have become vast complexities operating in widely different economic and political environments.

Specialization of Skills

There has been a growing tendency toward specialization and division of labor within the organizational structure. Specialization at the worker level was a result of mechanization and the scientific-management movement. The trend toward specialization of managerial skills has been given less emphasis. Witness the rise in the use of management specialists over the past few decades—the personnel expert, the risk manager, the quality-control manager, the operations-research team, public-relations expert, and a myriad of other specialists. With this increase of specialization, the problems of integrating the people in a modern business organization into an effective operating unit have multiplied geometrically.

Diversity of Objectives

Another characteristic of modern business organization is the diversity of objectives of the various people and organizational units. While it is generally accepted as a norm that the business organization operates for long-run profit maximization (the current discussion of the responsibilities of business for social well-being have even questioned this concept), there are the many subsystems operating within the business organization, each having its own unique objectives and goals. Indeed, every individual participant within the business organization brings to his work activity a multitude of personal goals, motives, and objectives which influence his organizational behavior. To speak of the enterprise as having one single, unique goal does not give recognition to the organization as a social institution. The diversity of objectives of the individual participants and subsystems within the organization creates problems of goal integration. Here again, the systems concept provides a basis for integrating these various objectives into a systematic whole.

Meeting Change

A further characteristic of business enterprises is the necessity of accepting change. Increasingly, the environment within which organizations are operating makes demands for change and evolution. It is impossible to think of the organization as a static system. It has to be a dynamic, adaptive system in order to meet the challenge of change. The impact of technological change upon business organizations is apparent. We are less aware of the underlying sociological, moral, and ethical changes which are influencing business organizations. The growing interest of the social scientists in the study of the business enterprise is indicative of the awakening to the importance of social and cultural norms in the organization.

External Demands

The modern business organization does not operate in a vacuum. It is an integral part of society as a whole. There have been a number of forces tending to restrict or change the role of the business organization. The growth of labor unions has placed restrictions upon business decisions, as has the increase in governmental regulations and control. The environmental influences will continually evolve and provide an important reason for maintaining the business organization as a viable system.

TRADITIONAL ORGANIZATIONAL CONCEPTS

In order to place organization theory in proper perspective in relation to general systems theory, it is desirable to look at some of the primary concepts about the business organization. They have evolved over an extended period and represent a transition in the study of organizations. Some of the most important of these views come from traditional, or classical, organization theory, while others have evolved from the neoclassical, or "human relations," school, and still others have come from modern organization theory. Some of the more important of the traditional concepts are discussed briefly in the following sections. This is followed by a discussion of the neoclassical and modern organizational views.

Structure

Structure is the relationship of the various functions or activities in an organization. Efficient management requires that the structure be in balance and adapted to the objectives and primary operations of the enterprise. The basic organizational structure provides the pattern around which more detailed administrative functions are interrelated. Organizational structure can be compared to the skeleton structure of animals—it provides the basic framework around which the various parts or units are related and function.[6] Furthermore, the structure provides for known and established relationships between participants in the organization. Simon emphasized this idea as follows:

> The organization structure establishes a common set of presuppositions and expectations as to which members of the organization are responsible for which classes of decisions; it establishes a structure of subgoals to serve as criteria of choice in various parts of the organization; and it establishes intelligence responsibilities in particular organization units for scrutinizing specific parts of the organization's environment and for communicating events requiring attention to appropriate decision points.[7]

Hierarchy

Closely related to structure in the organization is the concept of hierarchical relationships. Large organizations are almost universally hierarchical in nature. Almost any organization—the church, university, or business organization—is divided into units, which are subdivided into smaller units, which are in turn subdivided into smaller units. In classical organizational theory this concept of a hierarchical structure is the scalar principle, initially referred to by Mooney and Reiley.[8] The scalar principle refers primarily to the vertical division of authority and responsibility and the assignment of duties to organizational units.

Hierarchical structure has important implications for the general systems concept. Almost every system, both human and natural, has a hierarchical structure. Even the universe is made up of a complex array of subsystems—the earth with its own system is a subsystem of a galaxy, which is perhaps a subsystem of an infinite number of other large systems. Smaller units, such as the atom, are a combination of a number of subsystems organized into a larger system unit. Hierarchy appears to be a natural order of nature. According to Simon:

> The near universality of hierarchy in the composition of complex systems suggests there is something fundamental in this structural principle that goes beyond the peculiarities of human organization. . . . *There are*

---

[6] For a discussion of structure, see William H. Newman and Charles E. Summer, Jr., *The Process of Management,* Prentice-Hall, Inc., Englewood Cliffs, N.J., 1961, chap. 6.

[7] Herbert A. Simon, *The New Science of Management Decision,* Harper & Brothers, New York, 1960, p. 10.

[8] James D. Mooney and Allen C. Reiley, *Onward Industry,* Harper & Brothers, New York, 1931.

strong reasons for believing that almost any system of sufficient complexity would have to have the room-within-room structure that we observe in actual human organizations. The reasons for hierarchy go far beyond the need for unity of command or other considerations relating to authority.[9]

Again we see the similarity; one of the fundamental aspects of organization theory, the hierarchical structure, is also fundamental to any general systems theory.

Specialization

The principle of functional specialization is another important part of organization theory. Frequently it is encountered under the theories or concepts of departmentation, the division of the organization into specialized units which are assigned the performance of particular functions. Traditional departmentation into production, distribution, and finance departments is an example of functional specialization. The concept of specialization is closely related to the scalar concept. However, the difference is that the scalar concept deals with the vertical superior-subordinate relationship whereas the functional concept is related to the differences in duties assigned to various units or people within the organization.

Span of Control

The span-of-control, or span-of-supervision, concept relates to the number of subordinates a superior can supervise effectively. It relates closely to the hierarchical structure and to the concepts of departmentation. Implicit in the span-of-control concept is the necessity for the coordination of the activities of the subordinate by the superior. Span of control emphasizes the necessity for establishing a superior-subordinate relationship which allows for the systematic integration of activities. In formal organization theory the span-of-control principle recommended a narrow span in order for the executive or superior to provide adequate integration. However, this recommendation did not give recognition to the relationship between a narrow span and number of vertical levels within the organization. Thus a narrow span of control results in an elongated vertical structure and often creates problems for the systematic integration of activities on a horizontal level. Many of the modern writers have been critical of the usefulness of the span-of-control concept as a means of building organizations.[10]

[9] Simon, *op. cit.,* pp. 41–42. (Italics by authors.)

[10] For an interesting criticism of the span-of-control concept, see Herbert A. Simon, *Administrative Behavior,* The Macmillan Company, New York, 1957, 2d ed., pp. 26–28. A good reply was presented by Lyndall E. Urwick, "The Manager Span of Control," *Harvard Business Review,* May–June, 1956, pp. 39–47.

Line and Staff

In classical organization theory, the line organization is vested with the primary source of authority and the staff functions support and advise the line. The traditional concept of the staff was as an aid to the executive, an extension of his personality. Through the use of special staffs reporting directly to the executive, it was possible to increase his span of control without sacrificing his coordinating abilities. But this concept of staff has changed greatly with advancing specialization and complexities within business enterprises. Staffs have come to play a much more important role, providing service, information, and even control over other organizational units. With the expansion of the role of the staff, the clear delineation between line and staff relationships is no longer possible. This is particularly true in functional-staff operations. Functional authority refers to the authority which resides within a specialized staff and is exercised within other operational units. Quite frequently the industrial-relations department has functional authority over the labor-relations activities in all departments throughout the organization. The concept of functional authority represents a substantial variation from the traditional hierarchical organization, where the relationships are based upon the unity-of-command concept, with authority directed from only one superior and with each subordinate responsible to only one superior for his total activities. The enterprise with functional staffs does severe damage to the unity-of-command concept. With functional staffs, a number of specialists in each of the functional areas exercises an authoritarian relationship which results in multiple rather than unified supervision. The growth in the use of functional authority has complicated the clear-cut organizational relationship existing under traditional concepts.

The foregoing concepts of structure, hierarchy, specialization, span of control, and line and staff relationships come mainly from traditional organization theory, where the primary concern was one of grouping work in the most efficient way. Given the general objectives for an organization, it sought to identify the tasks necessary to reach this goal. Then the problem was to group these jobs into administrative units, to group the units into larger units, and finally to establish the top-level departments.

BUREAUCRATIC MODEL

A view of the formal organization which is traditional with the social scientist rather than with the management-oriented student was postulated by Max Weber at the turn of the century. In Weber's view, the bureaucratic form was the most efficient type of organization in a modern society. Basically, he wanted to construct an ideal organization which would provide a maximum of rationality in human behavior. This is obviously a far cry from the label "bureaucratic" often attached to large-scale, cumbersome government or business units which do not seem to recognize individual bidding. In speaking of the technical advantages of bureaucracy, Weber said:

> The decisive reason for the advance of bureaucratic organization has always been its purely technical superiority over any other form of organization. The fully developed bureaucratic mechanism compares with other organizations exactly as does the machine with the nonmechanical modes of production.
>
> Precision, speed, unambiguity, knowledge of the files, continuity, discretion, unity, strict subordination, reduction of friction and of material and personal costs—these are raised to the optimum point in the strictly bureaucratic administration, and especially in its monocratic form.[11]

A second aspect of Weber's theory of bureaucracy was its emphasis on universality. He suggested that this form of organization would result in the greatest efficiency for a wide variety of organizational units, ranging from the business enterprises, to governmental units, to military operations, and to such associations as labor unions. Basically, it was Weber's contention that man was unpredictable, often emotional, not necessarily rational, and would interfere with efficient organizational performance. He therefore set forth as an ideal model of bureaucracy a depersonalized form of organization which would minimize the impact of human diversities. He anchored his bureaucratic mechanism in the institutionalization of authority by society, a type of power legitimized by society that "makes a man do what he does not want to do." Weber's bureaucratic model had much in common with the traditional concepts discussed previously. It was mechanistic and impersonal, in sharp contrast to later concepts.[12]

NEOCLASSICAL MODEL

The neoclassical, or human relations, model of organizational behavior evolved as a reaction against the more mechanistic and impersonal bias of the classical school. This view, stemming from the well-known Hawthorne–Western Electric studies during the 1930s and reported by Roethlisberger and Dickson in *Management and the Worker* in 1938, transformed the focus from the rational model of traditional theory to a behavioristic model which accepted man as he is. Basically, this school accepted the

---

[11] H. H. Gerth and C. Wright Mills, *From Max Weber: Essays in Sociology,* Oxford University Press, New York, 1946, p. 214.

[12] For an interesting discussion of bureaucracy and its role in modern society, see Peter M. Blau, *Bureaucracy in Modern Society,* Random House, Inc., New York, 1956.

structural aspects of organization as discussed previously but modified the concepts regarding human resources and informal-group relationships within the organization. Perhaps the major contribution of the human relations group was their interest in and study of the informal-group relationships within the formal structure. The Hawthorne studies provided the first clinical insight into some of the implications of this heretofore neglected area. In general, the thesis of this school is that informal organizations grow out of social needs—the needs of people for interpersonal association with others—and that these informal organizations have considerable impact upon organizational behavior.

Shepard identified five key differences between traditional and human relations organizational theory:

1. Wide participation in decision making rather than centralized decision making.

2. The face-to-face group rather than the individuals as the basic unit of organization.

3. Mutual confidence rather than authority as the integrative force in organization.

4. The supervisor as the agent for maintaining intragroup and intergroup communication rather than the agent of higher authority.

5. Growth of members of the organization to greater responsibility rather than external control of the members' performance of their tasks.[13]

The human relations view brought to the forefront the concept of the organization as a total system encompassing individuals, informal groups, intergroup relationships, and formal relationships. In effect, this school put the human element back in the organization—the element which the traditional school had so carefully attempted to minimize.[14]

DECISION-MAKING MODEL

Simon focused the attention of organization theorists on the decision-making processes within the organization.[15] He rejected most of the traditional concepts and placed emphasis on the human problem-solving processes and decision mechanisms as primary forces in organizational behavior. According to this thesis, organizational participants should not be

[13] H. Shepard, "Superiors and Subordinates in Research," *Journal of Business,* October, 1956, p. 261.

[14] An interesting play on words aptly expresses the distinction between classical organization theory and the human relations approach to organizational behavior. Bennis has called the traditional theory "organizations without people" and the human relations approach "people without organizations." Warren G. Bennis, "Leadership Theory and Administrative Behavior," *Administrative Science Quarterly,* December, 1959, pp. 263–266.

[15] Simon, *Administrative Behavior.*

viewed as mere mechanical instrumentalities. They should be perceived as individuals with wants, motives, aspiration levels, and drives, who have limited rationality and capacity for problem solving.

Simon uses the term decision making as though it were synonymous with "managing." In this sense, decision making has three principal stages: *intelligence*—searching the environment for conditions calling for decision; *design*—inventing, developing, and analyzing possible courses of action; and *choice*—selecting a particular course of action from the available alternatives.[16] In a book in collaboration with March, Simon later used the decision-making process as a frame of reference to set forth a more general theory of organization. A key concept of this book is illustrated by the following:

> The basic features of organization structure and function derive from the characteristics of human problem-solving processes and rational human choice. Because of the limits of human intellective capacities in comparison with the complexities of the problems that individuals and organizations face, rational behavior calls for simplified models that capture the main features of a problem without capturing all its complexities.[17]

Such concepts greatly augment traditional and neoclassical organization theory with current knowledge from social sciences about the motivational aspects, conflicts of interest, perception, and restrictions on rationality, all of which influence organizational behavior significantly.

MODERN ORGANIZATION THEORY—A SYSTEMS CONCEPT

Traditional organizational theory generally emphasized parts and segments of the organization and was concerned with the separation of activities into tasks or operational units. The traditional theory did not give sufficient emphasis to the problem of interrelationships or integration of activity. Nor did the neoclassical, or human relations, approach move in this direction. Its approach was aimed at interjecting back into the mechanistic traditional models human motivations, aspirations, desires, and limitations. Neither of these approaches provided a basis for an integrated, systematic organizational model.

Increasing attention is being given to the notion that the most useful way to study organizations is to consider them as systems. This modern view tends to treat the organization as a system of mutually dependent parts and variables, and the business organization is thought of as a social system within the broader, more inclusive system of society. Parsons's definition of the organization expresses this view:

[16] Simon, *The New Science of Management Decision*, pp. 1–4.
[17] March and Simon, *op. cit.*, p. 169.

It seems appropriate to define an organization as a social system which is organized for the attainment of a particular type of goal; the attainment of that goal is at the same time a performance of a type of function on behalf of a more inclusive system, the society.[18]

Modern organization theory and general systems theory are closely related, with organization theory a special element of general systems theory. Systems theory and organization theory are both concerned with the investigation and performance of the organization as an integrated whole. However, general systems theory is concerned with all nine levels of systems as described in Chapter 1, whereas organization theory focuses primarily upon human social organizations. However, many general systems concepts, taken from the investigation and study of other types of systems, are meaningful to the study of human organizational systems. For example, the concepts of the cybernetic system, with its closed sequence and automatic adjustment, are important in the study of the human social organization.[19]

Most organized systems involve the following components: planners, administrators who carry out plans, human and material resources, controllers, outsiders who are affected by the organization's activity, and the social environment in which these components operate. The business organization also has a number of components or subsystems, which take the following form:

1. *Management,* which directs
2. *Men,* who control and operate
3. *Machines,* which convert
4. *Materials* into products or services made available to
5. *Consumers,* whose purchases are also sought by
6. *Competitors*
7. *Government* and the *public* [20]

---

[18] Talcott Parsons, "Suggestions for a Sociological Approach to the Theory of Organizations," *Administrative Science Quarterly,* September, 1956, p. 238.

[19] For an interesting discussion of the relationship between organizational theory and general systems theory, see William G. Scott, "Organizational Theory: An Overview and an Appraisal," *Journal of the Academy of Management,* April, 1961, pp. 7–26. Scott suggests the interrelationship between general systems theory and organizational theory as follows:

> Modern organizational theory leads, as it has been shown, almost inevitably into a discussion of general system theory. A science of organization universals has strong advocates, particularly among biologists. Organization theorists in administrative science cannot afford to overlook the contributions of general system theory. Indeed, modern organization concepts could offer a great deal to those working with general system theory.

[20] C. West Churchman, Russell L. Ackoff, and E. Leonard Arnoff, *Introduction to Operations Research,* John Wiley & Sons, Inc., New York, 1957, pp. 109–110.

These separate components of the business enterprise become a viable, operating system by virtue of *organization*. All man's more complex relationships are established in a systematic arrangement through the process of organization, or organizing. Thus organization concepts are vitally important to systems concepts. The *organizing function* is the means, or bonding agent, by which separate human and material resources are fused together to form an integrated, operating system.

THE SYSTEMS APPROACH AND ORGANIZING

The function of management in today's complex business organizations is to coordinate the activities of the various operational units and optimize the goals of the total enterprise. The manager should understand the business, not as a number of isolated parts, but as a system; he must have knowledge of the relationship between the parts and be aware of their potential interactions. Essentially, the business manager must bring these individual, often diverse, functions together into an integrated, organized *system* with all the parts working toward the common organizational goal. With growing specialization, size, and complexities of business organizations, this problem of integration has increased rapidly over the past few decades and will be of even greater importance in the future. In adopting the systems approach to the function of organizing, we should look at the following concepts.

Elements of the Business

In the business organization the elements, or parts, of the system are comprised of the individual, the informal work group or informal organization, the formal organization, and finally the environmental systems which have a direct impact upon the business organization as a system. There are also numerous subsystems which are established to perform specific organizational functions, such as the production system, the distribution system, the control system, and the information system. Thus every business enterprise is a systems hierarchy with many interrelated subsystems.

Interrelationships between Parts

The second fundamental step in the systems approach to organizing is to consider the interrelationships between the various elements, or parts, of the system. There are many interactional patterns which exist between the individual, the informal group, the formal organizational structure, the functional subsystem, and the various environmental groups. In interrelating the various subsystems, there should be a comprehensive framework, or general systems reference. Bakke has set forth a useful criterion for looking at the interrelationships between the various parts in a social organization, as follows:

1. The parts should be recognizable as variables essential to the achievement of end-result characteristics of an organization or its parts (such as flexibility, stability, etc.).

2. The parts should be related to the whole by reference to a common characteristic (or characteristics) having a necessary and logical functional relation to the performance of the organization's function.

3. The parts should be so defined as to indicate their logical and necessary functional relation to each other and to the whole, and not merely to suggest their usefulness as a set of categories for classifying variables.

4. Major parts should be capable of subsuming all elementary parts necessary to the explanation of organizational behavior.

5. The parts should have a necessary relation to the behavior of all participants in the organization.

6. The kind and pattern of interaction among the parts should indicate an unbroken continuity of reciprocal relations from individual participants, through systems of activity, to the surrounding environment.[21]

Bakke talks about the *fusion process,* which attempts to reconcile or fuse these various parts and bring them into harmony with each other. This fusion process, in effect, maintains the objectives of the organization in face of the divergent interests of individuals, groups, other organizations, and the organization itself.

Information and Communication Processes

Basic to the integration of the various parts to a system is the concept of a communicative, or informational, network. Communication stimulates action within the organization and provides the coordinating mechanism for relating the parts of the system into a synchronized pattern. Deutsch suggests that organizations are composed of subsystems which communicate with each other, receive and transmit messages with the outside world, and store information. Taken together, these communication networks constitute a configuration representing the total system.[22] The cybernetics model is primarily concerned with communication and information flow in complex systems. Although cybernetics has been applied primarily to mechanistic engineering problems, its model of feedback, control, and regulation has a great deal of applicability for biological and social systems as well.

[21] E. Wight Bakke, "Concept of the Social Organization," in Haire, *op. cit.,* pp. 35–36.

[22] Karl W. Deutsch, "On Communication Models in the Social Sciences," *Public Opinion Quarterly,* 1952, pp. 356–380.

Growth and Viability

The problems of growth and adaptation are basic to the concept of the organization as a system. Every system is subject to forces which make it necessary to adapt to a changing environment. Human systems, or social organizations, are subjected to substantial pressures for change. Witness the rather important changes which have taken place in the social ethic regarding the responsibilities of the business organization to general society. How does the organization provide for adaptability and change and at the same time ensure continuing growth? Maintaining a viable organization is an important part of the systems concept.

The homeostasis model, very important in physiology, biology, and the natural sciences, is a process of balancing the parts of the internal system to meet different environmental changes. Essentially, this is similar to the cybernetic mechanism of the engineer. The system is able to adapt through feedback information to a wide variety of situations; that is, it is able to reach an organizational equilibrium in a variety of environments.

Decision Making

Another part of general systems theory relating to the organizing function is that concerned with the location of decision points within the organization. The decision-making process becomes more complicated as we move up the hierarchy of systems from the physical, mechanistic systems to the higher-level social systems. Large social organizations, such as business and government, have developed complex information systems which attempt to facilitate decision making and focus it toward goal accomplishment. Many modern techniques, such as computers and data-processing applications, have helped provide a basis for applying systems concepts to decision making within the organization.

The foregoing discussion shows how the modern business organization is a system. The chief characteristics of the organization as a system are division into units, interaction of these units between themselves and with their environment, the maintenance of a structure of information flow and communications, the assurance of growth and viability, and a requirement for integrated and effective decision-making processes.

SUMMARY

General systems theory implies an interconnected complex of functionally related components, or parts. The business organization and other institutions of human interrelationships are unstructured, open-sequence systems. They are social, or man-made, systems. It is only through the process of organization that the vast complex of men, materials, machines, and other resources are combined into an efficient, effective, and viable business enterprise.

A simple but easily understood definition of the business organization is: *The organization is an assemblage of people, materials, machines, and other resources geared to task accomplishment through a series of interactions and integrated into a social system.* Systems concepts emphasize the integration of all activities toward the accomplishment of over-all objectives, but also recognize the importance of efficient subsystem performance.

One of the characteristics of modern life is the pervasiveness of human organizational relationships. As man has evolved more complex cultural, technological, and social institutions, so has he increased his organizational relationships. The large, complex organization is built upon the foundation of a number of more informal, interrelated group activities. Here again, the over-all system—the business organization—is a composite resulting from the interaction of a number of subsystems. The growth of large-scale, complex organizations has been one of the main characteristics of the evolution of modern industrial societies.

The business organization, with the primary objectives of production and distribution of physical products or services, represents one of the most complex forms of man's social organizations. These organizations generally have the characteristics of increasing size, growing complexity, specialization of skills, increasing diversity of objectives, viability to meet change, and adaptation to external demands.

Modern organization theory has developed from traditional organizational concepts which placed emphasis upon the organizational structure, hierarchical relationships, specialization, span of control, and line and staff relationships. This traditional theory was modified substantially by the human relations school, which placed greater emphasis upon personal and social needs of organizational participants. The human relations view brought to the forefront the concept of the organization as a total system encompassing individuals, informal groups, intergroup relationships, and formal structures.

Neither the traditional nor the human relations approach provided a basis for an integrated, systematic organizational model. The modern view is to treat the organization as a system of mutually dependent parts and variables, and the business organization is thought of as a social system within the broader, more inclusive system of society. The manager should understand the business, not as a number of isolated parts, but as subsystems; he must have knowledge of the relationships between the parts and be aware of their potential interaction. Essentially, the business manager must bring these individual, often diverse, functions together into an integrated, organized system, with all the parts working toward the common organizational goals.

Under the systems concept, the business organization is viewed as a series of parts which include the individual, the informal work groups, the formal organization, and finally the environmental systems, which have a direct impact upon the business organization. Furthermore, under the systems concept, consideration must be given to the means for interrelating and coordinating these various subsystems. These parts are integrated through various processes such as the information and communications network, the decision system, and built-in equilibrium mechanisms which exist in every organization.

Thus modern organization theory, as it has evolved, inevitably merges into concepts of general systems theories. Scientific investigation and research findings using general systems theory as a frame of reference can provide important understanding of the most complex of man-made systems —his large-scale social organizations.

Chapter Four

CONTROL AND SYSTEMS CONCEPTS

Many systems are designed to include the element of control, which is the means of ensuring the performance of the system within the limits described by the plan. Control can provide flexibility and effectiveness to the system. However, it also increases design and operating costs.

In this day of automation the term *control* may bring to mind visions of self-regulated electronic systems. The theory of control is by no means so restrictive; it applies to all systems, structured or unstructured.

Our discussion of control and systems concepts will cover the following topics:

Definition of Control
Elements of Control
Characteristics of Control
Kinds of Control Systems
Relationship between the Elements and Medium of Control
Examples of Administrative Control
Systems Concepts and Control

DEFINITION OF CONTROL

The concept of control is not new or difficult to understand. However, it has been used in different ways and to different degrees of sophistication.

For example, Newman and Summer apply the concept of control to the management of business firms as follows:

> 1. Standards that represent desired performance. These standards may be tangible or intangible, vague or specific, but until everyone concerned understands what results are desired, control will create confusion.
>
> 2. A comparison of actual results against the standards. This evaluation must be reported to the people who can do something about it.
>
> 3. Corrective action. Control measurements and reports serve little purpose unless corrective action is taken when it is discovered that current activities are not leading to desired results.[1]

Wiener, a mathematician, defines control in a very straightforward manner: "Control . . . is nothing but the sending of messages which effectively change the behavior of the recipient. . . .[2] Where a man's word goes, and where his power of perception goes, to that point his control and in a sense his physical existence is extended." [3]

We shall define control as *that function of the system which provides direction in conformance to the plan, or in other words, the maintenance of variations from system objectives within allowable limits.*

Control is maintained through a network of information which serves as the medium of control. When information is dormant or static, it is of little value to a control system. On the other hand, information in motion is the vital flow of intelligence which establishes the basis for controlling a system. The flow of such intelligence is necessary for the proper operation of a business enterprise.

ELEMENTS OF CONTROL

There are four basic elements in every control system. They always occur in the same sequence and have the same relationship to each other. They are:

1. A controlled characteristic or condition

2. A sensory device or method for measuring the characteristic or condition

3. A control group, unit, or equipment which will compare measured data with planned performance and direct a correcting mechanism in response to need

4. An activating group or mechanism which is capable of bringing about a change in the operating system

---

[1] William H. Newman and Charles E. Summer, Jr., *The Process of Management,* Prentice-Hall, Inc., Englewood Cliffs, N.J., 1961, pp. 561–562.

[2] Norbert Wiener, *The Human Use of Human Beings,* Houghton Mifflin Company, Boston, 1950, p. 124.

[3] *Ibid.,* p. 8.

Figure 1 illustrates the relationships among the four elements of control. The first element is the characteristic or condition of the operating system which is to be measured. This element may be the output of the system during any stage of processing, or it may be a condition which has resulted from the output of the system. For example, it may be the heat energy produced by the furnace, or the temperature in the room which has changed because of the furnace output.

The second element of control (sensor) involves the measurement of performance. The system should be engineered to provide a sensory device or method for measuring the controlled item (characteristic or condition). In a home heating system this could be a thermostat, and in a quality-control system this may be the visual inspection of a product by a worker.

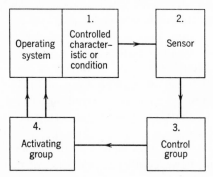

Fig. 1. The four elements of a control system.

The third element (control group) includes the determination of the need for correction and the release of corrective information. An allowable deviation from plan is usual and expected. As deviations are recognized, information is released to correct the output of the system. Often, it is possible to trace trends in performance and uncover problem areas before they become serious. Corrective action during the operation stage is characteristic of good control.

When there is a significant difference between output and plan, the situation may be "out of control." This would mean that the objective of the system is not feasible in terms of the capabilities of the system. If such a situation occurred, the objectives of the system would have to be reconsidered in terms of the capacity of the system, or the system would have to be redesigned. For example, a manufacturing plan could specify output of 1,000 units per month, but the actual output might be less than half of this amount. The goal of 1,000 units was not reasonable even though the employees worked overtime. If the planned output were essential, the system would have to be redesigned.

The fourth element of control is the implementation of corrective action. The kind of a device or method used to direct corrective input into the operating system takes a wide variety of forms. It may be a hydraulic controller positioned by a solenoid or electric motor in response to an electronic error signal from the control-group element, or it may be an employee directed to rework the parts which fail to pass quality inspection. When a plan is perfect, corrective action is not necessary, but theoretical perfection seldom occurs.

CHARACTERISTICS OF CONTROL

There are two characteristics of control which have particular significance. First, unlimited quantities of input may be controlled by a switch, valve, or some other device. A small amount of energy, therefore, can control jet airplanes, automatic steel mills, and hydroelectric power plants. The pilot presses a button, and the landing gear of the airplane goes up or down. The steel-mill operator pushes a lever, and a ribbon of white hot steel starts racing through the plant. A worker at a control board directs the flow of electrical energy throughout a regional network of stations and substations. In other words, it takes a small amount of control energy to release large units of the three basic inputs of systems: information, materials, and energy.[4]

Second, the control unit may be located far from the operating system. This does not mean, however, that all elements of control may be apart from the operating system. For example, there must be a means of measuring the output (the sensory element) at the point of operation. This measurement information can be transmitted to a distant point (the control group) for comparison with a standard, and when deviations occur, the correcting input can be released from a distant point. The input unit (activating group) would, however, be located at the site of the operating system. What does this mean? It means that planes can be flown by remote control; dangerous manufacturing processes can be controlled from a safe distance; and the marketing system of a national organization can be directed from a central office in a single city.

KINDS OF CONTROL SYSTEMS

There are two kinds of control systems: open-sequence and closed-sequence. The basic difference between these two types of control depends on whether or not the control unit is an integral part of the system it regulates. A kitchen fan is an illustration of an open-sequence circuit. The

---

[4] Inputs in systems have been broken into three categories in Eric W. Leaver, "How Automatic Can We Get?" in *Keeping Pace with Automation*, American Management Association, Special Report 7, 1956.

controlling action, turning the fan "on" or "off" as needed, requires energy from a person or device independent of the ventilating equipment.

Another example of an open-sequence system is a street-lighting system controlled by a timing device. At a certain time each evening the timing device closes the circuit and energy flows in the electric lines and the bulbs are lighted. It should be noted that the timing device is an independent unit and is not measuring the system being controlled. If on a dark stormy day the lights should be needed, the timing device would not recognize the need for light.

An open-sequence system depends on the correct properties being built into the controller, e.g., a street-light timing device which modified the time the lights are turned on as the days grow shorter or longer. When a system is regulated by a person, it requires that the person be attentive to the job of controlling the system effectively.

If control is exerted in terms of the operation rather than because of outside or predetermined arrangements, it is a closed-sequence system. The home thermostat is the classic example of a control device in this kind of system. When the room temperature drops below the desired point, the control mechanism closes the circuit to start the furnace and the temperature rises. The furnace operating circuit is turned off as the temperature reaches the selected level. The significant difference is that the control device is an element of the system it serves and measures the performance of the system. *In other words, all four control elements belong to the same system.*

An essential part of a *closed-sequence system* is *feedback;* that is, the output of the system is measured continually in terms of the item controlled, and the input is modified to reduce any divergence or error to zero. Sometimes the automatic system is not capable of complete correction:

> A system will cease to function when variations in its intake of energy or changes in its external and internal environment become too large. What distinguishes an automatically controlled system is that it possesses working components which maintain at least some of its typical processes despite such excessive variations. As need arises, these components employ a small part of the energy supplied to the system to augment or diminish the total volume of that energy, or in other ways to compensate for environmental changes. Even these elementary notions provide fruitful clues for understanding not only inanimate automatically controlled systems, but also organic bodies and their interrelations.[5]

Many of the patterns of information flow in a business are found to have the nature of closed loops. The reason for such a condition is apparent

[5] Ernest Nagel, "Self-regulation," in *Automatic Control* by the Editors of *Scientific American,* Simon and Schuster, Inc., New York, 1955, p. 3.

when one recognizes that any system, if it is to achieve a predetermined goal, must have available to it at all times an indication of its degree of attainment. In general, every goal-seeking system employs circuits, or feedback.

The relationships of the feedback loop may be illustrated by Figure 2. It involves measurement, comparison, and corrective input.

Figure 2 is consistent with Figure 1. Input is the activating element; the processor is the operating system; output represents the accomplishments of the system; the measurement channel is the sensor element; the comparator-and-control channel is the control-group element; and the objective, or standard, is the controlled item.

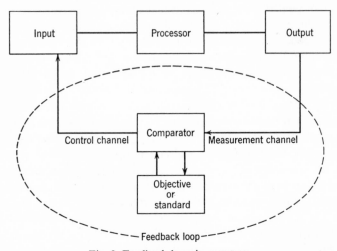

Fig. 2. Feedback loop in a system.

Feedback control operates in a system expected to make errors, for the error is depended upon to bring about correction. The objective of such a system is to make the error as small as possible within practical limits.

RELATIONSHIP BETWEEN THE ELEMENTS AND MEDIUM OF CONTROL

Information is the medium of control, for it is the flow of measurement information and later the flow of corrective information which allows a characteristic or condition of the system to be controlled. In order to ascertain how information actually influences control, it is necessary to review each element of control once more.

Controlled Characteristic or Condition

As noted earlier, the primary requirement of a control system is to maintain the level and kind of output necessary to achieve the objectives of the system. Usually, it is not practical to control every feature and condition associated with the system's output. Therefore the choice of the controlled item is of extreme importance. There should be a direct correlation between the controlled item and the operation of the system. In other words, successful control of the item should be indicative of the success of the operating system. To meet this requirement, the controlled item should be stated in the language used in the feedback loop. This is why it is important to understand what is to be transmitted before any information is transferred.

Further, the language should be selected in consideration of the effects of distortion in the latter stages of transmission. If there appears to be a possibility of distortion, the controlled-item information should be expressed in a language which lends itself to be checked by adding extra bits of information. For example, an extra column in punched-paper tape can be used to check the validity of the information contained on the tape.

Sensor

The relation of communication to measurement also is significant. Again we point to the importance of measuring only the characteristics that are representative of the standards desired and are the most economic to obtain. Information to be compared with the standard must be expressed in the same terms as the standard in order to facilitate managerial decision making. If machine methods are used, and sometimes even if they are not, extensive translation may be required. Optimum languages for computation and for human review are not the same. This fact should not be overlooked, as the relative ease of translation may be a significant factor in selecting the language for the units of measurement.

In many instances it is possible to sample output. The purpose of a sampling procedure is to estimate some characteristic of a group without a complete examination of all the items constituting the group. Statistical sampling is based on probability theory, and therefore the subjectivity and arbitrary nature of judgment in selecting the sample are controlled, and results can be evaluated by objective means.

The fundamental assumption underlying statistical theory is that the observed values follow some pattern. Once this pattern is ascertained, the probability that the variable will take on certain values or fall within a certain range can be computed.

Control Group

Information from the sensor element becomes the basis for control activity. Output information is compared with the controlled item, significant deviations are noted, and corrective information is released.

A frequency distribution (a tabulation of the number of times a given quality characteristic occurs within the sample of products being checked) may be used to show the average quality, the spread, and the comparison of output with standard.

Control charts are a vehicle for illustrating the comparison of actual product characteristics with the controlled item. Probably the most notable proponent of charting as a means of control was Henry L. Gantt. By drawing on his years of engineering experience and keeping in close contact with the shops where actual production processes were carried on, he was able to design and construct charts on which the output of men and/or machines could be related to the controlled item in a meaningful way.

Activating Group

The activating group responds to the information received from the control group. Inasmuch as every control system has a finite action time, certain problems arise where this time is an appreciable portion of the period of such a cycle.

Any system with negative feedback will maintain a continuous oscillation when disturbed if (1) the time delays in response to some frequency add up to half a period of oscillation, and (2) the feedback effect is sufficiently large at this frequency.[6]

The most critical problem arises where the delay is exactly one-half cycle, for then the corrective action is superimposed upon a deviation which at the moment is in the same direction as that of correction. This oscillatory behavior, known as *hunting,* causes the system to overcorrect, then to correct too much in the other direction, and so on, until the oscillations become very pronounced (Figure 3). One solution to this problem rests on *anticipation,* which involves measurement not only of the change, but of the rate of change as well.[7] The correction is directed as a factor of the type and the rate of the error. The difficulty can also be combated by reducing the time lag between the measurement of the output and the correction of the input. Better still, a time lead can be introduced to compensate for the time lag, bringing about consistency between the need for correction and the type and magnitude of the initiated correction.

EXAMPLES OF ADMINISTRATIVE CONTROL

Examples of control in business are infinite in variety; however, the concepts we have discussed apply to all of them. Five examples of control are reviewed by definition, objectives, and scope to illustrate the structure

[6] Arnold Tustin, "Feedback," in *ibid.,* p. 16.

[7] R. H. MacMillan, *Automation,* Cambridge University Press, London, 1956, p. 39.

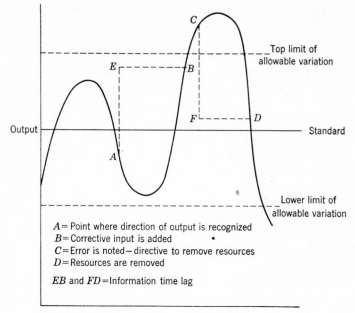

Fig. 3. Oscillation and feedback.

of each control system and to provide a basis for integrating control and systems concepts.

Production Control

"Production control is defined as the task of co-ordinating manufacturing activities in accordance with manufacturing plans so that preconceived schedules can be attained with optimum economy and efficiency." [8]

An effective system of production control will tend to (1) create better customer relations (orders are completed on schedule), (2) reduce the per-unit direct labor and material cost, (3) reduce the per-unit overhead cost (a larger flow of production can be handled in the same period of time), and (4) stimulate better management (executives can direct a larger portion of their time to more creative duties).

The detailed production planning necessary to yield a specific product includes a determination of what materials and work operations are necessary, where and how these operations will be accomplished, the path and sequence of operations, the kinds of machines and operators required, the time required to do the job, and the proper scheduling of work. After the

[8] William Voris, *Production Control*, Richard D. Irwin, Inc., Homewood, Ill., 1956, p. 3.

plan has been completed, the order is released or dispatched to the operating units. This is a description of the first element of control, the controlled item.

The follow-up function in production measures the progress of materials and parts through the production process. This function is best described as the job of reporting work status and investigating those orders which have varied from the prearranged plan. The follow-up group works in cooperation with the operating departments. It does not override these departments; it keeps check on progress, bringing delays to the attention of the section concerned. This is the measurement, or sensory element, of control.

The production-control function as it usually is outlined does not include all the elements in the control cycle. It does not plan production or activate a change, and probably would not initiate corrective action. This point is significant. The group measuring the performance of the system and identifying variations from the controlled condition has limited, if any, authority to institute correction. In other words, the control operates independently of the system it controls.

Quality Control

"Quality control is the function of insuring that the attributes of the product conform to prescribed standards, and that their relationships to one another are maintained." [9] It involves the maintenance of dimensions and other product characteristics within the specified plan—a responsibility which is broader than rejecting unsatisfactory parts.

A sound quality-control program can make significant savings in both direct and indirect costs. For example, effective control of the quality of raw materials can prevent defective materials from being processed. Production time which has been spent in producing or reworking defective parts now can be used to increase the quantity of production. A good product tends to build customer goodwill and increase sales volume. Moreover, most workers take pride in producing quality products, or in being associated with a company which cultivates a policy of producing high-quality goods.

Quality is always relative to other considerations: (1) to the manner in which the product will be used (e.g., a lathe might be of good quality for a home work shop but would be inadequate as a production machine); (2) to a measurable and definable characteristic (e.g., size, hardness, content, and viscosity); (3) to the economics of manufacturing (there is

---

[9] Robert B. Fetter, *Analysis for Production Management,* Richard D. Irwin, Inc., Homewood, Ill., 1957, p. 9.

a direct relationship between quality demanded and manufacturing costs); and (4) to quantity of output (the higher the quality the more difficult it becomes to achieve quantity output).

In the final analysis the quality standards for a product are established by the customer. The sales department represents the consumer's demands, and every effort is made to satisfy these demands within the limits set by engineering design and the ability to manufacture the product economically. In certain cases quality standards may even by dictated by the government, e.g., pure food and drug regulations. In one of these ways the controlled item is established.

The inspection group (the sensor element) must determine when and what number to inspect. It is seldom feasible to inspect every part after each operation; neither is it good policy to wait until the product has been completed before making an inspection. The economic balance lies somewhere between these two extremes. Usually, inspections are made on purchased materials at the time they are received, on materials in process at strategically selected points, and on finished goods ready for shipment.

The amount to inspect involves consideration of the characteristics to be controlled and the cost. The extremes can be 100 per cent, or sample inspection. Acceptance or rejection is only one phase of effective quality control. Records and charts of quality performance are kept, and these records are analyzed so that trends in product characteristics can be detected and the necessary corrections made in the production operation.

The typical quality-control group operates a more complete control cycle than production control. It has a part in determining the controlled item, measures performance, rejects faulty parts, and initiates corrective action.

Inventory Control

"The materials used in the manufacture of the products of industry as a whole amount to 50 to 55 per cent of the total cost to manufacture." [10] It is no wonder that so much attention is directed toward the control of materials. The maintenance of the optimum amounts of raw materials and finished goods is referred to as inventory control.

A company must maintain an adequate stock of proper quality materials and finished goods to ensure continuity of operation and sales. Each time a machine must be shut down for lack of materials, or each time a sale is postponed or canceled for lack of finished goods, a company loses money. However, it is important to stock materials and finished goods in the minimum quantities necessary to maintain the operation. Large

[10] Richard N. Owens, *Management of Industrial Enterprises,* Richard D. Irwin, Inc., Homewood, Ill., 1957, p. 536.

inventories are subject to deterioration and obsolescence, additional warehousing costs, and additional costs of record keeping and accounting.

The kind of materials to be used in building the product usually is determined by engineering design. Whenever a stock of materials is maintained it becomes necessary to determine the lot quantity to purchase. The quantity to purchase is dependent upon the *minimum* (the smallest quantity to be on hand at one time—the safety margin); the *maximum* (the largest quantity to be on hand—as determined by need requirements and practical storage limits); the *reorder point* (the quantity on hand when the materials are reordered—as determined by the vendor's location and reliability and the transportation time involved); and the *economic lot* to buy (the most economical order—a balance between the cost of ordering and the cost of receiving and storing).

Planning the maximum, minimum, reorder point, and the economic-lot quantity is not difficult for a single item, but when such planning is necessary for thousands of items with different characteristics, the job becomes complex. Many companies simplify this problem by grouping the various materials in classes, with a lot increment designed for each class of materials. Planning also includes the determination of methods for receiving, storing, and issuing materials and finished goods. This, in total, is the item to be controlled.

The measurement of performance is a constant job. Quantities received, stored, and issued must be checked. Any deviations from plan require review. Potential shortages are pointed out so that they may be eliminated before they interfere with production or sales. Records of inventories should also point out whether or not proper accountability of inventories is being maintained.

Inventory policies depend on many changing factors. As these factors change, the plan must be adjusted accordingly (e.g., sales increase, product specifications change, vendor's prices change, and economic conditions vary). Control suffers when a change of plan is not communicated promptly to those people who are controlling the operation. The control group finds itself using a standard which is no longer applicable—an impossible situation.

Cost Control

"Cost accounting is the process of ascertaining and interpreting the cost of manufacturing a product, of rendering a service, or of performing any function or operation in an enterprise." [11] It involves the preparation of a cost plan (standard costs), a means of measurement and comparison

[11] Lawrence L. Vance, *Theory and Technique of Cost Accounting,* The Foundation Press, Inc., Brooklyn, N.Y., 1953, p. 1.

(cost accounting), and the corrective action by management to bring costs in line with the plan.

The main objectives of cost control are to measure operating efficiency and to keep costs within a specified range. Standard costs are carefully worked out estimates of basic costs. These estimates are based largely on data of past performance. With such information it is possible to predict costs and establish prices as the controlled item.

The job of measuring performance depends on operating conditions, the size and complexity of the business, and the practices of the accounting department. It seldom is possible to make accurate distribution of costs among the many operations, nor is it practical to measure costs to an exactness where the benefits are offset by the increasing cost of the measurement.

Once the information is collected, it can be broken down into units of comparison. Such comparison should point out any variations from plan. When management action is indicated it might include (1) changing the selling price, (2) discontinuing a product, (3) revising the advertising program, or (4) instituting a campaign to motivate the workers. The action might vary from a change in major policy to a little extra administrative effort.

If it were possible to distribute costs more accurately, it would also be possible to maintain better control. Most problems arise because of the inability to plan or to measure cost performance accurately. These difficulties seem to increase in direct ratio to the number of operations and the size of the company. Further, the measurement of costs often is "after the fact" and not in time to institute corrective measures.

Military Control Systems

During the past few years the military services have created several sophisticated control systems which utilize computers in real-time applications. The computer is used as the centralized nervous system to process and analyze input information, make and communicate appropriate decisions, and develop information output in a form appropriate for human decision makers.[12]

SAGE (Semi-Automatic Ground Environment) is a control system which receives input information from a vast interconnected network of stations, processes this information against a schedule of planned air flights, and issues information to activate defense weapons if necessary. The SAGE system may be categorized relative to the four elements of control: the

[12] Donald G. Malcolm, "Exploring the Military Analogy: Real-time Management Control," in D. G. Malcolm, A. J. Rowe, and L. F. McConnell (eds.), *Management Control Systems*, John Wiley & Sons, Inc., New York, 1960, pp. 187–208.

controlled characteristic or condition is the prevention of flight over the continental United States and other parts of North America by hostile aircraft. Unauthorized flights are noted by *sensors* such as radar units or picket ships. This information is forwarded to the *control group,* where the computer processes the information. The output of the computer provides the information for the military officials, *the activing group,* to make a decision relative to the correct military action. The *operating groups,* the interceptor squadrons and missile bases, respond according to the instructions released by the activating group.

Notice that the effectiveness of this control system depends on the rapid feedback of information concerning unscheduled flights, the instant processing of information to determine the need for action, and the prompt and effective allocation of operating weapons to restrain the enemy.

SYSTEMS CONCEPTS AND CONTROL

The perfect plan could be outlined if every possible variation of input could be anticipated and the operating characteristics of the system could be predicted with accuracy. This kind of a plan would not be economical or feasible for business systems. In fact, the planning requirements (if feasible) would be so complex that the system would be out of date before it could be installed.

Instead, we engineer control into systems. This requires more thought in the systems design, but allows more flexibility of operation and makes it possible to operate a system of unknown components and undetermined inputs, with meaningful results.

The objective of the system is to perform a specified function, while the objective of control is to maintain the output which will satisfy the system requirements. The objective of control-system design, therefore, is to determine the relevant characteristics which, when controlled, maintain the function of the system within allowable variations. This is not easy to do:

> Too often, there is no one within a business that can clearly define the operation to be controlled, and usually the present data-handling system is rambling and redundant. The systems engineer must define for himself what the control system must be able to do.[13]

It is one thing to design a system containing elements of control, and quite another to make it operate true to the objectives of design. "In control" or "with plan" does not guarantee optimum performance. The plan

[13] Richard G. Canning, "Controlling a Business Process," in Byron K. Ledgerwood (ed.), *Control Engineering Manual,* McGraw-Hill Book Company, Inc., New York, 1957, p. 14.

may not make the most effective use of the inputs of materials, energy, or information, or the system may not be engineered to operate efficiently. Systems engineers look to the new sophisticated tools for processing and transferring information as one approach toward improving systems design:

> The Sage system has proven that an on-line, direct read-in-read-out, integrated computer operation is possible. This is an important technical achievement that can have significant implications in the management controls area.[14]

System breakdowns are another cause of ineffective operation. Systems designers have attempted to solve this problem by designing simplicity into the systems, adding redundant components, and building systems with greater potential than required. Eventually, control systems may be designed which repair themselves:

> What other solutions are there to automatic repair except redundancy? This is an area which is begging for research. . . . The problem is threefold: first, there must be means for detecting failure; next, a knowledge of what is needed to complete the repair; and lastly, the equipment required to do so.[15]

The ultimate goal of the systems designer is to create control elements which compensate for environmental changes and still maintain the system in operation regardless of excessive variations in input. The principles of design will be presented in Chapter 13.

Feedback control determines how automated a system can become. For example, when a system is designed as an open-sequence system, human intervention is required to maintain the system "in control." The control is outside of the operating system. When the control system becomes a part of the system it controls, we have a closed-loop system capable of performing the objectives of the system without human intervention. Feedback control, therefore, has added a new dimension to the capabilities of machines to simulate and replace the human nervous system.

SUMMARY

There are four elements of every control system: (1) the controlled item; (2) the sensory device, or method of measurement; (3) a control group, unit, or equipment for comparing measured data with planned performance and directing corrective information; and (4) the activating group or mechanism which is capable of bringing about a needed change.

[14] Malcolm, *op. cit.*, p. 205.
[15] "Automatic Repair with Manipulators," *Automatic Control*, August, 1960, p. 29.

A small amount of energy can trigger corrective information and release vast amounts of input, and this can be accomplished at great distances from the operating system.

Systems may be open-sequence: where one or more of the elements of control is not an integrated part of the system it controls. Systems may be closed-loop: where the elements of control are integrated into the operating system.

Information is the medium of control; it is the flow of measurement information and later the flow of corrective information which allows an item to be controlled. This information should be in a language common to the plan, accurately measured and transmitted to the control group for comparison, and processed rapidly. It is possible to control any situation (1) if it is possible to measure and compare the performance situation with a standard, (2) if the required changes can be activated, and (3) if both the measurement and the regulation are rapid enough to make a correction before the factors of the situation have become inconsistent with the correction.

Systems can be created with features of good control. However, the system must be capable of accomplishing the objective of control, i.e., to maintain the output which will satisfy the system requirements.

Chapter Five

COMMUNICATION AND SYSTEMS CONCEPTS

Communication plays an integral role in the managerial functions of planning, organizing, and controlling. It is a key ingredient which allows organizations to function as open systems, including some degree of feedback control. It involves information flow, a vital element in managerial decision making. Much attention has been focused on person-to-person, individual-to-group, group-to-individual, and group-to-group communication. In short, the term means many things to many people.

While there are many avenues which could be explored under the heading "communication," our concern in this chapter will be the broad (or macro) aspects of communication in business and industry. We shall investigate communication systems (or, as we prefer, systems of information flow) in organizations. Also, we shall discuss the integration of the communication system and decision making via an information-decision system. The following topics will be covered:

Terminology
Communication Systems
Communication Problems
Communication and Organization
Communication, Organization, and Decision Making
Information-decision Systems

Before proceeding into the main discourse on these concepts it will be helpful to discuss the terminology surrounding the communication process. The purpose will not be to develop a composite definition. Rather, it will be to place the various terms in proper perspective and provide a basis for subsequent discussion.

TERMINOLOGY

Numerous definitions (or connotations) of the term communication have been set forth according to the purpose of various writers or researchers. For example:

> *Communication* comes from the Latin *communis,* common. When we communicate we are trying to establish a "commonness" with someone. That is, we are trying to share information, an idea, or an attitude. . . . The essence of communication is getting the receiver and the sender "tuned" together for a particular message.[1]

An Air Force pamphlet states:

> In its broadest sense the term "communication" refers to the whole process of man's life in relation to the group. It covers a vast and varied field of human action. All the basic social institutions—numbers, language, music, graphic art, science, religion, government—have the function of creating a community of thought, feeling, or action among people. The word "communication" is therefore merely one way of designating the subject matter of education. Language, however, is the chief means of communication.[2]

Communication is intercourse by words, letters, or similar means, and it involves interchange of thoughts or opinions. It also presents the concept of communication systems, for example, telephone, telegraph, or television. Communication implies information; the terms are part of the same family.

Information

In the broadest sense information has been defined as "that which is communicated." Information is the communication of knowledge or intelligence. Another common definition of information is a "patterned relationship between events." As such, information takes on many forms. For example:

> Information is what is transferred in telephony or television: it is not events as such, but a patterned relationship between events. Information

[1] Wilbur Schramm, *The Process and Effects of Mass Communication,* University of Illinois Press, Urbana, Ill., 1954, p. 3.

[2] *Communications Techniques,* Air University, USAF Extension Course Institute, 1954, p. 3.

has physical, "material" reality: without exception, it is carried by matter-energy processes. Yet it is not subject to their conservation laws: it can be created and wiped out, although it cannot be created from nothing nor destroyed completely into nothingness. Finally, it differs from the classical notion of "form" in that it can be analyzed into discrete units which can be measured and counted.[3]

Information is the substance of communication systems. In its various forms—electronic impulses, written or spoken words, informal or formal reports—information provides a basic ingredient for decision making. The concept of information for decision making will be developed in more detail later in this chapter.

Information Theory

The science of information theory, or the mathematical theory of communications, has been described as a powerful tool for studying various systems. The foundations of information theory are generally attributed to Claude Shannon.[4]

By invoking certain basic assumptions (ignoring semantics or meaning) a simplified set of mathematical relationships was developed which is useful primarily in the technical aspects of information transmission.

Information theory is used as a tool in determining the rate at which information can be transmitted under certain specified circumstances. Some of the factors affecting transmission might be the nature of the signal source, whether the signal is discrete or continuous; the nature of the channel and, in particular, its capacity for transmitting information; the nature of the noise, if any, which perturbs the transmission; and the fidelity criterion by which the adequacy of the transmission is judged.[5]

Information theory, in the sense employed by Shannon, Weaver, and others, has a much narrower concept than might be connoted by the term. For example, if we assume that a theory (according to the dictionary definition) is a body of theorems presenting a clear, rounded, and systematic view of a subject, and further, if we assume that information is "that which is communicated," then information theory would necessarily be an extremely broad subject. Although a wide range of applications are claimed for information theory, most of these are in the technical aspects of transmission. Some of the subdisciplines claimed are filtering theory,

---

[3] Karl W. Deutsch, "Mechanism, Teleology, and Mind," *Philosophy and Phenomenological Research,* December, 1951, pp. 196–197.

[4] Claude Shannon and Warren Weaver, *The Mathematical Theory of Communication,* University of Illinois Press, Urbana, Ill., 1949.

[5] Harry H. Goode and Robert E. Machol, *System Engineering,* McGraw-Hill Book Company, Inc., New York, 1957, p. 428.

detection theory, and the analysis of signal statistics. Information theory is cited as an integral part of such areas as the theory of communication, the theory of automata, the theory of automatic control systems, the analysis of languages, and informational aspects of physics. There are fields where information theory is cited as operative and unifying, e.g., thermodynamics, statistical mechanics, photography, language, models, gambling, cryptology, pattern recognition, and computer technology.

One author divides information theory into three principal areas: communication systems, mathematical theory (a branch of probability theory and statistics), and various considerations of entropy and uncertainty applied to physical and biological systems. He goes on to say:

> The one thing information theory does not pertain to is "information"! The sense in which the term is used in the theory is quite arbitrary in that it has almost no relation to the term as popularly understood.[6]

For our purpose the concept of communication systems or information flow must be broader than that represented by information theory in its technical sense. Therefore we shall try to avoid the terminology used in information theory, or at least broaden the connotation as needed.

Information Technology

Another concept that has developed in the general area of communication is information technology. Technology is defined as applied industrial science or as systematic knowledge of the industrial arts. When applied to the broad connotation of information—that which is communicated—information technology would seem to cover a wide spectrum. An even broader connotation for this phrase is indicated by several authors. For example, Whisler and Shultz state:

> Within the last decade we have seen rapid and extensive progress in the application of quantitative techniques to the analysis of management problems. Three areas of activity are involved: (1) the use of mathematical and statistical methods, with or without the aid of electronic computers; (2) the use of computers for mass integrated data processing; and (3) the direct application of computers to decision-making through simulation techniques. These areas are clearly interdependent, although the nature and the degree of interdependence are still undergoing exploration. We will lump these areas together here under the heading "information technology," a phrase used by one of the authors in an earlier paper.[7]

[6] Robert C. Hopkins, "Possible Applications of Information Theory to Management Control," *IRE Transactions on Engineering Management,* March, 1961, p. 41.

[7] George P. Shultz and Thomas L. Whisler (eds.), *Management Organization and the Computer,* Free Press, Glencoe, Ill., 1960, p. 3.

Without question, problems of information flow or communication are of vital concern in each of the three areas outlined above. If management decision making is viewed as the focal point in the application of quantitative techniques of analysis, then information flow becomes an integral part of the total system. However, many additional factors are involved in the question of management decision making; therefore the use of the phrase "information technology" to encompass the entire field is misleading.

Systems of Information Flow

Information flow is one of the several integral systems in a business or industrial organization. And the systems concept is the over-all framework within which communication or information flow logically fits. Furthermore, we visualize the systems concept as a vital aspect of the entire managerial process, including planning, organizing, and controlling. Communication systems, or systems of information flow, will be presented as the vehicle through which the key management functions can be integrated and administered.

COMMUNICATION SYSTEMS

In their early writings on information theory Shannon and Weaver presented a basic symbolic representation of a communication system as

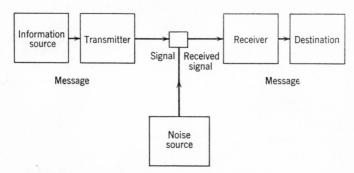

Fig. 4. Symbolic representation of a communication system. Source: Claude E. Shannon and Warren Weaver, *The Mathematical Theory of Communication,* University of Illinois Press, Urbana, Ill., 1949, p. 98.

shown in Figure 4. This basic model has been adapted by other writers since that time by changing some of the terminology or by making the model more elaborate. In all cases there is an information source which provides the raw material for a message which is to be transmitted to a destination. The general model includes a transmitter and a receiver, with the receiver connected directly to the destination. Also involved is the concept of a noise source which theoretically interferes (to some degree) with information flow between the transmitter and receiver. With a larger system, noise or interference obviously could come at numerous junctures within the subsystems. Regardless of the size or sophistication of the system, communication always requires three basic elements—the source, the message, and the destination. Noise transmission and reception are elements which also can be considered in the basic model. Yet these items can take on so many forms that it is useful to think of an even more abstract model of source, message, and destination. Some writers substitute the words encoder and decoder for transmitter and receiver in order to depict a more general process.

Everyday examples of communication systems can be abstracted in terms of the model shown in Figure 4. The usefulness of such an approach is explained by Schramm as follows:

> Now it is perfectly possible by looking at those diagrams to predict how such a system will work. For one thing, such a system can be no stronger than its weakest link. In engineering terms, there may be filtering or distortion at any state. In human terms, if the source does not have adequate or clear information; if the message is not encoded fully, accurately, effectively in transmittible signs; if these are not transmitted fast enough and accurately enough, despite interference and competition, to the desired receiver; if the message is not decoded in a pattern that corresponds to the encoding; and finally, if the destination is unable to handle the decoded message so as to produce the desired response—then, obviously, the system is working at less than top efficiency. When we realize that *all* these steps must be accomplished with relatively high efficiency if any communication is to be successful, the everyday act of explaining something to a stranger or writing a letter, seems a minor miracle.[8]

By checking day-to-day experiences in either face-to-face communication or organizational communication it is easy to find instances where *all* the steps indicated above are not in effect, and hence where a communication system is not working optimally. Visualizing the complexities involved in modern organizations, it is not to be expected that such conditions can be developed for all communication processes. However, these conditions can provide goals which can be used as a frame of reference in designing and implementing systems of information flow.

Communication Apparatus

Three types of communication have been set forth which involve human beings: (1) intrapersonal, (2) interpersonal, and (3) mass communication. In addition, there are examples of man-machine or even

[8] Schramm, *op. cit.*, pp. 4–5.

machine-machine communication systems. Ruesch and Bateson describe the communication apparatus of man as follows:

(a) His sense organs, the receivers
(b) His effector organs, the senders
(c) His communication center, the place or origin and destination of all messages
(d) The remaining parts of the body, the shelter of the communication machinery [9]

This model can be integrated with the general symbolic representation of a communication system by physically locating information source and destination in contiguous positions. Furthermore, phase d of the above listing could be broadened to include organizations and institutions of varying size and complexity, or it could involve an entire society in the case of mass communication. Thus the various types of communication can be depicted by the basic model set forth above.

Man uses his communication system:

(a) To receive and transmit messages and retain information
(b) To perform operations with the existing information for the purpose of deriving new conclusions which were not directly perceived and for reconstructing past and anticipating future events
(c) To initiate and modify physiological processes within his body
(d) To influence and direct other people and external events [10]

Human beings are involved in communication systems of various sizes and degrees of complexity. They are involved in their intrapersonal communication system, which is a part of their own physiological and mental processes. They are involved in interpersonal systems when communicating to one or more people. In the area of mass communication the individual can participate to varying degrees, depending on the particular issues and his involvement.

The same hierarchy can be built up for one machine communicating with itself in the sense of automation or feedback control; a machine controlling a group of machines (numerical-control applications); or more complex man-machine systems of communication and control. In all cases, the concept of systems being developed as over-all frameworks for subsystems can apply. All the various levels and types of communication indicated can be analyzed or developed in their own context, and yet each must be considered in terms of its relationship to a whole. Thus over-all systems concepts should be recognized when analyzing communication

[9] Jurgen Ruesch and Gregory Bateson, *Communication*, W. W. Norton & Co., New York, 1951, pp. 16–17.
[10] *Ibid.*, pp. 17–18.

in general, and the same principles apply when considering detailed aspects of systems or subsystems.

COMMUNICATION PROBLEMS

There are three levels of communication problems:

Level A. How accurately can the symbols of communication be transmitted? (The technical problem.)

Level B. How precisely do the transmitted symbols convey the desired meaning? (The semantic problem.)

Level C. How effectively does the perceived meaning affect the conduct in the desired way? (The effectiveness problem.) [11]

The narrow applicability of information theory (to technical aspects of transmission) was mentioned previously in the discussion of terminology. Communication systems for management decision making must be concerned with semantics and effectiveness. In fact, all problems must be considered; semantics and effectiveness would certainly be affected if technical aspects could not be solved. Progress in technology makes it feasible to consider problems of meaning and content.

The question of semantics in communication is one which has been long recognized, receiving considerable attention from researchers and writers.[12] While such questions obviously are important from a standpoint of information flow and decision making, they are not central to our discussion, namely, systems concepts as a frame of reference for carrying out managerial functions.

Similarly, questions on the interaction level or questions of evaluation of the effectiveness of information transmission have received some attention. For example, the central theme in the whole field of cybernetics is that of communication and control.

In giving the definition of Cybernetics in the original book, I class communication and control together. Why did I do this? When I communicate with another person, I impart a message to him, and when he communicates back with me he returns a related message which contains information primarily accessible to him and not to me. When I control the actions of another person, I communicate a message to him, and although this message is in the imperative mood, the technique of communication does not differ from that of a message of fact. Furthermore, if my control is to be effective I must take cognizance of any messages from him which may indicate that the order is understood and has been obeyed.[13]

[11] Shannon and Weaver, *op. cit.*, p. 96.

[12] S. I. Hayakawa, *Language in Thought and Action,* Harcourt, Brace and Company, Inc., New York, 1949.

[13] Norbert Wiener, *The Human Use of Human Beings,* Houghton Mifflin Company, Boston, 1954, p. 16.

In this sense, unless there is effective control, the communication process has not been complete. It is evident that there are several large problem areas in the general theory of communciation systems. Yet communication is a vital element in everyday existence. For our purpose, we are concerned primarily with its role in group activity, specifically the business or industrial enterprise. Therefore let us consider the relationship between communication systems and organizations.

COMMUNICATION AND ORGANIZATION

Communication has been receiving more and more attention as a critical aspect on the industrial scene. Management has long been concerned with "getting its message across" to the workers, that is, communicating downward throughout the organization. In terms of the problem areas cited previously, management often is concerned with its lack of effectiveness in the communication process and may not be entirely familiar with the semantic problems involved. In other cases, in industrial organizations, management is concerned with upward communications, that is, soliciting the attitudes and feelings of the lower echelons and encouraging their transmission upward through the hierarchical structure. In addition, management is interested in communicating its message outward to other institutions in the form of public-relations efforts beamed at customers, stockholders, and the general public.

Organization structure definitely is tied to communication systems. Whether it is the formal organization structure and the formal channels and types of media, or whether it is informal organization structures and informal types of communication systems or information flow, the relationships are evident. However, a direct relationship is not apparent; that is, communmication does not necessarily follow stated organizational arrangements, or vice versa. Numerous overlaps and gaps are evident in most organizations, phenomena which cause problems. Deutsch explains these relationships in the following manner:

> Communication and control are the decisive processes in organizations. Communication is what makes organizations cohere; control is what regulates their behavior. If we can map the pathways by which communication is communicated between different parts of an organization and by which it is applied to the behavior of the organization in relation to the outside world, we will have gone far toward understanding that organization. . . .
>
> Generally speaking, the communications approach suggests lines of attack in the study of organizations. First, instead of concentrating on the ostensible purpose of the organization, it will concentrate on two ques-

tions: how are the formal and informal communications channels of the organization connected, and how are they maintained? [14]

These suggestions for research indicate that organization structures might follow the development of communication systems rather than vice versa. For many organizations, communication systems have been designed to follow organizational lines without recognition of the fact that this may not provide for optimal flows of information for decision making. This concept of organizing and communicating for decision making will be explored in more detail in the next section.

Some of the problems in communication systems for decision making have resulted from changes in organizational relationships in recent years. Companies have been faced with dynamic world conditions, rapidly changing technology, changing markets, and other similar phenomena which have required adaptation on their part. Such adaptations have been made, but without recognition, in many cases, of the impact of the organizational changes on communication systems. Thus much information that was appropriate under older arrangements now has become obsolete. Furthermore, additional types of information are urgently needed in order to plan and control current operations. According to Daniel:

> Unfortunately, management often loses sight of the seemingly obvious and simple relationship between organization structure and information needs. Companies very seldom follow up on reorganizations with penetrating reappraisals of their information systems, and managers given new responsibilities and decision-making authority often do not receive all the information they require.[15]

Granting that organization structure and communication systems are inextricably intertwined, there remains the problem of which comes first. Although this problem does not seem important from the standpoint of research or analysis, it becomes increasingly significant as one attempts to design either an organization or a communication system. This question will be considered in more detail in Chapter 13, Systems Design (implementing the systems concept). At this point, however, it will be helpful to bring the subject of decision making into the discussion.

COMMUNICATION, ORGANIZATION, AND DECISION MAKING

In this section several points of view will be presented concerning the interrelationships of these three topics. There are scholars and writers who

[14] Karl W. Deutsch, "On Communication Models in the Social Sciences," *Public Opinion Quarterly,* Fall, 1952, pp. 367–368.

[15] D. Ronald Daniel, "Management Information Crisis," *Harvard Business Review,* September–October, 1961, pp. 112–113.

view organization as the fundamental element for consideration; others who look upon decision making as the key activity to analyze; and still others who would point to the communication system as the underlying framework. We hold no brief for any particular point of view; rather, we are interested in integrating the various ideas by means of the concept of information-decision systems.

Pfiffner and Sherwood describe the relationship between decision making and communication systems as follows:

> The relationship between the communications system and decision-making is extremely important. If decision-making and communication processes are not identical, they are so interdependent they become inseparable in practice. As a result all studies of communication inevitably involve decision-making.[16]

As indicated in Chapter 3, there have been several relatively distinct approaches to the study of organizations: (1) the traditional view, characterized by emphasis on some logical arrangement for dividing the work, hierarchical structure, and specialization; (2) the behavioral view, developing the concept of cooperative relationships, participation, and informal organization; (3) the decision-making view, focusing on the study of an organization as a decision-making unit; and (4) the systems view, the integration of subsystems into an operational whole. The decision-making system (or organization) would include information, objectives, strategies, alternatives, probabilities, and consequences. The function of the organization would be to facilitate the flow of information and the making of appropriate decisions. In this view, the communication system appears paramount, with organization structured around it as a frame of reference. In turn, the communication system is considered primarily as a supplier of information for decisions. More and more attention has been devoted to organizations as decision-making units. In a pioneering work in this area Simon states:

> The anatomy of the organization is to be found in the distribution and allocation of decision-making functions. The physiology of the organization is to be found in the processes whereby the organization influences the decisions of each of its members—supplying these decisions with their premises.[17]

If organizations are complex networks of decision processes, there must be decision points throughout, ranging from individuals at the lowest

---

[16] John M. Pfiffner and Frank P. Sherwood, *Administrative Organization,* Prentice-Hall, Inc., Englewood Cliffs, N.J., 1960, p. 308.

[17] Herbert A. Simon, *Administrative Behavior,* The Macmillan Company, New York, 1959, p. 220.

levels to boards of directors at the top. The primary aspect of the physiology of the organization is the communication system, which supplies premises for decisions at various points in the organization; that is, each decision point can be considered an information-processing unit with input, processing, and output. Such an arrangement fits the formal, symbolic representation of the communication system shown in Figure 4. Thus the decision process can be considered an extension of the communication process; it can be a relatively simple intrapersonal communication or decision system or range through interpersonal communication or decision systems of varying size and complexity. This connection between decisions and communications is stressed by Dorsey as follows:

> Thus decision may be conceived of as a communication process, or a series of interrelated communication events. A decision occurs upon the receipt of some kind of communication, it consists of a complicated process of combining communications from various sources, and it results in the transmission of further communication.[18]

This analogy to the intrapersonal communication or decision process can be expanded to the interpersonal decision-making situation.

A manager decides issues based on the current information received in conjunction with previously developed strategies, procedures, or rules. Depending on the level in the organization and/or the type of decision (programmed or unprogrammed), the decision maker has several alternatives. If the matter is fairly commonplace and routine, he can dismiss it quickly, particularly if there are rules or procedures covering the situation. If the matter at issue is more complex, more of an unprogrammed nature, the decision maker may require additional inputs and may request some consultation on the part of subordinates, superiors, or peers. In any case, the communication process is obviously important and the flow of proper information to the decision points throughout the organization appears vital. If administration or management were thought of primarily as decision making and if the decision process were considered as essentially a communication process, including a network of communication systems, then administration or management could be viewed as a communication process. According to Dorsey:

> Structurally, administration can be viewed as a configuration of communication patterns relating individuals and collectivities of varying sizes, shapes, and degree of cohesion and stability. Dynamically, administration appears as a patterned swirl and flow of communications, many of them

[18] John T. Dorsey, Jr., "A Communication Model for Administration," *Administrative Science Quarterly,* December, 1957, p. 309.

channeled through transactional "circuits" between persons and persons, persons and groups, and groups and other groups.[19]

For our purposes, concepts of communication patterns and flows are particularly important. The patterns relate communication to organization, and the flow concept relates to decision making. Thus the several concepts —communications, organization, and decision making—are inexorably interwoven.

INFORMATION-DECISION SYSTEMS

The concept of information flow is central to the development of systems concepts and communication. Since a system by definition requires interrelationship among parts to constitute a composite whole, a system of information flow would necessarily provide information throughout various subsystems and would entail some feedback mechanism in order to represent a closed-loop system. A simplified system is represented by Figure 5,

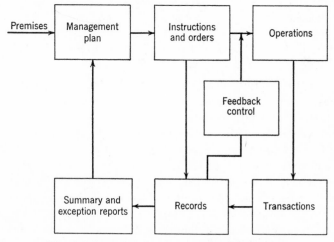

Fig. 5. Information flow in a business organization.

an elementary model of a business enterprise showing the flow of information necessary to accomplish the programmed tasks.

The term *information-decision system* is used to emphasize the fact that information developed should be requested in light of the decisions to be made throughout the organization. Thus an information-decision system should be designed as a communication process relating the necessary inputs to the stored information and the desired decisional outputs. It is likely that decisions at a given stage in the organization represent

[19] *Ibid.*, p. 310.

output from one communication process and information for a subsequent decision at the same level, a lower level, or a higher level. The over-all information flow must be regarded as a system with many interdependent elements and subsystems.

Information-decision systems should be considered in conjunction with the fundamental managerial functions: planning, organizing, and controlling. If organization is to implement planning and control, if organization is tied inextricably to communication, and if communication is represented by an information-decision system, then the key to success in planning and controlling any operation lies in the information-decision system. Its importance cannot be overemphasized.

In his discussion of the management information crisis caused by too rapid organizational change, Daniel states:

> The key to the development of a dynamic and usable system of management information is to move beyond the limits of classical accounting reports and to conceive of information as it relates to two vital elements of the management process—planning and control. . . . We hear more and more these days about new techniques for inventory, cost, and other types of control, but information systems for business planning still represent a relatively unexplored horizon.[20]

He goes on to describe several kinds of information required for planning: environmental information, competitive information, and internal information. While most companies have some systematic approach to development of internal information for planning purposes, few have formal systems for developing information concerning competitor's plans, programs, and past performance. Nor do they deal in a systematic fashion with the social, political, and economic environment of the industry or industries within which they operate. Formal recognition of the decisions which must be made at various points and of the type of information required to do an optimal job in that decision process should point the way toward development of information flows which will be helpful.

Differences in the type of information needed for planning, on the one hand, and control, on the other, should be recognized. The contrast can be seen in terms of the following attributes of information:

> 1. *Coverage*—good planning information is not compartmentalized by functions. Indeed, it seeks to transcend the divisions that exist in a company and to provide the basis on which *integrated* plans can be made. In contrast, control information hews closely to organizational lines so that it can be used to measure performance and help in holding specific managers more accountable.

[20] Daniel, *op. cit.,* p. 113.

2. *Length of time*—planning information covers fairly long periods of time—months and years rather than days and weeks—and deals with trends. Thus, although it should be regularly prepared, it is not developed as frequently as control information.

3. *Degree of detail*—excessive detail is the quicksand of intelligent planning. Unlike control, where precision and minute care do have a place, planning (and particularly long-range planning) focuses on the major outlines of the situation ahead.

4. *Orientation*—planning information should provide insights into the future. Control information shows past results and the reasons for them.[21]

This emphasis on the differences between information appropriate for planning purposes and that appropriate for control purposes indicates the importance of carefully designing information-decision systems. Blind adherence to organizational patterns for the flow of information will often hamper the development of an optimal system. Particularly where there have been organizational adjustments and there is a mixture of functional organization and program or product organization, the development of an information-decision system becomes critical. Key decision points must be identified and the concept of flows of material and information must be kept paramount when designing over-all systems of information flow. In such systems, the planning function can be carried out with the necessary information and premises, the organization can be adjusted to reflect the decision-making activities involved, and control information can be readily developed along appropriate lines.

SUMMARY

Throughout history the transmission of information has been a key to progress. Efficient communication is important in all fields of human endeavor. However, as society has become more complex, as technology has increased at an accelerating rate, and in spite of improvements in communication media, it is becoming more and more difficult to communicate effectively. The growth of organizations and increased specialization and functionalization have developed barriers to communication in many spheres of activity. Scientists and researchers find it more and more difficult to communicate on a broad scope. Managers of business and industrial organizations find communication an increasing problem in their day-to-day operations.

On the other hand, technical breakthroughs in data-processing equipment have provided an opportunity for development of integrated systems of information flow. In spite of this opportunity, however, few organizations have really capitalized on it. In order to do so, management must be cog-

[21] *Ibid.*, pp. 117–118.

nizant of the role of communication in the primary managerial activities: planning, organizing, and controlling.

Information-decision systems can be developed which provide the proper flow of information among decision points in the organization. The organization can then be structured around such systems of information flow. Both formal and informal communication must be recognized. Management might well analyze informal communication patterns in some detail because the information-decision system may follow "natural" patterns or systems, even though they are not recognized in the formal organization structure. Once the over-all information-decision system has been established, the functions of planning and control are greatly facilitated.

Systems concepts are vital to the establishment of communication or information flow. Over-all systems are comprised of subsystems of communication processes which are represented as flows of information through a decision process. A hierarchy of such processes can be established and fitted to the framework of an over-all, integrated, information-decision system.

Chapter Six

INTEGRATION OF
SYSTEMS CONCEPTS

In the preceding chapters we have reviewed the concepts of planning, organization, control, and communication as they apply to systems. In this chapter we integrate these functions into the *systems concept,* a concept which is structured to serve a dynamic situation, identify responsibilities and effectiveness, discourage empire building, and adjust activities as situations change.

The only thing certain about the future is change. Few business firms can expect to survive and grow without a comprehensive plan to cope with the dynamic nature of the society they serve. The philosophy of management by system is developed through the following topic areas:

Systems Theory and Management
Principle of Integration
Systems Defined
A Model of the Systems Concept
The Systems Concept and Management Functions
Characteristics of Effective Systems

SYSTEMS THEORY AND MANAGEMENT

During the past few years there have been several new approaches toward improving the management of business firms, e.g., organization theory, decision theory, planning theory, and the behavioral theory of the firm. Each of these philosophies has helped to sharpen management skills; however, there is still a need for an operative theory of management—a theory which will provide a conceptual framework for better business design and operation.

The need for an integrative philosophy of management has been dramatized by the recent increase in world-wide competition in the market and by the increasing complexity of operating the typical business firm. Further, the conflict between specialists and generalists has not been resolved, i.e., the paradox of requiring more skills in special areas in contrast to the more general and integrative knowledge needed to manage. Moreover, the choice between centralization or decentralization of activities swings back and forth like a pendulum.

The management of a business firm can solve many of its problems and improve its operating efficiency by adopting the systems concept and operating the business as a system. The theory of systems is not new, for much of it has been developed and used in the natural sciences for many years. Further, it is being used to some degree in business. For example, systems theory is used in administering certain military programs where specification and time requirements are critical, and in some single-venture programs, e.g., construction projects. There is no reason, however, why this concept is not equally applicable to an appliance manufacturer, a retail department store, or a bank.

The systems concept is not a substitute for progressive management; rather, it depends on such leadership. It provides the opportunity for ambitious and creative managers to prove themselves. First, management decides on a specific job to be accomplished, the facilities and manpower are supplied, and technical assistance is provided to help design the system. The management of the project must take complete responsibility, however, for designing the system, planning the operating strategy, and redesigning as conditions change. The success or failure of the operation is dependent upon the management.

Systems theory is analogous to the principle of integrating parts within a whole. Therefore the principle of integration is vital in the systems concept.

PRINCIPLE OF INTEGRATION

The best way to view the business system is by describing the flow process, analyzing each segment, and investigating the relationships and contributions of the parts to the whole. In this way it is possible to direct attention and study to those segments which fail to optimize their contribution to the total system.

Integration means to make whole or complete; to bring parts together into a whole. The *vitalist* theory of deduction or philosophical reasoning proposes the following points:

1. The whole is primary and the parts are secondary.

2. Integration is the condition of the interrelatedness of the many parts within one.

3. The parts so constitute an indissoluble whole that no part can be affected without affecting all other parts.

4. Parts play their role in light of the purpose for which the whole exists.

5. The nature of the part and its function is derived from its position in the whole and its behavior is regulated by the whole to part relationship.

6. The whole is any system or complex or configuration of energy and behaves like a single piece no matter who complex.

7. Everything should start with the whole as a premise and the parts and their relationships should evolve.[1]

The whole renews itself constantly through a transposition process; the identity of the whole and its unity is preserved, but the parts change. This process continues endlessly; sometimes it is planned and observed, while at others it occurs without notice; often it is encouraged, but other times it is resisted.

A business firm is an integrated whole where each system, subsystem, and supporting subsystem is associated with the total operation. Its structure, therefore, is created by hundreds of systems arranged in hierarchical order. The output of the smallest system becomes input for the next larger system, which in turn furnishes input for a higher level.

SYSTEMS DEFINED

A system will be defined as *an array of components designed to accomplish a particular objective according to plan.* There are three significant points in this definition. First, there must be a *purpose,* or *objective,* which the system is designed to perform. Second, there must be design, or an *established* arrangement of the components. Finally, inputs of information, energy, and materials must be allocated according to *plan.*

Leaver classifies the basic ingredients of a manufacturing process (information, energy, and materials) as they relate to the operation or to the output (product).

1. "Information" is used in the broad sense to mean shape, pattern, or arrangement (static) or instructions (dynamic). It cannot exist in the prac-

[1] L. Thomas Hopkins, *Integration: Its Meaning and Application,* Appleton-Century-Crofts, Inc., New York, 1937, pp. 36–49.

tical sense unless it is associated with either energy or materials. Information associated with differences between product and raw material in form, structure, or state may be called "product" information in contrast to that associated with the structure or state of the manufacturing equipment used to make the product or with instructions to the manufacturing elements, which may be called "operational" information in that it determines the actual operations on the product. If the product reacts to this information in a linear way, the product information can be a linear function of the operational information. Otherwise, one will be a resultant of the other but not have one-to-one correspondence, as the characteristics of the workpiece itself will contribute to the final product form. (In molding, for example, some materials will shrink, so that finished form does not correspond exactly to the mold.)

2. Energy is used for the movement of the workpiece, tool, and assembly devices; heat, etc., used in the fabricational process. In most factories, energy is generally all "operational." The product rarely contains stored useful energy (product energy) as a result of the manufacturing process. An interesting exception is compressed-gas plants, where such substances as carbon dioxide may contain a considerable amount of stored energy.

3. Materials are both "operational" and "product." Operational materials are those embodied in the machines and plant, while product materials are those converted into useful output by the action of the operational information, energy, and material on the raw-material input.[2]

These same ingredients are basic to every system, manufacturing or any other. However, the emphasis in the systems concept differs slightly. Information, energy, and materials are classified in terms of whether they are used (1) to create the system or (2) to operate the system.

A basic system is illustrated in Figure 6. It consists of input, according to plan; a processor for converting inputs into goods or services; and output, the measurable achievement of the system.

Design and Operation

First, a system must be designed; that is, components must be arranged in some combination to produce a desired goal. For example, a system designed to prepare invoices for mailing would include billing machines and operators. These components would be arranged in a planned order to provide optimum utilization. Notice that it requires information to determine the exact and proper way to accomplish the objectives (design and procedures); materials in the form of machines; and energy, in terms of the time spent designing the system.

After the system has been designed it is ready to operate. There will

[2] Eric W. Leaver, "How Automatic Can We Get?" in *Keeping Pace with Automation,* American Management Association, Special Report 7, pp. 1–2, 1956.

be inputs of information (e.g., customer data, quantities, prices, discounts, and delivery dates); inputs of materials (e.g., invoice forms and machine ribbons); and inputs of energy (energy exerted by the workers and the electrical energy supplied for the machines).

The operating inputs are allocated according to a plan. For example, a supervisor may determine which kind of invoice to use, when various customers should be billed, when the operators should work overtime, and when the machines should be repaired.

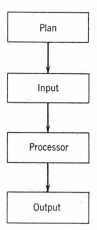

Fig. 6. The design of a basic system.

It is possible to eliminate parts of the planning required during operations by designing systems with predetermined input allocations, structuring the system to operate in a specified fashion and with more predictable results. The more the operation of the system is preplanned, the more automatic it becomes. There always are two stages of planning: first relative to the design and then to the operation of the system.

Systems and Procedures

Often systems and procedures are considered to be the same because the two terms are so closely related. However, procedures are only an information resource related to systems design. In order to implement a system, detailed instructions must be prepared delineating duties, responsibilities, and operating instructions. This implementation is accomplished by the procedure—the formal instruction for implementing the system.

The procedure (or method) tells how to do the job, what processes to use, and other general information about the job. The procedure is task-oriented; it normally is written as a formal document segmenting the tasks to be performed. The primary purpose of the procedure is instructional in nature. It is not designed or intended to represent job flow except with the task covered. It is not expected that the procedure will relate the task at hand with those preceding or following.

Systems with Control

Basic to the theory of systems is the premise that given certain inputs, the processor will give certain outputs or operate within established limits. However, the business firm, as a whole, is not a structured or predictable system. Its equilibrium cannot be determined by equation, and it will change, within limits, as the components of the system are rearranged or as the inputs are reallocated.

In more advanced form, a system will include some means of control, i.e., a sensor for measuring output or related characteristics, a means of comparing the measurement with a standard, and an activating group to adjust inputs to correct the indicated deficiencies. The objective is to control variables so the system will tend to stabilize near the ideal equilibrium point. This objective is possible only if the ideal standard can be determined and if the operating values can be measured. A complete system, including control, is illustrated in Figure 7.

Figure 7 illustrates the flow of planning information as it releases resources of materials, energy, and processing information. A record of the plan is stored where it can be used as a standard for control purposes. The resources are released by an activating group. For example, detailed schedules are planned (processing information), workers are assigned to specific tasks (energy), and the necessary raw materials or purchased parts are provided (materials). The combination of these inputs into the system results in the performance of a task (processing), and output is produced.

Sensory devices are placed at strategic points in the system flow to measure performance or output. These measurements are fed back to a control group, and this information is compared with the standard. As significant deviations from plan are recognized, information to correct the situation is released to the activating group, which in turn will change the release of resources of information, energy, or materials.

If this diagram represented a system used by an insurance company to pay accident claims, the system could be outlined as follows:

1. The system may be designed to make sure valid claims are paid *promptly* and *accurately* (objective).

2. The policy concerning the kind of protection and payment schedule would be planned (planning information).

3. Claims would be received (processing information) and filed (information storage).

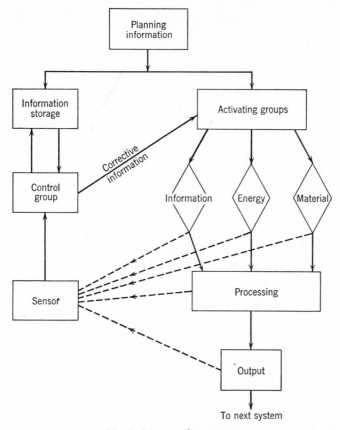

Fig. 7. An operating system.

4. Workers would be assigned to process the claims. Heat, light, and power would be used in the office area (energy).

5. Claims blanks, typewriter ribbons, etc., would be used (materials).

6. The claims would be reviewed and paid (processing).

7. Claim payments would be measured against the time in process and against the standards or criteria for judging correct payment (control).

The resources of the system must be allocated in a manner which will provide the maximum utility to the concern. Each input is variable, and in addition, the operating characteristics of certain components of the system may vary. The greatest amount of variation among components is likely to be found in the behavior pattern of individuals; therefore, if human behavior can be predicted, variations between plan and operations can be reduced considerably. In any ongoing process, where actions taken in one area relate to and depend upon actions taken in another area, it is likely that a smoother and more efficient operation can be provided when these actions are repetitive. Activities can be routinized to the extent that the choice can be simplified or eliminated. As the degree of repetitiveness decreases, the less likely, or the more difficult it becomes, to have an efficient operation. The activities which are not repetitive will vary in relation to their frequency of occurrence. The more infrequent they become, the less possibility there is that they can be controlled within the finite limits of the operation.

A MODEL OF THE SYSTEMS CONCEPT

Traditionally, business firms have not been structured to utilize the systems concept. In adjusting the typical business structure to fit within the framework of management by system, certain organizational changes will be required. The best way to describe these changes is to illustrate by means of a model. The relationships which would exist among the top-management positions, if the business used the systems approach, are shown in Figure 8.

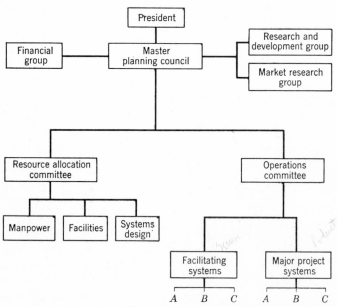

Fig. 8. The systems model: top management.

The master planning council would make decisions relative to the products or services the company supplied. Further, this council would establish the limits of an operating program, decide on general policy matters relative to the design of operating systems, and select the director for each new project. New-project decisions would be made with the assistance and advice of the product research and development, market research, and financial groups. Once the decision was made, the resource-allocation committee would provide the facilities and manpower (components) for the new system and supply technical assistance for systems design. After the system had been designed, its management would report to the operations committee as a major project system or as a facilitating system.

Facilitating systems would include those organized to supply a service rather than a finished product. Each project system would be designed with a view to making it self-sufficient. However, in many cases this objective may not be feasible or economical. For example, it may not be feasible to include a large automated mill as a component of a major project system, but the organization as a whole, including all the projects, could support this kind of facility. A facilitating system would be designed, therefore, to produce such an operating service for the major project systems. The output of the facilitating system would be material input for the project system, and a fee should be charged for this input, just as if the input had been purchased from an outside source.

A soap manufacturer could have, for example, major project systems in hand soap, laundry soap, kitchen soap, and tooth paste. A facilitating system might be designed to produce and *sell* containers to the four project systems.

Operating Systems

These systems would have one thing in common: they would all use a common language for communicating among themselves and with higher levels. In addition, of course, each system designed would be structured in consideration of company-wide policies. Other than these limits, each operating system would be created to meet the specific requirements of its own product or service. A model of an operating system is shown in Figure 9.

Figure 9 is designed to illustrate the relationship of the functions to be performed and the flow of operating information. The operating system is structured to (1) direct its own inputs, (2) control its own operation, and (3) review and revise its own system design as required. Input is furnished by three different groups: technical information is generated as input into the processing system, and in addition, technical information is the basis for originating processing information. Both technical and processing information are used by the material input system to determine and supply materials for processing. Each operating system has its own control unit. The control group measures the inputs and outputs of the processing

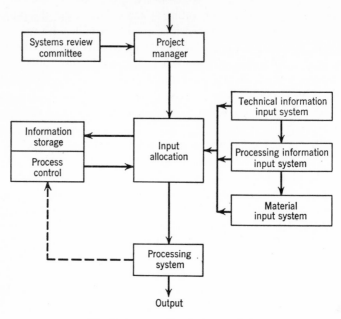

Fig. 9. An operating-system model.

system. However, corrective action, when necessary, would be activated by input allocation.

This model can be related to any business situation. For example, if this represented a system to produce television sets, the technical information would refer to the design of the product, processing information would include the plan of manufacture and schedule, and the material input would pertain to the raw materials and purchased parts used in the processing. These inputs of information and material would be processed and become output. Process control would measure the output in comparison with the standard (information storage) obtained from input allocation and issue corrective information whenever the system failed to function according to plan. The design of the system would be reviewed continually, and the components rearranged or replaced when these changes would improve operating efficiency.

THE SYSTEMS CONCEPT AND MANAGEMENT FUNCTIONS

Structuring a business according to the systems concept does not eliminate the need for the basic functions of planning, organization, control, and communication. However, there is a definite change of emphasis, for the functions are performed in conjunction with operation of the system and not as separate entities. In other words, everything revolves around the system and its objective, and the function is carried out only as a service to this end. This point can be clarified by reviewing each of the functions in terms of its relation to the systems concept.

Planning

Planning occurs at three different levels in the systems concept. These levels are shown in Figure 8. First, there is top-level planning by the master planning council. Second, the project and facilitating systems must be planned and resources allocated to them. Finally, the operation of each project and facilitating system must be planned.

The master planning council establishes broad policies and goals and makes decisions relative to the products or services the company supplies. It decides upon general policy matters concerning the design of the operating systems and selects the director for each new program. It is the planning council which receives informational inputs from the environmental and competitive systems. It combines these inputs with feedback information from the internal organizational system and serves as the key decision-making center within the company. Much of the decision making at this level is nonprogrammed, unstructured, novel, and consequential. While some of the new techniques of management science may be helpful, major reliance must be placed upon mature assessment of the entire situation by experienced, innovative top executives.

Once these broad decisions have been made, the planning function is transferred to the resource-allocation and operating committees. They plan and allocate facilities and manpower for each new system and supply technical assistance for individual systems design. At this planning level it is possible to utilize programmed decision making—operations research and computer techniques.

The third level, planning the operations of each project or facilitation system, is concerned primarily with the optimum allocation of resources to meet the requirements established by the planning council. This planning can most easily be programmed to automatic decision systems. However, the project director would still have to feed important nonquantifiable inputs into the system.

Under the systems concept of planning there is a direct relationship between the planning performed at each of the three levels. The first planning level receives informational inputs from the environment and competitive system and feedback information from within the organization. It translates this into inputs for the next planning level, which in turn moves to a more detailed level of planning and provides inputs for the third, or project, level. One of the major advantages of this systems concept is to provide a clear-cut delineation of the responsibility for various types of planning.

This concept facilitates integrated planning on a systems basis at the project level within the organization. Given the inputs (premises, goals, and limitations) from the higher levels, the project managers are delegated the function of integrated planning for their project.

One of the basic tenets of the systems concept is to have the people associated with an operating system do their own planning. This is a basic change from traditional management wherein the planners are physically separated from the doers and report to different departments. The planning information created and the spirit of the task to be accomplished often lose their effectiveness in this transition. Under the systems concept each project or facilitating system would include both functions of planning and doing. This arrangement improves planning through the availability of feedback information and corrective input.

Organization

Traditional organization theory emphasizes parts and segments of the structure and is concerned with the separation of activities into tasks or operational units. It does not give sufficient emphasis to the interrelationships and integration of activities. Adapting the business organization to the systems concept places emphasis upon the integration of all activities toward the accomplishment of over-all objectives but also recognizes the importance of efficient subsystem performance.

The traditional concept of organization deals primarily with people and their interrelationships. Systems design is broader and includes all components, arrangements, and operations of the business. The systems concept considers the organization as a complex man-machine system.

The systems basis of organization differs significantly from traditional organization structures such as line and staff or line, staff, and functional relationships. As shown in Figure 8, there are three major organizational levels, each with clearly delineated functions. The master planning council has broad planning, control, and integrative functions; the resource-allocation committee has the primary function of allocating manpower and facilities and aids in systems design for the facilitating or project systems. One of the major purposes of this type of organization is to provide an integration of activities at the most important level, that is, the individual project or program.

Staff specialization of skills is provided for the master planning council through such groups as financial, research and development, and market research. Their activities, however, are integrated and coordinated by the planning council. There are specialists at the operating level who are completely integrated into each project system. Thus the activities of these specialists are geared to the effective and efficient performance of the individual project system. This type of organization minimizes a major problem associated with staff and functional personnel—their tendency to associate their activities with specialized areas rather than with the optimum performance of the over-all operation.

There are other advantages of the systems concept. Business activity is dynamic, yet the typical organization is structured to perpetuate itself rather than change as required. There is generally resistance by the various specialized functions to change in order to optimize organization performance. For example, Parkinson's law states that there is an ever-increasing trend toward hierarchies of staff and functional personnel who are self-perpetuating and often do not contribute significantly to organizational effectiveness, or in extreme cases may be dysfunctional. In contrast, a system is designed to do a particular task. When the task is completed, the system is disbanded.

Systems are created from a central pool of resources. Facilities, machines, and manpower are assigned to specific projects or programs. The approach is to create and equip the project system with a complete arrangement of components to accomplish the job at hand. This may result in the duplication of certain activities in more than one operating system; however, this disadvantage is not as serious as it may seem. For example, it may be more efficient to have several typewriters assigned to each system rather than a central pool of typewriters. In the first instance, the typewriters may be utilized less than 100 per cent of the time, but the problems of scheduling the work at the central pool, delays, accountability, measurement of contribution, etc., would soon offset the advantages of centralizing equipment. Too much effort may be spent in creating processing information which accomplishes no objective other than keeping the machines utilized. A reasonable amount of redundancy or extra capacity will provide more flexibility, give protection against breakdowns, reduce flow time, require less planning, eliminate many problems associated with interdepartmental communication, and reduce the amount of materials handling.

Obviously, there are situations where it is impractical to decentralize a particular facility, because individual systems cannot utilize it sufficiently to warrant its incorporation into each separate operation. In these instances, a facilitating system would be created which would sell its services to any or all of the major project systems. These service systems would have to justify their existence and compete with outside vendors as suppliers to the major project system.

One of the great advantages of the systems concept for organizing pertains to the decentralization of decision making and the more effective utilization of the allocated resources to the individual project system. This has the merit of achieving accountability for performance through the measurability of individual systems of operation.

Control

The systems concept features control as a means of gaining greater flexibility in operation and, in addition, as a way of avoiding planning operations when variables are unknown. It is designed to serve the operating system as a subsystem of the larger operation. Its efficiency will be measured by how accurately it can identify variations in systems operation from standard or plan and how quickly it can report the need for correction to the activating group.

We must conclude that error is inevitable in a system which is subject to variations in input. When the lag in time between input and output is great, more instability is introduced. Feedback can reduce the time lag; however, corrective action which is out of phase will magnify rather than overcome the error. Every system should be designed to make its own corrections when necessary; that is, a means should be provided to reallocate resources as conditions change. The systems review committee (Figure 9) should be aware of any change in operating conditions which might throw the system out of control. Replanning or redesign may be required.

Design is important in control; the sensor should be constructed to measure the characteristics which are indicative of the operating system's performance and the characteristics which can be measured economically. Further, the control elements must be arranged to achieve the rapid processing and transmission of data.

In controlling a system it is important to measure inputs of information, energy, and materials and outputs of products and/or services (Figure 7). This will determine operating efficiency. In addition, it may be important to establish points of measurement during critical or significant stages of processing. Such measurements would be used principally to help management analyze and evaluate the operation and design of individual components. The best approach is to spotlight exceptions and significant changes. Management can focus its attention on these areas. One important thing to remember is that the control group is not a part of the processing system; it is a subsystem, serving the operating system. Cost control can be used as an example to illustrate this point. The cost accountant must understand that his primary objective is to furnish managers with information to control costs. His task is to inform, appraise, and support; never to limit, censure, or veto. The same principle applies to every control group serving the operating system.

The systems concept fosters better control of the most variable and unpredictable resource—people. This occurs because the systems concept identifies the responsibilities and accomplishments of people. When people know that their activities can be measured, they tend to produce in a more consistent manner.

Communication

Communication plays a vital role in the implementation of the systems concept. It is the connecting and integrating link within the systems network. The flows of information, energy, and material—the elements of any processing system—are coordinated via communication systems. As shown in Figure 7, an operating system requires information transmission to ensure control. At the outset, information flows to storage to be used as a control mechanism, and to activating groups for use in planning the actual processing function. In order to control the operating system, information is fed back to the control group, thus generating information for making corrective adjustments. For example, a means of communication can be established to feed back information on the final output in order to check its quality or appropriateness. Similarly, the processing operation itself is monitored in order to ensure that it is "in control." Communication systems should be established to feed back information on the various flows—information, energy, and material. Information on the effectiveness of the planning and scheduling activities (as an example of information flow) would be helpful in adjusting the nature of this activity for the future. Similarly, reports on absenteeism are examples of communication concerning the energy flow (the people in the system) to the processing activity. Information on acceptance inspection is an example of information stemming from the material-flow aspect of an operating system. All these feedback communication systems provide for information flow to a sensor and a control group. Comparison between the information received and the information stored (the master plan for this particular operating system) would result in decisions concerning the transmission of corrective information to the appropriate points.

Relationships within and among various project systems and between the levels of the system as a whole are maintained by means of information flow, which also can be visualized as a control device. Moreover, any operating system maintains contact with its environment through some sensory element. Referring to Figure 8, the sensory elements in this case are the groups reporting to the master planning council. The master planning council makes decisions concerning the product or service the organization will supply, based on information gained from market research, research and development, and financial activities. In a sense, these activities function as the antennas of the organization, maintaining communication with the external environment. The master planning council combines the information received through these activities with other premises covering the internal aspects in order to make decisions about future courses of action. Here again, communication, or information flow, can be visualized as a necessary element in controlling the course of action for the enterprise as a whole. Based on the feedback of information concerning the environment in general, the nature of competition, and the performance of the enterprise itself, the master planning council can continue its current courses of activity or adjust in light of developing circumstances. Thus communication, or information flow, facilitates the accomplishment of the primary managerial functions of planning, organizing, and controlling.

A common language among a network of systems facilitates integration and improves the efficiency of the whole. This does not mean that information must be kept in a common form at all times. Rather, the system language must be in a standard form or medium at designated input and control points. The critical decision points in the system should be identified. Also, the necessary information for the decision-making process must be set forth explicitly. On the basis of such analysis, information-decision systems can be planned which will process various types of data available with the intent of reducing such data to meaningful information for decision making.

The communication, or information-decision, system can facilitate implementation of the systems concept. Communication by definition is a system involving a sender and a receiver, with implications of feedback control. This concept is embodied in the lowest-level projects or subsystems, in all larger systems, and in the system as a whole. Information-decision systems, regardless of formal charts or manuals, often flow across departmental boundaries and are often geared to specific projects or programs. The systems concept focuses on this approach and makes explicit the information-decision system which might be implicit in many of today's organizations.

The systems concept does not eliminate the functions of management, i.e., planning, organizing, control, and communication. Instead, it integrates these functions within a framework designed to emphasize their importance in creating more effective systems.

CHARACTERISTICS OF EFFECTIVE SYSTEMS

Why is one system effective and another ineffective? In general, the effectiveness of systems is a factor of design and operation. First, the system should be designed with certain characteristics, and second, it must be accepted by the people who will be operating it. Characteristics associated with effective system operation include simplicity, flexibility, reliability, economy, and acceptability.

Simplicity

A system does not have to be complex to be effective. On the contrary, a simple system can be understood and followed better than a complex system. Learning will take place faster, and the operation will be more efficient. It should be pointed out, in addition, that there is usually a direct, positive correlation between simplicity and reliability. In other words, there are fewer things to go wrong.

A system becomes complex when the boundaries between systems and/or subsystems are not defined. It is important, therefore, to make the limits of operation definite. For example, a facilitating function should not be attached to more than one system.

Flexibility

Businessmen know that conditions change and that they must be prepared to adjust their operation to meet these changes. There are two ways to meet the evolution in operating environment: new systems can be designed, or operating systems can be modified. We are not suggesting that an existing system should be converted to meet a basic change in the objectives of the system; however, it should be flexible enough to absorb changes in certain environmental conditions or input factors. For example, a company should not use the same system for building missiles as they used for building airplanes; or the same system for selling appliances as the one designed for selling groceries. However, it should be possible to modify an existing system to produce different sizes, varieties, or types of the same product or service.

To be effective and simple, the system must be well defined, but to be practical, it cannot be rigid. There will always be minor variations, and the system should be able to accept these changes without breaking down.

Reliability

System reliability is becoming a more important factor in business operation. By reliability we mean the consistency of operation of the components. This can vary from zero output (a complete breakdown or work stoppage) to a constant and predictable output. The typical business system would operate somewhere between these two extremes. A greater degree of reliability can be designed into the system by a careful selection and arrangement of the operating components. Where the requirements of a particular component are critical, it may be necessary to design redundant or stand-by components. In all situations provision should be made for repair and recovery, to overcome any failure. One valid approach toward solving the reliability-maintenance problem is the use of the modular construction to permit maintenance by substitution of submodules. This should be considered when the system is designed. How serious are failures of individual components, and how soon could specific failures be repaired or replaced?

Economy

A system may be effective without being economical. For example, an operating service system can control the output of the system by using a large task force of expeditors. However, the cost of achieving this kind of performance would not be economical. In another example, inventories can be controlled by a comprehensive system of storekeeping; however, if the cost of the storekeeping is more than the potential savings from this degree of control, the system would not be economical. It is a diseconomy of design to develop one segment of the system with much greater capacity than some other part. Further, it is impossible to build in redundancy or provide for every contingency. This would destroy the operating economy of the system.

Acceptability

Any system, no matter how well designed and thought out, is worthless if it is not accepted by the people who operate it. If the people affected do not believe it will benefit them, if they are opposed to it, if they are pressured into using it, or if they think it is not a good system, it will not work. Two things can happen: the system will be altered by the people who are using it, or the system will be used ineffectively and fail. This is why it is so important for the project manager and his management team to help in designing the system. Decentralization of responsibility also tends to foster acceptance of the system. The relation of people to systems will be discussed in detail in Chapter 14.

SUMMARY

The business firm is an integrated whole, where each system, subsystem, and supporting subsystem is associated with the total operation. All these parts must be brought together as a whole. The management of a business firm can solve many of its problems and improve its operating efficiency by adopting the systems concept and operating the business as a system.

A system is defined as an array of components designed to accomplish a particular objective according to plan. First, there must be a purpose, or objective, which the system is designed to perform. Second, there must be design, or an established arrangement of the components. Finally, inputs of information, energy, and materials must be allocated according to plan.

First, a system must be designed; that is, components must be arranged in some combination to produce a desired goal. Detailed instruction must be prepared delineating duties, responsibilities, and operating instructions —these are the procedures. After the system has been designed, it is ready to operate. Inputs of information, energy, and materials are used in processing output.

Most systems include some means of control, i.e., a sensor for measuring output, a means of comparing the measurement with a standard, and an activating group to adjust inputs to correct indicated deficiencies. The objective is to control variables so that the system will tend to stabilize near the ideal equilibrium point.

A model of the systems concept would include a master planning council to make decisions relative to the products or services the company supplied; a resource-allocation committee to provide the facilities, manpower, and technical assistance for design; and operating systems, including major project and facilitating systems.

Planning occurs at three different levels in the systems concept. First, there is top-level planning by the master planning council. Second, the project and facilitating systems must be planned and resources allocated to them. Finally, the operation of each project and facilitating system must be planned. One of the basic tenets of the systems concept is to have the people associated with an operating system do their own planning.

A system is designed to accomplish a particular task. When the task is completed, the system is disbanded. The approach is to make each system self-sufficient to the degree this is economically feasible. A reasonable amount of redundancy or extra capacity will provide more flexibility, afford protection against breakdown, reduce flow time, require less planning, eliminate many problems associated with interdepartmental communication, and reduce the amount of materials handling. Whenever it is not feasible to add a component to the system, the service is performed outside of the project system, within the same company (facilitating system), or by another company (vendor).

The systems concept features control as a means of gaining greater flexibility in operation and, in addition, as a way of avoiding planning operations when variables are unknown. The best approach is to spotlight exceptions and significant changes. Control is a subsystem of the project system; its only function is to serve.

Communication is the connecting and integrating link within the systems network. The flow of information, energy, and materials—the elements of any processing system—must be coordinated via communication systems. A common language within a network of systems facilitates integration and improves the efficiency of the whole.

The effectiveness of a system is a factor of design and operation. First, the system should be designed to include specific characteristics, and second, it must be accepted by the people who will be operating it. Characteristics associated with effective system operation include simplicity, flexibility, reliability, economy, and acceptability.

The body travels more easily than the mind,
and until we have limbered up our imagination
we continue to think as though we had stayed home.
We have not really budged a step until
we take up residence in someone else's
point of view.

John Erskine, *The Complete Life*

Part Two
APPLICATIONS
Introduction

It can be enlightening to look at the world around us through the eyes of others. In this section of the book the reader is invited to play the role of a "systems analyst" and review these chapters with reference to the concepts developed in Part One.

Four different kinds of systems are illustrated: weapon systems, distribution systems, production systems, and data-processing systems. We have selected these examples because they are of general interest to the business and/or scientific world. However, our purpose in reviewing these applications is more than descriptive; it is our belief that these illustrations will help cement the philosophy of managing by system.

Chapter 7 discusses the weapon-system management concept, a philosophy of management which emphasizes the importance of timely integration of all aspects of a weapon system or support system, from the establishment of operational requirements (perception of need) through design, production, delivery, and utilization. This chapter illustrates the application of the systems concept in managing large-scale, complex projects.

Chapter 8 explains the proposal to integrate the functions of production and marketing into a single material-flow system. This approach has been called rhochrematics, the science of managing product flow from raw materials, through the various stages of processing, to the distribution of the product to the customer. This example serves to illustrate the relationships between systems, i.e., how the output of one system will change the structure of the system receiving the output as input, or how the input demands of the second system will change the operating characteristics of the preceding system.

Chapter 9 discusses automation and describes a recent development in producing machines: numerical control. In this system the operation of machines is planned and controlled through programmed instructions recorded on tape, usually as a digital code. It is an example of a structured, closed-loop system where inputs are measurable and outputs are predictable.

Chapter 10 reviews the activity of data processing, a system for managing information. A data-processing system—collecting, processing, comparing, and deciding—provides information for instruction, comparison, and control. Electronic data processing can be a sophisticated system provided it is used as an integral component in a system capable of utilizing its potential. Integrated data processing and real-time processing are set forth as the systems of the future.

Chapter Seven
WEAPON-SYSTEM MANAGEMENT

Part One explained the systems concept and its relationships to the primary functions of management—planning, organizing, controlling, and communicating. In this chapter, the application of the systems concept in its most complex form—the development, production, and utilization of large-scale man, material, and machine systems—will be presented. Generally, the discussion will focus on large systems which are integrations of a number of major subsystems. We shall discuss several civilian applications of large-scale systems; however, because of their enormity and importance, we shall concentrate upon military and space systems.

The development of the systems concept in weapon and space programs has been one of the significant evolutions in our industrial society and promises to be increasingly important as we spend more energy conquering space. This chapter will cover the following topics:

Impact of Advancing Technology
Large-scale Integrated Systems
Definition of Weapon-system Management Concept
Evolution of Concept
Product Missions
Basic Functions Required for Mission Accomplishment
Factors Contributing to Growth of Concept

Impact of Weapon-system Concept
The Polaris System

IMPACT OF ADVANCING TECHNOLOGY

Prior to the industrial revolution in Western Europe and America, increasing scientific knowledge was rarely, or at best slowly, translated into useful forces for the material betterment of man. Since 1850, however, the lag between discovery and utilization of scientific knowledge has been decreasing. Moreover, a growing share of scientific and technological effort has been devoted to applied research. Thus science has become a pervasive force in modern society, having widespread influence over all man's activities. Technological advances in the United States have progressed at an ever-increasing rate. This has been particularly true since the end of World War II. A substantial part of the advancing technology is due to the great increase in expenditures for research and development. Information from the National Science Foundation indicates a research boom. In 1947 research and development expenditures totaled $2.1 billion; by 1960 they had risen to $12.4 billion.[1] The amount of funds contributed for research and development by private industry and educational institutions has increased, but Federal participation in research and development is even greater. In 1960 the Federal government provided a staggering $7.7 billion, nearly 70 per cent of the nation's research funds.

The rapidly advancing technology has taxed man's organizational and administrative abilities. As major scientific projects become more complex, the problems of management increase geometrically. Scientific advancement in a complex society has required increasing specialization among men and organizational units. The integration of specialized functions into an optimum organizational performance is a critical management responsibility; this is where the systems concept has its greatest usefulness. Furthermore, the growing specialization of functions, although having the advantage of superior performance, does create inflexibility in organizational relationships.

Rapidly advancing technology has emphasized the need for more effective management. With new-product ideas continually pushing the state of the arts, plus rapid obsolescence, the management functions of planning, organizing, controlling, and systems integration are crucial. Figure 10 shows the relationship between useful product life and the time required for research and development behind that product.[2] Accelerating technol-

[1] *Research and Development in the Gross National Product,* National Science Foundation, Washington, D.C., February, 1961.

[2] Melvin E. Salveson, "Planning Business Progress," *Management Science,* April, 1959, p. 226.

ogy has led throughout history to shorter and shorter life spans for each new generation of products. Planned obsolescence has become a byword in modern industrial society. In addition, the amount of time and money required to design and develop the product and set up production facilities has increased. This longer development cycle has made the management function of long-range planning and systems integration mandatory in order to minimize the risk of expending valuable resources on a project with little or no chance of success.

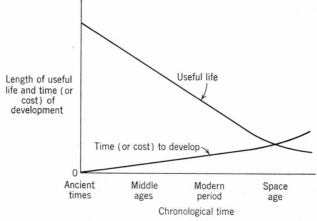

Fig. 10. Relationship of useful product life to length of time (or amount of money) it takes to develop and produce the product.

This relationship is apparent with military weapons. Cost of research and development for the newer missiles and space systems has skyrocketed. Furthermore, advances are so rapid that some missiles are obsolete even before they are operational. Although not as spectacular, the rapid pace of change in the civilian sector is also apparent. For example, within a period of less than ten years, black-and-white television went through the cycle of market introduction to market saturation. Market expansion and demand for new products, together with increasing research and development and technological advancements resulting in product innovations, have been major forces fostering an environment of change and the attendant necessity for more effective systems management.

LARGE-SCALE INTEGRATED SYSTEMS

There have been numerous examples of the application of the systems concept to complex problems of integration of human and material resources. A good example of the necessity for systems management for the successful accomplishment of a large venture can be seen in the development of the nation's transportation facilities. In establishing railroads, for example, it was necessary to weld such diverse functions as the securing of railways, rolling stock, and fuel; the building of lines, bridges, tunnels, stations, terminal facilities, and many construction projects; the training of personnel and the accomplishment of this under political and competitive pressures. Successful establishment of the nation's transportation network required successful systems management of all these and many more components.

As another example of the necessity for considering the broad systems concept, we might examine the early stages of commercial television. It was not sufficient for manufacturers to design and produce a workable television set; standardization of frequencies and other aspects had to be achieved among manufacturers, broadcasting had to be standardized, network cables had to be installed, interest and demand had to be stimulated (with early programming by manufacturers), and distribution and service channels had to be established. With all these functions necessary for successful performance of the entire system, it is little wonder that there was more than twenty years' time lag between the first successful receiver and its widespread use.

We could point to many other applications of the systems-management concept as it has been applied to civilian sectors in our society, such as the construction of roads or the building of dams and other large-scale, complex activities. Even though these civilian projects are of major magnitude, they do not approach the complexities involved in the management of weapon systems.

One of the earliest and most successful applications of the systems concept in the military sphere was in the development of the atomic bomb— perhaps one of the major scientific efforts in history—which covered a period of five years, cost over $2 billion, and required the energy and talents of many of America's leading scientists. In 1939, the theory of an atomic bomb already had been established through the cooperative efforts of many scientists on an international basis. Manufacturing the bomb was mainly a matter of converting theory into practice. Under the guidance of Vannevar Bush, Director of the Office of Scientific Research and Development, it was decided (in 1941) to begin a program of scientific research and development that reached tremendous complexities. General organization and management of the engineering phases of the atomic-bomb project were set up in 1942 under Brig. Gen. L. R. Groves of the Corps of Army Engineers and became known as the Manhattan Project. General Groves had the primary over-all systems-integration responsibility. It was his job to keep the various parts of the project in step, to see that raw materials were available for the various plants, to determine production schedules, to make sure that the development of the bomb design kept up with the production schedules, and to maintain an adequate system of security. In short, he was charged with the functions of managing the atomic-bomb project. Certainly, the scientific and technological achievements were indispensable in making the project successful. However, the importance of the management functions in bringing together the vast complex of materials and human resources should not be underestimated. A combination of scientific and technological knowledge, together with competent managerial and organizational abilities, was integrated into a coordinated system to reach the goal.

These examples of the application of the systems concept to broad managerial problems were forerunners of what has come to be termed the weapon-system management concept. This concept called for the systematic integration of a vast number of technologies, industries, human and material resources, and other subsystems into an integrated whole toward the accomplishment of objectives.

DEFINITION OF WEAPON-SYSTEM MANAGEMENT CONCEPT

Basically, the weapon-system management concept calls for the integration of all activities necessary for successful mission accomplishment. According to the Air Force, weapon-system management is a rather broad term covering several approaches to the implementing of the *weapon-system concept*. The weapon-system concept is a philosophy of management which emphasizes the importance of timely integration of all aspects of a weapon system or support system, from the establishment of operational requirements through design, development, production, personnel training, operation, and logistic support. A weapon system, as contrasted with the weapon itself, is a total entity consisting of an instrument of combat, such as a bomber or an intercontinental ballistics missile, together with all related equipment, supporting facilities, services, and trained personnel required to bring the instrument upon its target or to the place where it carries out the function for which it was built. The Department of Defense defined the term weapon system as follows:

> The term "weapon system" comprises facilities and equipment in combination which form an instrument of combat to be used by one or more of the military departments.
>
> The proposed definition is necessarily broad, as are all aspects of weapon system concepts, because the outstanding feature of the concept is flexibility. To fall within the weapon system concept an instrument of combat is designated as a weapon system at high levels of the military department. Thus not all instruments of combat are weapon systems even though technically the definition might be applicable. . . .
>
> Clear examples of what might be designated as weapon systems are

missiles, aircraft, and ships which consist of vehicles or in some case massive facilities, guidance or navigational systems, complex electronic gear, armament, communications equipment, and which require specialized, varied, and integrated logistic support and training.[3]

This definition suggests that the weapon system itself is an integrated system composed of equipment, skills, and technique, which, combined together, form a major instrument of combat or support.

The development, production, and employment of a weapon system involve the integration and cooperation of many military and industrial activities. Several management approaches have been utilized to implement the weapon-system concept, depending upon various factors such as the nature of the item, the state of the art, contractor capability, and degree of urgency. Although numerous interpretations have developed, depending upon the agency involved, two basic connotations of this concept stand out.

1. On the one hand, the weapon-system management concept implies the organization and integration of executive management responsibility by a specific agency within the military service. The military agency given this responsibility is required to coordinate, expedite, and integrate all functional effort of the military department, as well as to integrate military-industry relationships necessary to assure the timely delivery and support of the complete weapon system.

2. On the other hand, the weapon-system management concept has been applied to the various methods to procure weapon systems. Generally, under this concept, private industry has been delegated a broader range of responsibility for seeing that the weapon system is produced and delivered.

The foregoing descriptions of the weapon-system management concept give the impression that it is relatively new—even revolutionary—when, in fact, the basic managerial functions have been performed for many types of complex systems. To understand this concept it is necessary to trace its evolution and impacts.

EVOLUTION OF CONCEPT

The weapon-system management concept has evolved from systems-engineering approaches employed to meet complex industrial- and military-product applications over a number of years. Systems engineering—the invention, design, and integration of the entire assembly of equipment as distinct from the invention and design of the components, and geared to the

[3] *Military Procurement, Hearings on Senate Bills 500, 1383, and 1875 before a Subcommittee of the Committee on Armed Services,* U.S. Senate, 86th Cong., 1st Sess., 1959, p. 546.

accomplishment of a broad objective—is a concept which has been fundamental to practical engineering since the beginning of the industrial revolution. One of the earliest applications of systems engineering in the United States was geared to military procurement. During the War of 1812 Eli Whitney was commissioned to provide rifles for the young republic and developed a complex system (for that time) for the design of component parts for interchangeability. This fostered, much as modern systems engineering, the design of new equipment and methods of production.

The term *systems engineering* has been utilized in recent years to describe engineering systems which are larger, more complex, and more difficult to engineer than any of those in the past. For industrial and military products up through World War II, systems engineering was involved mainly in integrating existing subcomponents into a final product. Design was geared to steady improvement rather than explosive breakthroughs. Interchangeability between components became a major consideration in design and engineering.

One of the key elements in systems engineering today is the design of the product for a mission without complete assurance that the necessary components will be forthcoming. The systems-engineering function now involves—whether for military or industrial products—the coordination of research and development of subcomponents, as well as the integration of these subcomponents in the production phase.

One of the major problems in systems engineering for a large-scale, highly complex product such as a weapon system lies in coordinating machines and materials and in establishing organizational relationships for the necessary decision making and dissemination of information to the complex array of groups whose efficient performance is vital to the project. This coordination is achieved through a *system of information flow*. The system of information flow is of necessity complex and less rigidly established when there are rapid technological changes and product innovations.

In general, weapon-system management includes the combination of systems engineering—the integration of the physical components of an assembly—and information systems—the establishment of a communications and informational network between the various functions whose performance is necessary for a successful product mission.

PRODUCT MISSIONS

A convenient step in understanding the evolution of the weapon-system management concept is the *product-mission concept*. Any product, civilian or military, can be thought of as having a mission to perform. Often, in the civilian economy, one of the problems is the determination of the right product mission and the development of promotional materials which will enhance the ability of the product to fulfill its mission in the eyes of the consumer. Briefly, to fulfill the product mission it is necessary for the manufacturer to perceive a need, to design or develop a successful product, to produce it efficiently, to stimulate demand for this product, to provide for distribution through channels necessary to reach the consumer, and perhaps to educate the potential users to proper utilization of the product. The accomplishment of a successful mission for the product can be viewed as a systems-management problem much broader than just physical production.

The product-mission concept has a counterpart in the military. The tremendous technological innovations that occurred in the twentieth century, primarily in aircraft utilization, caused major shifts in military concepts. With aircraft, for example, it became more necessary for design and manufacturing to be undertaken with a more definite understanding of the basic product mission. The post–World War II era has seen the introduction of technological developments which have radically changed not only the weapons themselves, but also the military missions utilizing them. For example, nuclear bombs and the B-47, the first jet bomber, caused revision in planning for the role of the Air Force. Medium-range aircraft facilitated the extension of the Strategic Air Command and implementation of the mission of massive retaliation. The development of the intercontinental jet bomber, the B-52, necessitated the emergence of an even more complex approach to the military mission. In addition to the more critical systems-engineering requirements for the aircraft itself, there was the need to develop and integrate advanced support facilities such as in-flight fueling. Advancements in atomic and hydrogen bombs enhanced the striking power of the systems but also increased the problems of integration. As the state of the art advanced, it became increasingly apparent that more coordination between the military and industry was essential in order to optimize the chance of fulfilling a military mission.

BASIC FUNCTIONS REQUIRED FOR MISSION ACCOMPLISHMENT

The same functions have to be performed for successful mission accomplishment for the simplest weapon and for the most complex weapon systems. The major differences are not in the types of functions to be performed, but rather in the complexity and integration of these functions. There are five basic functions necessary for successful mission accomplishment:

1. Perception of need
2. Design
3. Production

4. Delivery

5. Utilization

Within each of these primary functions there are numerous subfunctions, many of which have increased so much in complexity and importance that they are frequently considered to be separate functions; however, it is useful to think of broad functions first and then to discuss more detailed subfunctions so that the interrelationships can be discerned.

Perception of Need

Perception of need for a new or different weapon system is influenced by many strategic and political considerations. Consideration has to be given to the current and possible future technological military capabilities of potential enemies. It also requires a thorough assessment of the political situation, particularly the implications of military preparedness upon foreign policy. The broad perception of need must be narrowed by consideration of what is desired, tempered with an evaluation of the current state of the art, a forecast of future technological feasibility, and a consideration of economic factors. There is a strong likelihood of conflict between the various objectives. This conflict must be resolved at a high national level.

Design

Once the initial stage of perception of need is accomplished, the next stage is research, development, and design. Given a broad military mission, there are generally numerous alternative solutions for the successful accomplishment of that mission. The design function includes setting forth alternative solutions, developing designs, evaluating alternative solutions, and selecting the final design. Obviously, experimentation and testing of components and over-all systems are performed in each of these stages. Once the design has been determined, the next step is production.

Production

The function of production includes the establishment of manpower and physical facilities, selection of component suppliers and sources of raw materials, testing and inspection of parts and components to meet quality specifications, assembly of components into final products, and testing and performance analysis of final products. The coordination of all these subfunctions is a vital part of the production process.

Delivery

This is the function of physically transferring ownership from producer to user. In military production, particularly of complex weapons, this function is accomplished by an elaborate program of testing and reevaluation. In the civilian economy, distribution of the finished product is usually more complex, however, requiring major effort on the part of the producers. Military producers, on the other hand, deal directly with ultimate users.

Utilization

The function of utilization is most frequently performed by the military services, although private industry may participate to a limited extent. This function includes such things as training of personnel, development of facilities for operations, logistics, maintenance and repair, modernization, and retirement.

These five functions—perception of need, design, production, delivery, and utilization—are basic for mission accomplishment. Regardless of the weapon used or the time period, these functions have to be performed by some agency. Essentially, then, the weapon-system concept is an approach which envisions the performance of all these primary functions necessary for the successful military mission as an integrated whole.

The weapon-system management concept evolved from the necessity for the timely integration of all the functions necessary for successful mission accomplishment. Under less complicated mission requirements and weapons it was possible to separate the functions and have performance carried out by separate and distinct agencies. Emphasis was placed on maximization of the goals set forth for each function, with less consideration given to optimizing total weapon-system performance. The weapon-system concept seeks the optimization of over-all systems performance and may suboptimize performance of individual functions. Furthermore, this concept requires the establishment of a management structure to ensure managerial and technical integration.

FACTORS CONTRIBUTING TO GROWTH OF CONCEPT

To further comprehend the increasing emphasis on the weapon-system management concept it is useful to consider the impact of various forces which have been important in recent years.

Need to Integrate Technologies

One of the major forces leading to the necessity of the systems-management concept has been the dynamic technology of recent years. Although there have been gradual advances in military technology throughout history, these advances have accelerated in recent years and have blurred the distinction between basic functions for military accomplishment. The distinction between design and production, for example, is not precise for the newer, more complicated weapon systems. The design function continues in conjunction with the production function and even beyond. The determination of the feasibility of meeting a perceived need is often dependent on breakthroughs achieved in later stages of design and production. The functions of utilization, such as training and logistics, cannot be delayed until completed production, but must precede delivery and take place during the design and production phases. This suggests the necessity for integrating through a systems approach all the basic functions rather than using a piecemeal approach.

Advancing technology also has meant changes in the location of responsibility for performing the various functions. Previously, it was possible to achieve reasonable success by having closely related agencies perform these functions. With the newer weapon systems, it is vital to provide for a systems manager whose responsibility is over-all coordination of technological innovations.

Rise of Adverse World Power

One of the major forces leading to continued emphasis on military security has been the rise of the Soviet Union as a potential adversary. The apparent success of its build-up of military strength and technological advancement has focused attention upon the necessity for improving our own military and technological capabilities. The continued threat has forced our nation to maintain a high level of research, development, and production of weapons, all geared to the primary objective of a "force in being." However, even with continuing necessity for national security preparation, there are political and economic considerations which definitely limit the funds available. And the rapid technological innovations have made for many alternative weapon systems which could meet the need. Decisions on allocation of available funds to alternative systems require high-level planning and systems integration.

Critical Lead Time

As a result of dynamic advances in technology and the rise of an adverse world power, the time available for military preparations has become critical. During World War II and the Korean crisis it was possible to mobilize the nation after the start of hostilities. It is quite evident that this will no longer be possible; any all-out war will be fought basically with the force in being. The emphasis is on having the latest weapon systems in operational readiness.

Greater complexities in modern weapon systems tend to result in longer lead times, while technological advancements have also made for more rapid obsolescence. Because of the desire to keep the lead time as short as possible, from perception of need to operational readiness, it has been necessary to dovetail the basic functions required for mission accomplishment. By integrating the functions on a weapon-system basis, it is possible to keep lead time from increasing significantly. Thus the importance of lead time has focused attention on the weapon-system management concept as a need to coordinate the efforts spent on the basic functions.

Changing Industrial Complex

In past periods, defense industries generally were defined according to product lines. However, with newer weapon systems, these previously established industry functions have been changed significantly. Technological advancements have required that efforts of new producers be coordinated for systems accomplishment. The new complex of industries coming in the wake of technological advancements requires concerted effort in order to optimize their contribution to national security. New technology and the changing industrial complex have made it difficult to standardize parts and components, so that every new system has to be considered as a separate entity.

IMPACT OF WEAPON-SYSTEM CONCEPT

The weapon-system concept is thus a prime example of the applications of the systems-management approach to complex problems. It utilizes the basic systems concepts of integration, coordination, and optimization of over-all performance. In adapting to this concept, many new managerial and organizational relationships have been necessary. In order to understand the importance of this concept we shall briefly outline the impact which it has had in three areas: the military, the industry level, and individual companies.

Impact on Military Departments

The systems-management concept has had a major impact upon the national defense establishment. Although the military services have always performed the over-all integrating functions necessary for mission accomplishment, the traditional organizational structures within the military departments have not sufficed for the newer, more complex weapon systems. Historically, the military departments were organized on a functional basis, with separate bureaus or commands given the responsibility for certain functions. The Navy, for example, was organized on a functional basis, with agencies such as the Bureau of Ships, Bureau of Ordnance, Bureau of Personnel, and Bureau of Aeronautics having clearly defined areas of authority. The Air Force, although organized much later, carried through the functional concept with the Air Research and Development Command,

Air Materiel Command, Strategic Air Command, and others. These commands were given definite areas of responsibility and authority.

These organizational structures with primary departmentation on a functional basis had advantages. Often, this breakdown arises naturally because of the functions which must be performed. For example, in the Air Force the five primary functions for mission accomplishment discussed previously were performed by specialized agencies. The Air Staff had prime responsibility for perception of need; the Air Research and Development Command had responsibility for design engineering; the Air Materiel Command, for production and delivery; and the Strategic Air Command and the Tactical Air Command, for utilization. The chief characteristic and primary benefit of such a structure is specialization. By concentrating on a single phase or similar group of activities, these functional departments can make full utilization of special knowledge and skills. Furthermore, this departmentation provides for the clear-cut assignment of authority and responsibility on a line basis for the performance of specialized functions. It also enhances the ability to control performance and provides for definite accountability.

This organizational structure presupposes that there will be a continuous flow of weapon systems to meet changing mission requirements. Each weapon system normally would move through the basic functions required for mission accomplishment. Under the functional basis of organization, a specific command would be charged with the responsibility and authority for the performance of its functions during a certain time phase. This functional basis is most efficient when there is a substantial similarity in the task to be performed for each weapon system. Where there is dissimilarity in the task required for different weapon systems, the previously stated advantages no longer apply and the organization has difficulty in meeting the decision-making requirements.

A further limitation of functional specialization is the possibility of optimizing the performance of certain activities at the expense of over-all system efficiency. Thus we see the major conflict which presented itself in the organization of the military departments. A continuation of the functional departmentation provided for specialization but created major problems of coordination. Because of these problems the military services have moved generally in the direction of the systems concept.

With the event of the newer, more complex weapon systems, the military services have had to adapt their organizational structures to augment their traditional functional departments. Pressures of technological complexity and time requirements have made it necessary to set up centralized management agencies that provide over-all integration on a weapon-system basis.

There are many examples of this reorganization on a systems basis. The Navy has set up its Special Projects Office to provide over-all integration for the Fleet Ballistic Missile program and has merged the Bureaus of Ordnance and Aeronautics into a Bureau of Naval Weapons. The Secretary of Defense clearly outlined the reasons for the establishment of this Bureau of Naval Weapons as follows:

> Advances in technology and changes in weapon characteristics, particularly in the field of missiles, have tended to merge the areas of development now under the Bureau of Aeronautics and the Bureau of Ordnance to such a degree that the consolidation of the functions of these two bureaus into a single new bureau, and the subsequent abolition of the old bureaus is considered essential in order to expedite the timely development and procurement of effective weapons. . . .
>
> Such a consolidation would place the weapon system development effort of the Department of Navy under the direct authority and control of a single executive; would simplify the funding of major weapon systems; would ensure full utilization of the professional and technical talents available to the Navy; and would permit more effective use of facilities and laboratories. The result would be significant improvement in the total weapon system development effort of the Department.[4]

The establishment of this new bureau gives evidence of the acceptance of the systems concept by the Navy. Even greater utilization of the systems concept is seen in recent developments in the Air Force. In 1961, Secretary of Defense McNamara issued a directive, "Development of Space Systems," which outlines the responsibilities of the various services in the military portion of the national space program. Specifically, this directive assigned the Air Force the responsibility for research, development, test, and engineering of the Department of Defense Space Program.[5] This directive in effect made the Air Force the systems manager for the military space program. To facilitate the carrying out of this newly assigned responsibility, the Air Force has undergone a sweeping reorganization, another evolutionary step toward integrated systems management. Basically, the Air Force will concentrate development and procurement of all systems—space, aeronautics, electronic, and ballistic—in a single command, the Air Force Systems Command. Figure 11 shows the revised Air Force organization emphasizing the Air Force Systems Command and indicating how far the military services, particularly the Air Force, have moved toward the systems-management concept. This command was established

---

[4] *Authorizing Establishment of Bureau of Naval Weapons*, Senate Committee on Armed Services, Report 582, 86th Cong., 1st Sess., July 24, 1959.

[5] *Military Astronautics*, Report of the Committee on Space and Astronautics, House of Representatives, H.R. 360, 87th Cong., 1st Sess., May 4, 1961, pp. 10–11.

to coordinate and control the activities of many agencies during the research and development phases and through production.

These new systems-integration agencies have been superimposed upon the functional organizations, thus limiting the latter's authority. As could be expected, when there are changes in authority and control relationships, there is some evidence that these changes have resulted in interdepartmental friction. The imposition of an integrating agency tends to create new

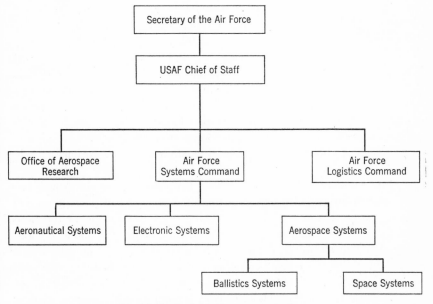

Fig. 11. Revised Air Force organization.

and more complex organizational relationships. Authority and responsibility for the performance of certain tasks is not as clear-cut as in the traditional functional structure. As the services gain more managerial experience under the new approaches, some of these frictions should be eliminated. The functional approach will be retained because of its many advantages. However, with continued complexities of new weapon systems, there will also be the need for the continued integration of these functions for each new weapon system.

In essence, the weapon-system management concept from the standpoint of the military services means the integration of the efforts of its functional units through the establishment of coordinating agencies. This function of integration and coordination is the primary systems-management function.

Impact on Military-Industry Relationships

Not only has the weapon-system concept had a major impact on the military services, but it also has influenced the relationships between the military and the national defense industries. The impact of this concept upon the military-industry relationship is centered primarily around the degree of delegation to private industry of managerial authority and responsibility for the performance of design engineering and production. The degree of delegation of this responsibility depends upon many factors, including complexity of the weapon system, capability of available development and production agencies, producibility, requirements for compatibility, and military urgency. Because of varying weights of these factors, numerous procurement patterns have emerged. The range may vary from total management of the program within the military department to contracting with a specialized agency for technical direction and systems engineering, or to having these functions performed by the prime defense contractor. One of the key issues in the weapon-system management concept concerns the technical and managerial capabilities of the various agencies involved.

For standardized weapons, where the military has developed proficiency over an extended period of time, the services tend to retain a substantial proportion of the decision-making responsibility for all functions, including design engineering and production. With the more complex weapon systems, however, the military has looked to private industry for the necessary skills. This has been true for aircraft production, with even greater delegation evident for missile systems.

Because it has dealt with relatively complicated air weapon systems, the Air Force traditionally has delegated greater responsibility to private industry than have the other two services. This was possible because of the development of strong managerial and technical capabilities within the airframe industry. With the advent of the highly complex ballistic missiles, the Air Force utilized the services of specialized organizations for systems integration and technical direction. For example, Space Technology Laboratories Inc. was utilized by the Air Force for the over-all technical direction and systems integration of the ballistic-missile program. For the newer space programs, the Aerospace Corporation has been established as a private nonprofit corporation to aid with technical direction and systems integration for the Space Division of the Air Force Systems Command. Primarily these agencies have specialized in the performance of the systems-management function. The emergence of these specialized agencies for the performance of systems-management functions is further evidence of the growing importance of the systems concept.

Impact upon Company

The weapon-system management concept has had a major impact upon military suppliers. The ever-increasing technology has made it difficult for the military to maintain capabilities for merging perceived requirements with technology. Indeed, for the more sophisticated weapon systems, the military must depend heavily upon industry for formulating requirements. Industry, in conjunction with the military, must have overall capability to perceive new military requirements and to relate these to technical capabilities.

Suppliers' ability to perceive needs and define requirements must begin with consideration of international relationships and capabilities of any adversary, and then must analyze national political, economic, and military requirements. Merging these broad systems requirements with the technical state of the art generally will result in a number of hypothetical solutions which must be evaluated to determine the optimum approach.

Rapid obsolescence of weapon systems has required new methods and innovations for minimizing the time cycle between need perception and operational availability. There is a trend toward limiting the volume of production of individual weapon systems to a relatively small number as compared with the production runs of aircraft such as the B-36, B-47, and B-52. However, there has been an increase in the number of separate programs in various stages of research, development, and production. Greater variety and smaller production are an apparent result of advancing technology.

Modern weapon systems have required state-of-the-art advancements in a number of previously unrelated technologies. Thus a weapon system such as Dyna-Soar requires the integration of manned aircraft technology, missile technology, space electronics, human physio-psychological considerations, and other technologies. And the system itself may not have any clearly defined military mission but may represent a broad advancement in basic technology. The weapon-system contractor therefore must develop technical integrative and managerial skills over a broad range of technology.

Weapon-system management requires the integration of a broad complex of diverse product and services. To meet this product responsibility it is necessary for the successful weapon-system contractor to develop technical know-how in all phases of the weapon system. For example, Boeing established an engineering force to work closely with an IBM group for the integration of the SAGE-Bomarc system. Lockheed established a similar relationship with the Bureau of Ships and other major subsystems contractors on the Polaris project. One of the results of this approach has been to broaden the technical know-how of the weapon-system contractor in a wider product spectrum.

For companies, one of the requirements is increased specialization of managerial and organizational resources to ensure maximum efficiency in their performance. For example, top management, with the aid of designated staff groups, must study and be cognizant of broad international considerations, political-economic forces, defense economics, and other environmental forces. This points up the necessity for special and continued emphasis by top management on long-range planning and on adapting the organization to a changing environment.

A weapon-system contractor, faced with the problem of successful integration of an increasing number of functions, and also doing this for a growing variety of programs, has found his managerial and organizational resources hard-pressed. Generally, in order to adapt to the new problems, the major weapon-system contractors have adopted the systems concept. Accordingly, a project or program manager has been designated and given broad responsibilities for the integration of all the functions necessary for total system accomplishment.

We have traced the impact of the weapon system upon the military, upon the defense industries, and upon individual companies. Now, in order to understand these changes more completely, we shall outline briefly the application of this concept to one of the nation's most complicated, modern, well-known weapon systems.

THE POLARIS SYSTEM

The development of the Polaris Fleet Ballistic Missile Weapon System was begun early in 1957. This is one of the more complex of the military weapon systems and includes the requirements of a nuclear-powered submarine, together with a long-range ballistic missile. The Polaris system is a basic part of the broader United States system of strategic deterrence.

In order to develop this complex weapon system effectively, the Navy found it desirable to establish a specialized management device to integrate the entire operation. The management structure for the Polaris system is special and unique in the organization of the Navy—a Manhattan Project type of organization. A Navy Special Projects Office was established, with a relatively small military and civilian staff which is essentially a task force with responsibility matched with authority to achieve specific high-priority goals in the shortest time possible. The Director of Special Projects Office, Vice-Admiral William F. Raburn, reports directly to the Secretary of the Navy, who is chairman of the Navy Ballistic Missile Committee. As shown in Figure 12, the Special Projects Office serves the role of an integrated program manager for the entire Polaris system. The Director of Special Projects is the weapon-system manager for Polaris and has discretion to specify and coordinate requirements and areas of work. This office has the authority and control of available funds required to implement the various decisions regarding alternative scientific and engineering courses

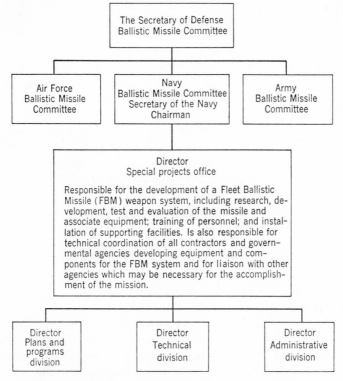

Fig. 12. Organization of the Navy Special Projects Office.

of action involved in the complex Polaris program. Basically, the Special Projects Office has the following seven major responsibilities:

1. Developing, testing, and producing the Polaris missile
2. Coordinating construction of nuclear-powered submarines and development of advanced communication systems
3. Developing, testing, and producing, launching and handling, fire control, and navigation systems
4. Training Fleet Ballistic Missile personnel, including crews and the nuclear assembly, storage, and issue facilities
5. Conducting tests to insure that fully operational weapon systems are turned over to the fleet on or before the required time
6. Constructing and equipping the over-all system production facili-

ties, including buildings, production, test and inspection tooling, and a maintenance facility

7. Management of fiscal and other resource matters for the entire Fleet Ballistic Missile Program [6]

With these many complex responsibilities the Special Projects Office has had to establish a management program which would provide a systematic orderly development. The Polaris management sequence consists of three principal phases: (1) definition of program objectives, (2) program planning and implementation, and (3) program evaluation.

Program objectives for Polaris are outlined by the Chief of Naval Operations in operational and performance requirements. These objectives are the basis for detailed planning by the Special Projects Office, together with a Special Steering Task Group from the Special Projects Office and scientific representatives of Lockheed, Aero-Jet, General Electric, Westinghouse, Sperry-Rand, Massachusetts Institute of Technology, Atomic Energy Commission, Chief of Naval Operations, Bureau of Ships, and Navy Ordnance Laboratories.

Program planning and implementation is based upon program objectives and defines in detail parameters and requirements for the Polaris weapon system, subsystems, and components. Before projects are undertaken, technical proposals are developed which outline and justify the work plant, funds required, key technical events, and supporting requirements. Major program proposals are reviewed and approved by the Director of Special Projects.

Program evaluation is accomplished and management decisions are made on the basis of information provided by the Polaris contractors and participating Naval agencies. Thus the management sequence calls for the establishment of objectives, implementation through planning, and finally program evaluation as shown in Figure 13.

In addition to assigning the prime responsibility and authority for the management of the Polaris system in the hands of the Special Projects Office to provide management with an integrated systematic concept, there are a number of major subsystems to which management responsibility and authority have been delegated. For example, the prime contractor for the Polaris missile system is the Lockheed Aircraft Corp., which serves as the missile-system manager. Aero-Jet General is the propulsion system manager, and General Electric is the missile-guidance system manager. Westinghouse Electric Corp. is the prime contractor for the design, development, and production of launching and handling systems. Contracts for

[6] *Polaris Management,* Department of the Navy, Special Projects Office, Fleet Ballistic Missile Program, 1961, p. 2.

submarine construction were awarded to the Electric Boat Division of the General Dynamics Corp. and to the Newport News Shipbuilding and Drydock Co. In addition, the Naval shipyard at Mare Island and at Portsmouth are each constructing a submarine. The precise navigation equipment for these submarines is being developed by a number of contractors, the major ones being Sperry-Rand and North American Aviation. Westinghouse is developing the submarine reactor components.

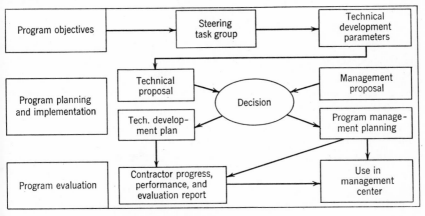

Fig. 13. Polaris management sequence.

The entire Polaris program has demanded the integration and coordination of a vast complex of military and industrial activities. The management approach was to break down the total system into subsystems and then to integrate these into the total operational units. This approach has been quite successful; the date for initial operational capabilities of the Fleet Ballistic Missile Weapon System was advanced from 1963 to 1960. The Navy anticipates that it will use this total systems concept in those projects which are very complex and require integration through special management unities such as the Special Projects Office.

Many other examples from the military could be given of the establishment of specialized agencies to perform the job of systems integration and technical direction. The Air Force in particular has made use of this systems concept in its most complex programs, such as the Dyna-Soar and the ballistic-missile programs. There seems to be a general consensus that although many difficulties have arisen in actual operation under this concept, its value has been proved in reducing delay and in more effective management.

SUMMARY

There have been numerous examples of the application of the systems concept to complex problems of integration of human and material resources. The development of the nation's railroad transportation system and, more recently, the introduction of commercial television are typical examples. One of the earliest and most successful applications of the systems concept in the military sphere was in the development of the atomic bomb during World War II.

These examples of the application of the systems concept to broad managerial problems were forerunners of what has come to be termed the weapon-system management concept. This concept calls for the systematic organization of a vast number of technologies, industries, human and material resources, and other subsystems into an integrated whole toward the accomplishment of objectives.

The weapon-system concept is a philosophy of management which emphasizes the importance of the timely integration of all aspects of a weapon system or support system, from the establishment of operational requirements through design, development, production, personnel training, operation, and logistic support. In general, weapon-system management includes the combination of systems engineering—the integration of the physical components of an assembly—and information systems—the establishment of a communications and informational network between the various functions whose performance is necessary for a successful product mission. It sets forth a managerial and organizational structure for integrated performance of the functions necessary for successful military-mission accomplishment. Rapid technological advancement, increasing complexity of modern weapon systems, pressure for keeping lead times as short as possible, and changing industrial structure are forces which have required the integration of technical and managerial skills in order to optimize performance.

We foresee that these trends will continue. There is little to indicate that we shall be able to simplify technology; rather, with major technical and managerial requirements stemming from space-exploration programs and military requirements, we anticipate an ever-increasing tendency toward greater technical and organizational complexities. The only efficient approach to the management of this kind of complex program is through the use of the systems concept. There is significant evidence that most of the agencies involved, both military and private-industry, have come to recognize the importance of this concept. It is impossible to manage a program of such magnitude by thinking of each operational unit separately. It is absolutely necessary to start with a broad systems concept and then to break down the total system into subsystems, and so on, in order to achieve optimum performance. This type of complex program, most apparent in military and space activities, is the vanguard of more complex systems which will evolve in the future.

Chapter Eight
RHOCHREMATICS

Converting raw materials into finished goods is a complex process. There are countless interrelationships among the many activities involved in the process of material flow. For example, decisions made in manufacturing affect the purchasing of raw materials and the sale of finished goods. Decisions made in selecting a mode of transportation may affect packaging, warehousing, and/or production. However, the typical business firm operates within functional walls; each function is carried out as an entity, and performance is measured by the departmental manager's success in reducing costs in his own particular activity.

Recently a number of companies have reorganized their operation to manage and control the movement of materials as a single integrated system, from the raw-material source through the many stages of processing and including the distribution of the finished product. In this chapter we shall review this concept (rhochrematics) under the following topic areas:

Rhochrematics—An Application of the Systems Concept
The Changing Pattern of Distribution
Increasing Problems in Distribution and Production
Need for a Different Approach
Applying the Rhochrematics Concept
Application of Rhochrematics

RHOCHREMATICS—AN APPLICATION OF THE SYSTEMS CONCEPT

During the past decade much has been written on the "new marketing concept," "distribution management," and "landed costs." Unfortunately, these concepts usually refer to the distribution of finished products and

136

do not include prior stages of material flow. A new term, rhochrematics,[1] was coined to include the entire system. It is defined as the *science of managing material flow,* embracing the basic functions of producing and marketing as an integrated system and involving the selection of the most effective combination of subfunctions such as transporting, processing, handling, storing, and distributing goods.[2]

The rhochrematics approach is (1) to review the need for the function in terms of the objectives of the business, and (2) to determine its cost and contribution in relation to other necessary functions. For instance, packaging costs could be reduced by using new kinds of materials or packaging machinery. However, a more basic approach would be to investigate the relationships among packaging, transportation, handling, and advertising; this may reveal the desirability of changing, or eliminating, the packaging function. In another case, it may be more profitable to allow manufacturing output to fluctuate, because selling costs may be reduced more under this kind of policy than the additional costs incurred when production is geared to demand. These are illustrations of relationships which exist among a few functions. The matrix of relationships among all the functions relative to converting and transferring raw materials to the market provides a whole new field of exploration. Forrester made this point in his writings on industrial dynamics.

> In other words, the company will come to be recognized not as a collection of separate functions but as a system in which the flows of information, materials, manpower, capital equipment, and money set up forces that determine the basic tendencies toward growth, fluctuations, and decline.[3]

Every activity in the flow of materials should be considered a component of the total system. The selection, arrangement, and operation of the components would be engineered as a system. The contribution of each component and subsystem could be ascertained by measuring its output. The efficiency of each component and subsystem could be determined by comparing this measure of output against a measurement of resource input. This kind of evaluation would point out areas of inefficiency and enable management to adjust its operation to meet changing conditions.

[1] From the Greek *rhoe,* meaning to flow, as a river or stream; *chrema,* meaning products, materials, or things; and the abstract *-ics,* for any of the sciences.

[2] See Stanley H. Brewer, *Rhochrematics: A Scientific Approach to the Management of Material Flows,* University of Washington, Bureau of Business Research, Seattle, 1960.

[3] Jay W. Forrester, "Industrial Dynamics," *Harvard Business Review,* July–August, 1958, p. 52.

THE CHANGING PATTERN OF DISTRIBUTION

A few decades ago, when the market for products was small relative to the present and the state of development of communications and transportation resulted in limited competition for the mass market, the variety of products manufactured was much less than today. Since then company policies and practices have resulted in a strong trend toward increased product variety. Causes of this trend include a shift to market orientation in company policy, sales-promotional activities, and the practice of dividing the market into small segments.

The New Marketing Concept

For many years following the industrial revolution, primary attention was directed toward production efficiency and manufacturing activities. Mechanization, specialization, and assembly-line methods were developed. Emphasis was placed on minimum unit production costs with the hope that products could be sold, but with limited thought given to the needs and desires of consumers. In many product lines the variety of colors, sizes, and models was kept at a minimum.

A significant trend in American industry today is increased attention to the market. Seldom has business management indulged in such introspection as is prevalent today in the marketing field. Companies of all sizes are conducting searching inquiries into consumer habits and motivations in attempts to determine what they can do to develop or maintain leadership in the marketplace. There is a new philosophy concerning the proper relationship of marketing to the other divisions of the company. Marketing personnel are playing an increasingly important role in product development and production scheduling. In short, increased emphasis is being placed on learning more about the needs, desires, likes, and dislikes of customers and using this knowledge as a primary basis for planning and organizing the entire company operation.

Sales-promotional Activities

Much of the incentive to expand the variety of products is traceable to the use of different colors, sizes, and models as a means of sales promotion. Sales and advertising personnel apply pressures constantly to encourage new products, variations in old products, more sizes, more colors, and new models, so that they will have something "new and different" to feature in their attempts to stimulate sales.

Thus annual model changes in automobiles, appliances, and other products have been common practice, justified as a device for sales promotion and market stimulation. Soap manufacturers, instead of distributing one size and one color of one or a few brands, as they did years ago, have expanded their product lines to more brands, several sizes, and several colors.

Market Segmentation

Mass production of a single product does not take into account the distinct differences in taste and desires within a market. As the size of the market has grown, segments of the market have become large enough to justify the development of separate products to meet specific needs. As a result of market-segmentation policies, companies which were producing one or a few products a decade ago are producing and distributing a greatly expanded variety of items to meet the desires of submarkets discovered through market-research activities. An extreme example may be found in the cigarette industry; in order to appeal to various segments of the market, companies distribute cigarettes of various lengths, with or without filters, with or without menthol additives.

Social and economic changes have transformed the American society from a homogeneous market of basic and simple needs to a substantial number of heterogeneous submarkets. When market research locates clusters of consumers with similar tastes and wants, companies are quick to develop products which appeal to them. Instead of one product which satisfies most customers but dissatisfies some customers, the variety of products is expanded in an attempt to satisfy all customers. Industrial progress has cycled from an age of custom production to mass production and now almost back to the degree of custom variation that economics and market segments permit.[4]

INCREASING PROBLEMS IN DISTRIBUTION AND PRODUCTION

The problems associated with efficient performance of distribution and production activities have expanded geometrically relative to the expansion in the variety of colors, sizes, and models of products being distributed. These problems may be grouped into areas of anticipating demand, dislocation of inventories, maintaining adequate stock for customer service, control of inventory, and production planning.

Problems of Anticipating Demand

The problems of anticipating demand, planning inventories, and planning production of a total product line are simple in comparison with similar problems associated with specific segments of the product line. More

---

[4] See Lynn H. Stockman (ed.), "The Strategy of Market Segmentation," in *Advancing Marketing Efficiency,* American Marketing Association, Chicago, 1959, pp. 128–165.

specifically, an appliance manufacturer can determine the sales potential for refrigerators based on past experiences and economic conditions. When this potential demand, however, must be translated into sales by size, model, and color, the problem becomes much more complex. Past experience has limited value, and it is difficult to evaluate trends effectively. Much of the overproduction and subsequent distress selling in appliances and other products is traceable to the difficulty of anticipating demand when a large variety of products is manufactured.

Dislocation of Inventory

Experience has shown that there is no pattern of consistency in the demand for various colors, sizes, and models of products within regions of the United States market. When regional inventory planning is based on past experience, it is not unusual to find that consumption patterns have shifted and inventories are in the wrong locations. Colors or models which sell in a region one year may not sell in the same proportion the following year. As a result, transshipments of inventories—with the additional costs —are necessary in order to balance supply with demand.

Maintaining Adequate Stocks

One of the specific problems associated with efficient performance of the distribution function is the maintenance of adequate stocks at regional warehouses, distributors, and retailers in order to serve the market rapidly. When the number of products to control is small, the problem is relatively simple. As the variety of products increases, however, the problem becomes more complex. Minimum inventories must be expanded in order to provide sufficient selection, but middlemen become reluctant to assume the risks associated with large inventories. To illustrate, two units of each model, size, and style of a single television manufacturer may represent an investment in excess of $50,000 for a retailer.

Control of Inventory

As suggested above, the problems associated with controlling inventories are intensified as the variety of items is increased. The growth and change in product-line characteristics in both consumer and industrial products has resulted in more items for the distribution system to handle and stock. More items mean less volume per item and correspondingly higher unit processing, handling, and transportation costs.

In a study to measure the effect of increased product variation on the amount of inventory required, it was concluded that an increase in variety from one to three items (with total sales remaining the same) necessitated an increase in field inventories of 60 per cent; in the same study, if total sales increased 50 per cent, inventory requirements increased 100 per cent.[5]

These figures, typical of companies with a wide market for their products, illustrate the effect of small-volume items on inventory control. Yet, as companies have expanded the variety of their product lines, the number of small-volume items has increased. Studies based on the records of a large number of firms distributing consumer and industrial products revealed that a relatively small percentage of items—usually 10 to 20 per cent—account for about 80 per cent of sales, while about half of the items account for less than 4 per cent of sales.[6] This is a critical factor in inventory control because the slow-moving items usually cause much more than their proportionate share of inventory cost.

Production Planning

The increased efficiency and reduced cost of mass production are recognized as significant contributions to increased standards of living in the United States. Mechanization, assembly lines, specialization, and, more recently, automation have resulted in productivity increases in manufacturing activities which have outstripped progress in distribution activities. The trends described above, however, tend to restrict the potential contribution of improved manufacturing techniques to over-all cost reduction.

As more and more companies succumb to the trends of market segmentation, product differentiation, and product variety, the opportunity for mass production—with its inherent advantages—is reduced. While the total number of units to be produced has increased, the number of identical units is reduced as a company increases the variety of colors, styles, sizes, and models. Instead of an assembly-line production of a large number of identical units, the manufacturing process becomes a series of shorter runs of dissimilar products. Economies of continuous runs are reduced as new setups and changes become normal procedure. Estimates of demand for the various products must be substituted for estimates of total demand in the determination of production planning and production scheduling. Liaison and communications between the manufacturing and distribution functions within companies become much more important than in the past.

An alternative to reducing the size of the run is to produce for inventory. However, this increases the risk and storage costs.

[5] John F. Magee, "The Logistics of Distribution," *Harvard Business Review*, July–August, 1960, pp. 90–91.
[6] *Ibid.,* p. 91.

NEED FOR A DIFFERENT APPROACH

It is evident that a more comprehensive approach is needed to solve the problems created by the changing patterns of distribution—a philosophy which considers the costs of production and of distribution in terms of total costs. In other words, the functions of production and marketing should be integrated into a total system, and the cost of operating each individual component should be measured in consideration of its contribution to the objectives of the system and to total system cost. Two things are occurring which tend to encourage this kind of an evaluation: (1) flow-cycle time is increasing, and (2) marketing and inventory costs are increasing.

Flow-cycle Time

Flow-cycle time is the time required to produce and distribute the product. Normally, production is planned to satisfy a market demand, and for most products this demand is estimated months to years in advance. For many items there is no turning back from a course of action which is established early in the production cycle. Firms commit thousands and even millions of dollars which may or may not produce a profit, depending on the acceptance of the product in the market.

A major reason for making production commitments far in advance of sales is the material flow cycle. Market planning provides the basis for production planning, which in turn establishes material requirements; materials are purchased, delivered to the plant, inspected, and transferred to stores. A protective cushion of time is added for each step of this flow process, tending to allow the maximum time which any step might take.

Finished products may got into temporary storage, then to the shipping department, sometimes to branch warehouses, to wholesalers and/or retailers, and finally to the customer. This outbound movement is replete with multiple handling and costly delay before the product is placed in the hands of the final consumer.

The longer the flow-cycle time, the further in advance the commitments must be made relative to producing a given item. The longer the cycle, the greater the opportunity for competitors to develop a new product which may enable them to capture a larger share of the total market.

Increasing Marketing and Distribution Costs

As products are differentiated and the variety of products increases, several elements of marketing cost increase. Advertising and sales-promotion expenditures are necessary to create desire and stimulate demand for the various products in the line. Under policies of product development for market segmentation, sales-promotional appeals must be directed at the various submarkets. In addition, it may be necessary to expand the sales force and increase expenditures for sales training.

The process of handling orders becomes more complex and costly because a larger number of relatively small orders are substituted for fewer large orders. Consequently, costs associated with order handling and filling back orders are increased.

Decreasing the size of orders often results in a larger number of small shipments from manufacturing plants and warehouses to the market. As a result, unit transportation costs are increased.

These examples illustrate the effect of the increased variety of products on marketing costs. Actually, the entire marketing process becomes more complex and therefore more costly. Goals of improving the efficiency or controlling marketing costs become more difficult to attain.

Inventory costs include warehousing, insurance, taxes, handling, capital costs, and obsolescence. These combined costs represent a substantial part of the total cost of distribution. Any steps that can be taken to reduce the amount of inventory required have an immediate and significant effect upon physical-distribution costs. Conversely, current trends of increased product variety lead to increased inventory requirements and add materially to these costs.

Much of the added inventory costs is traceable to the obsolescence that develops from the addition of new products, engineering changes, and the regular introduction of new models. Technological obsolescence as a result of these changes is a significant price to pay for the progress and sales-promotional values of regular style and model changes and has become an accepted cost of moving ahead in dynamic industries. No precise data are available on the cost of inventory obsolescence. There is no doubt, however, that this factor constitutes a definite problem and a major cost. To illustrate, one of of the daily activities at a parts depot of a large vehicle manufacturer is the scrapping, or returning to a central warehouse, of parts that have been designated obsolete.

The problems and costs of inventory obsolescence, while they vary considerably among different classes of products, also arise in relationships between manufacturers and middlemen. In general, when a product line is long, contains a variety of items, or contains slow-moving items, it is necessary to offer obsolescence protection and/or return privileges to distributors and retailers in order to get them to carry an adequate inventory.

APPLYING THE RHOCHREMATICS CONCEPT

Certain phases of the external distribution system have been studied intently, and optimal warehouse location patterns as well as optimal routing and scheduling patterns have been developed. In every case, however, the confines of the problem have been rather narrow, with simplifying assumptions being made concerning the effect of factors at either end of the system. The effect of changes within the system upon external elements usually has been ignored. Further, the broader aspects of the total system have not received much attention, principally because of the organizational structure of the typical business firm.

Traditionally, organization has been predominantly vertical and hierarchical, with authority and responsibility resting in individual functions. Superior-subordinate relationships have been established on a functional basis, with orders and instructions going down the line and reports and requests going up the line. Recently, this traditional approach has been questioned in reference to its suitability for over-all efficiency of the operation. For example, the flow of material and information in the typical manufacturing operation tends to be horizontal, cutting across the vertical structuring of functional authority.[7]

In discussing new technology and its impact on organization, Jasinski lists three ways in which change can be integrated:

> 1. Changing the technology to conform with the existing organizational structure
> 2. Changing the organization so as to define and formalize the relationships required by the technology
> 3. Maintaining both the existing organization and the existing technology, but introducing mechanisms to reduce or minimize the discrepancies between the two [8]

Rhochrematics involves the entire company operation. There may be a need to make significant changes in the organizational structure, facilities, or basic company policy. This kind of study should be started at the top; otherwise it may be a waste of time. Top management must be convinced of the value of the total-system approach and give full support to its implementation.

The problem is that most companies organized in the traditional functional fashion are not set up to take advantage of conceptualizing the total

[7] Stanley Brewer and James Rosenzweig, "Rhochrematics and Organizational Adjustments," *California Management Review,* Spring, 1961, pp. 52–71.

[8] Frank J. Jasinski, "Adapting Organization to New Technology," *Harvard Business Review,* January–February, 1959, p. 80.

flow process. Management must be willing to reevaluate its organization and reconstruct it as a network of systems.

In order to develop a scientific approach to the management of material and information flows, it is helpful to know which tools and techniques can be applied in this kind of analysis. A more comprehensive discussion of these tools and techniques will be included in Chapter 11.

Rhochrematics and Simulation

The best way to study material flow is by simulation. Since rhochrematics by definition is concerned with the over-all flow of material and information, and since it contains a number of separate and diverse functions, it would be extremely difficult to create a mathematical equation to define the total system. Therefore analysis structured toward optimizing the total system operation seldom would be meaningful. Simulation, on the other hand, would allow the researcher to reproduce the system under study via a series of simplified algebraic equations set up to represent the various levels and flows of material, information, and manpower.

A number of benefits accrue to the researcher and the manager when a simulation study is undertaken of the total flow from raw material to consumer. First of all, since those persons involved in making decisions in the operation as a whole must verbalize their decision-making process to the researcher, they cannot avoid becoming better acquainted with their own operation. The explicitness with which the activities and decisions must be set forth for a simulation model forces those involved to define their own functions clearly. Often this activity in itself can result in benefits which more than offset the time and cost involved in the research project. Once the system has been simulated via a number of simplified and fairly straightforward equations, a number of days, weeks, or years of activity can be generated, and the results of these operations can be compared with actual results for the same period. In this way the critical points in the model can be compared and its realism evaluated. The model as verbalized by the decision makers may turn out to be quite different from the actual operating system. When the simulation results are compared with some actual operating data, the decision makers involved see where their perception of the process was wrong.

In applying the rhochrematics concept, the model of the total system, including accumulation of raw materials, production, and distribution, can be used to evaluate the changes in given policies. A policy change can be made in any one segment of the total process, and the impact of this change can be evaluated through the medium of simulated operating results. This tool gives management an opportunity to test and evaluate proposals without running the risk of actually installing new approaches and absorbing the necessary costs associated with system changes.

Changes in the various segments of the total system can be programmed and "run" over a period of time in order to discover which parts of the total flow are most sensitive to change. If wide fluctuations result at a particular point because of what were considered minor policy changes in another area, management has a good clue for subsequent decision making and/or more detailed investigation.

Typically, the system simulation which can be used for describing an entire operation will be a relatively closed system. This means that the operation is simulated with little participation by outside individuals or other external variables; that is, policy changes or alternative decisions are programmed into the simulation model at relatively few points.

When the simulation program is used more for demonstration or training, it may allow for participation of outside decision makers. In this case the decision makers who are external to the simulation process must make key decisions which are then fed into the computer. In accordance with the basic program and the choices of the "players," the results of the operation are simulated. This can be a valuable exercise in that it forces the people involved to make decisions in a dynamic environment and also to think about all the various factors involved in the total system.

It is quite obvious that the use of simulation techniques, particularly for large-scale operations, would not be possible if it were not for the availability of large-scale electronic computing equipment. While the design of simulation systems is not overly complicated and does not involve a great deal of sophisticated mathematics, a vast quantity of variables and a large number of equations are involved. Although the equations are simple to manipulate, there can be many thousands of them and they all must be computed for each time period involved in simulating the operation. With the computer these calculations are simple and elaborate system simulations are possible.

The application of operations-research techniques in the science of material and information flow should complement the use of simulation techniques. As simulation studies provide clues concerning the most sensitive areas of decision making, these areas can be isolated and studied in more detailed fashion. The simulation approach is designed to help describe the total system and in many cases to point the way toward better operating approaches. However, system simulation does not have as an objective optimization of the total system or even any large segment. Operations-research techniques, on the other hand, can be applied where an optimum is desired: either the best-profit or the least-lost situation. The application of probability and statistics, linear and mathematical programming, queuing theory, Monte Carlo techniques, and dynamic programming can all contribute toward a science of material and information flow. If these techniques are applied within the over-all framework of a total-system concept, they can be useful to the researcher and ultimately to management (Chapter 11).

Some work has been done on simulation of the entire firm by a research group at MIT under the direction of Jay W. Forrester. He calls his approach "industrial dynamics," a mathematical model for analyzing stability and fluctuation of an industrial system.[9] The model has closed-loop, information-feedback characteristics and also incorporates decision-making procedures. There are five interacting subsystems: material flow, order flow, money flow, capital-equipment generation and usage, and manpower employment and mobility. The subsystems are all interconnected by information flow or a decision-making network. Although these studies in themselves are extremely complex, continuing efforts are being directed toward incorporating all the subsystems into one total system.

The situations to be studied can be represented realistically only by sophisticated mathematical systems. Likewise, if the real-life situation is unstable, then the system simulation program must represent this phenomenon. In order to describe a total system accurately, it often is necessary to evaluate hundreds of variables. The goal is to develop improved, but not "optimum," system design. There is no meaningful definition of an optimum system, nor is there any method of proving that the designated system is the best achievable.

A mathematical model should not be undertaken until every functional relationship is defined completely. This often leads to the omission of admittedly significant factors (most of the "intangible" influences on decisions) because they are unmeasured or unmeasurable. This approach is equivalent to saying that they have zero effect—an obvious oversimplification.

As long as attention is focused on the complete flow of material and information from the raw-material stage to the production process and through the distribution system, progress can be made in establishing rhochrematics as a science. No one particular technique will foster a science of material and information flow. The necessary body of theory and principles can be developed, however, by means of an integrated research approach involving all available tools and techniques in management science.

APPLICATION OF RHOCHREMATICS

It is possible to illustrate the philosophy of rhochrematics without sophisticated mathematical models and without including total material

[9] Forrester, *op. cit.*

flow. The following example shows how this kind of analysis points out significant relationships which are not always recognized.

The Service Cycle

It is common to think of service time as the time it takes for delivery from the warehouse to the customer. However, the service cycle in reality includes the total time after the need for goods is recognized until the goods are available for us. Figure 14 shows the complete service cycle.

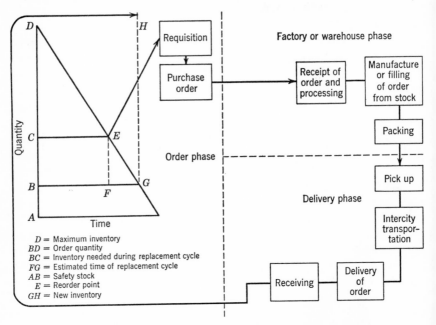

Fig. 14. The three phases of the delivery cycle.

This service cycle can be divided into three phases: (1) the order phase, (2) the warehouse phase, and (3) the delivery phase. The order phase includes all activities of the buyer necessary to transfer or communicate the need of a product to a seller at the place where the product is manufactured or stored. Specific activities include recognition of the need to order or reorder; the paper work involved in writing a requisition and purchase order; and the transfer of the order to the vendor. If the vendor's representative calls on the buyer and gets the order, the transfer of the order to the plant or warehouse would still be a part of the order phase of the service cycle.

The warehouse phase includes the activities needed to get the order ready for shipment, e.g., the receipt and processing of the order; the planning, scheduling, and manufacturing or the filling of the order from stock; and the packing of the order for shipment.

The delivery phase involves the physical transfer of the product from the seller to the buyer. The delivery from plant or warehouse to the shipper, the transfer to the buyer's location, and the receipt and processing of the incoming shipment are activities of the delivery phase of the cycle.

The lead time between recognizing the need and the satisfaction of that need therefore includes all the activities outlined. Some of these activities are carried out by the customer, some by the seller, and the rest by outside agencies. The buyer can reduce total lead time by accelerating the activities within his operation or by bringing economic pressure on the seller to improve that portion of the service cycle which the seller controls.

Delivery Service and Sales

Most customers would like to have manufacturers, or their representatives in the distribution system, maintain all inventories beyond current requirements and locate these inventories close at hand. This relieves the customers of carrying safety stocks; the reorder point could approach zero inventory. Customers need carry only those inventories consistent with ordering in economic quantities. The manufacturer has the prime responsibility of forecasting demand, maintaining safety stocks, and giving the customer prompt delivery service from decentralized inventories.

How much are sales influenced by the amount of service the seller provides? Or stated in other words, will there be an increase in sales if the seller provides better service? Klass interviewed 300 executives in 208 industrial companies across the country. Over all, the considerations which were rated as being most important to buyers included:

> Maintaining quality consistent with specifications
> On time delivery performance
> An honest and sincere attitude on the part of salesmen
> Price
> Keeping the buyer informed about new products and product developments
> Effective handling of requests for samples and information [10]

It is significant that "on time delivery performance" ranked as the second most important consideration. This is consistent with other studies which illustrate a direct correlation between sales and service, and the simplest representation of this is a straight-line, or linear, relationship. Figure 15 shows that an individual firm can increase its share of the market pro-

[10] Bertrand Klass, "What Factors Affect Industrial Buying Decisions?" *Industrial Marketing*, May, 1961, pp. 33–35.

vided it improves its delivery service relative to other companies in the industry.

The share of the market equals the service time multiplied by a constant. When the change in service time does not result in as great a change in sales, the constant is less than 1. Usually, this is the case, because a firm seldom operates at the extremes of no service or perfect service; reasonably good service is provided by the typical firm.

When a firm is operating at either extreme of the service-time cycle, there is no longer a linear relationship. As service time approaches zero, the curve tends to become horizontal; the increase in sales realized by a decrease in service time from near perfect to perfect probably would be less than a similar rate of improvement in the intermediate portion of the

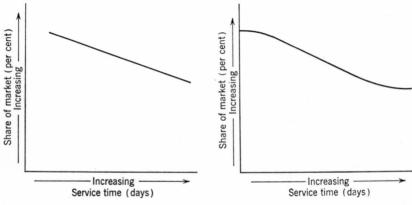

Fig. 15. Relationship between service time and share of the market.

Fig. 16. Relationship between service time and share of the market for extremes of service.

scale. Similarly, change in service from poor to very poor may have little effect on sales. Figure 16 illustrates the tendency of the sales-service curve to flatten out at either end of the scale.

Another factor also must be considered. Changes in sales as a function of service would not be constant or incremental, but would occur in steps. For example, a manufacturer would tend to initiate a significant improvement in service time in order to produce a psychological impact on the customer. A dramatic improvement, such as a reduction from ten to six days, would be more desirable than a gradual change from ten to six days over a long period of time. Figure 17, therefore, would be the most descriptive of the service-time–sales relationship.

The relationship of the change in sales to the change in service will vary in different industries, depending on competition and the possibility of product substitution. However, the important points suggested from this analysis are that (1) service changes at either extreme have little effect on sales, and (2) a service change must be significant to have a psychological impact on the customer.

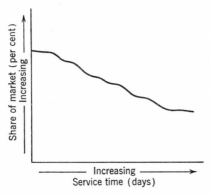

Fig. 17. Relationship of service time to sales with significant changes in service time.

A System of Improved Service

One method of improving customer delivery service is to reduce the time cycle by storing inventories in many locations close to the point of need. This implies, first of all, that someone has been able to forecast what and where the need will be. New techniques of forecasting are being developed. Rash writes:

> Forecasting is not crystal-gazing. In the past 20 years the art of forecasting has approached the stature of a science through the pooling of techniques and knowledge from the fields of mathematics, economics, and engineering.[11]

The real test of forecasting is the accuracy of the forecast in comparison with what happens and the ability to isolate distinct variables so that major errors may be recognized and corrected. As variables are added, the problem of measurement becomes more complex and the accuracy of the forecast more doubtful. For example, it may be possible to forecast the demand for refrigerators in this country for next year, but forecasting the demand for brand X, model Y, yellow, automatic-defrosting refrigerators in Omaha next year obviously is more difficult.

It becomes apparent, therefore, that when inventories are decentralized and the amount of inventory stored depends on the forecast for that region, additional inventories must be stored to offset the unreliability of the fore-

[11] Wayne Rash, "10-step Plan for Forecasting an Industrial Market," *Industrial Marketing,* March, 1961, p. 40.

cast. In fact, inventories must increase more than proportionally to provide for all contingencies. Table 3, a probability table prepared by the Bell Telephone Company, illustrates this point.

TABLE 3   Service-policy Effect on Order Point and Inventory Shows Order Point for Each Service Policy

| Demand during lead time | Order point, order-service policy, per cent | | | | |
	50	90	95	99	99.9999
1	1	3	3	4	9
10	10	15	16	19	29
100	100	113	117	124	153
1,000	1,000	1,037	1,050	1,075	1,158
10,000	10,000	10,112	10,152	10,232	10,500

If the demand during the lead time is 1 and the product is ordered when the stocks have declined to 1 unit, 50 per cent of the time there will be a stockout. When a company wants to provide stock in almost every situation (99.999 per cent of the time), the reorder point would occur when the stocks are reduced to 9 units. However, the rate of increase of the order point is not as great when the demand during lead time is larger. Therefore, as service is improved by increasing the number of decentralized storage units, the inventories necessary to provide this service increase dramatically and the cost increases accordingly. W. Clay Hill, of the General Electric Company, used a hypothetical but realistic example to illustrate the high cost of decentralized storage. He indicated that in a company whose sales were $50 million, nearly $3 million could be saved by reducing the number of distribution points from 100 to 25, by cutting warehouse replenishment time from 25 to 10 days, by storing slow-moving stocks in only 5 key warehouses, and by reducing the manufacturing cycle from 3 weeks to 1 week.[12] Magee reached the same conclusion:

> To suggest the size of the opportunity, one analysis with which I am familiar showed that cutting the number of field distribution points for a national product line from 50 to 25 would increase total transport costs by 7% but cut inventories 20% and cut total physical distribution costs 8%.[13]

A second and more logical approach to the customer-service problem is to maintain customer-service levels consistent with the demand of most customers, but accomplish this objective through a more efficient system of distribution. One plan is to centralize distribution points and gain sav-

[12] "The Case for 90% Satisfaction," *Business Week*, Jan. 14, 1961, pp. 82–85.
[13] Magee, *op. cit.*, p. 89.

ings through smaller inventories, less paper work, and greater control and still maintain equivalent service levels. This can be done by improving each phase of the service cycle and combining the three phases into an effective total system.

When the total service is considered, a business firm may find that it is not getting prompt service from decentralized storage points. A study was made of the service cycle of a firm which supplied products to retail stores. Orders were traced from the time the customer dispatched the order until the goods were delivered to the customer. The results were rather startling. Table 4 shows the cycle time necessary to complete 50, 90, and 100 per cent of the orders sampled.

TABLE 4   Number of Days for 50, 90, and 100 Per Cent
of Orders to Flow through Service Cycle

	50 per cent completed	90 per cent completed	100 per cent completed
Order phase	1.0	3.0	11
Warehouse phase	8	4.3	6
Delivery phase	2.0	3.7	5
Total service cycle	4.7	7.5	14

The company believed that it was providing daily deliveries to its customers, but the study indicated that only 50 per cent of the orders were in the hands of the customer 4.7 days after the customer placed the order. It was 7.5 days before 90 per cent of the orders completed the service cycle, and 14 days before all deliveries were made.

Improvements in the Ordering Phase

The ordering phase can be streamlined by using better techniques for recognizing the need to reorder and for accomplishing the ordering procedure. Electronic-data-processing equipment makes inventory management by exception a reality. The equipment can be programmed to report only those items which require attention. For example, in the manual system, items ready for reordering usually are found by time-consuming periodic review or by recognizing the need through a minimum-stock system. Either method leaves innumerable possibilities for costly stockout or overstocks. With electronic data processing, this problem can be eliminated. A machine can be programmed to review every item after each activity and report those items which have reached the reorder point. Thus only the items at the reorder point need be reviewed by people, and more time is available for routine planning and analysis. At the same time, accuracy is improved and better control maintained.

High-speed data transmission is a proven means of transferring data rapidly and accurately. It reduces the time required to transfer information concerning the need for inventory from the customer to the supplier and thus reduces the length of the service cycle by reducing the order phase of the cycle. The Raytheon Company uses Western Union's Tele-originator to transmit order data from district offices directly to the processing center in a way which provides simultaneous reproduction of data-processing cards.[14]

Improvements in the Warehouse Phase

Electronic data processing also is applicable to the warehouse or manufacturing phase of the cycle to process incoming orders for rapid action, to schedule manufacturing operations, or to process the information needed to fill the orders from inventory. The physical task of filling orders from stock can be streamlined by using conveyor systems, automatic warehouse flow systems, and so forth. The objective is to reduce the time lag between the receipt and shipment of the order.

The Reliance Electric Company of Cleveland has developed an automated storage warehouse which makes it possible for one man to supervise a storage area of over 5,000 square feet. The new system is capable of transporting loads to and from a central loading dock at the touch of selective electrical controls.[15]

The Maytag Company of Newton, Iowa, a manufacturer of home laundry equipment, wanted one-day service in filling parts orders. Sales studies revealed that 75 to 80 per cent of the total parts volume was made up of 352 items. These items were concentrated in a compact area and prepacked in quantities of ten for fast processing.[16]

Improvements in the Delivery Phase

Fast forms of transportation are available to reduce delivery time. Air-freight service is a reality and represents a challenge to both rail and over-the-road haulers. Airline officials estimate that jet-powered cargo planes will make it possible to reduce freight rates substantially.

Delivery time from New York to San Francisco can be a few hours instead of several days; goods in special orders can be put on a plane in New York in the morning and be delivered in San Francisco before noon.

[14] Speech by John T. Thompson, General Manager, Distribution Products Division, Raytheon Company, at the Distributors Management Conference sponsored by the AMA, Inc., San Francisco, Apr. 13, 1960.

[15] "Automatic Storage Cuts Space and Labor," *Distribution Age,* August, 1959, p. 43.

[16] *Distribution Age,* "A Prepacked Solution to Order-picking Problems," September, 1960, pp. 36–37.

As air-freight volume increases, there will be more scheduled flights and better pickup and delivery service. All these things will help to transfer shipments promptly.

We have attempted to point out the relationship of one activity (level of service) to inventory requirements, which in turn affects production planning and raw-material procurement. The rhochrematics approach is to create a new system to accomplish the desired level of service and to innovate by integrating the system through the different levels of production and distribution.

SUMMARY

Rhochrematics is the science of managing material flow from the raw-material stage through the many stages of processing and including the distribution of the finished product.

There have been numerous changes in the patterns of marketing products. The shift to market-oriented company policy, sales-promotion activities, and the segmentation of markets has brought about the manufacture of numerous new products, models, sizes, and colors. Consequently, demand is hard to predict, inventories often are stored in the wrong market area, inventories must be larger than before, and production planning becomes more difficult. The objective of rhochrematics is to reduce the material-flow cycle and the total costs associated with this flow.

A new conceptual scheme is a necessary antecedent of the effective application of rhochrematics on the industrial scene, i.e., the adoption by management of the view that movement of goods from raw material to consumer is a flow process which must be planned, organized, directed, and controlled as an integrated system. Acceptance of this viewpoint by top management is an essential prerequisite to the pursuit of work designed to develop and implement rhochrematics. Such management support is crucial to what must be essentially an introspective staff function concerned with describing, simulating, analyzing, and ultimately changing the major flow of material and information throughout the entire business.

If rhochrematics is to be of benefit to practicing management, it must provide a better solution to the problem of over-all material flow. System simulation (industrial dynamics or some similar approach) can be employed as a basic tool of analysis. However, much work needs to be done in order to refine this approach and maximize its usefulness.

At the same time, the more narrowly oriented techniques of management science and operations research can be employed in areas which are pointed up as sensitive, based on the over-all analysis. It is important that these techniques be applied whenever possible without assumptions which destroy the realism and meaningfulness of the results.

As we become more sophisticated in the application of management science and operations-research techniques to the problems of material flow, and as these techniques are fitted neatly into an over-all analysis based on system simulation, we can move ever closer to an excitingly new science of material and information flow, rhochrematics.

Chapter Nine
AUTOMATION AND NUMERICAL CONTROL

Automation represents an important application of the systems concept in business and industry. It is a term which describes the control of machines by machine—a natural evolutionary step in man's continuing efforts to achieve technological progress. Before automated operations are designed, it is essential to consider the entire operation as an integrated system and relate the impact of new tools on other subsystems of production and distribution.

Numerical-control machines are one example of automatic processing. These machines are engineered to achieve standards of performance impossible under other forms of manufacture. Further, they provide a degree of flexibility and efficiency unparalleled in man-operated machines.

We have selected numerical control as an example of an automated production system because it illustrates the concepts of planning, organizing, control, and communications as they pertain to a closed-sequence system. Further, this is an example of automation which offers promise as a production system of the future. The following topics will be covered in this chapter:

Automation and Systems
Numerical Control Defined
Historical Development

157

AUTOMATION AND SYSTEMS

Automation is one of the best-known applications of the systems concept. It requires an over-all systems approach to integrate all the operations of the business firm (e.g., perception of the product mission, product research and development, engineering and design, manufacture processing, distribution methods, and other facilitating activities) into an operational man-machine system. Successful automation is more than adopting a new production process for an existing product; it may require, for example, a complete redesign of the product to complement the automated system. One of the best-known examples of the need to redesign has occurred in the production of electronic equipment, where printed circuits and dip soldering have replaced more conventional assembly operations.

Distribution also is affected by the automation of production lines. Automation often results in the standardization of the product and limits the flexibility of output. Consequently, the distribution system of the organization must integrate its activities closely with those of the automated production system. Further, fixed costs increase as the company substitutes capital goods for direct labor. Therefore the automated plant should be operated at high capacity for an extended period of time in order to recover the capital investment.

The design of meaningful systems requires long-range planning. The master planning council (as set forth in the organizational model in Chapter 6) determines the product missions the company will initiate and the basic policy the company will follow to integrate the subsystems.

Definition of Automation

We have discussed the broad philosophy of automation as an application of the systems concept. Inasmuch as automation represents a philosophy or concept rather than the specific application of certain techniques, it is difficult to present a precise definition—it is a word of many meanings. It was coined by Del Harder of the Ford Motor Company in 1946 to denote the introduction of a new type of mechanized equipment. To Harder this term described the automatic transfer of in-process work from one machine to the next without human aid. Diebold has described automation as a basic change in production philosophy—a frame of reference which considers an industrial process as an integrated system from the introduction of the raw material to the packaging of the complete product. He defines automation as:

> . . . a new word denoting both automatic operation and the process of making things automatic. In the latter sense it includes several areas of industrial activity, such as product and process redesign, the theory of communication and control, and the design of machinery.[1]

Karsh defined automation as "the accomplishment of a work task by an integrated power-driven mechanism entirely without the direct application of human energy, skill, intelligence, or control." [2]

These definitions of automation range from a description of super-mechanization to continuous flow, where machines replace the energy of man in the direction, operation, and control of processing. Rather than limit the discussion to a single definition of automation, it is preferable to think of automation as a total concept. Using this idea, the basic features of automation are:

1. The replacement of the human operator in a step or steps of a process. Man appears outside the process—as a designer, planner, monitor, and maintainer—the machine does the work. This concept of increased mechanization was the first to be associated with automation.

2. The increased employment of feedback control—both theory and techniques—to the design and operation of automation systems. Mathematics is becoming an essential tool of business and industry.

3. The use of sensing, decision, and computing elements to replace human operators, implying machines with a higher "intelligence" content and ability to control a process. The computer is becoming a more and more common component.

4. A broad "systems" approach to new developments, viewing operations as a complex of men, materials, machines, methods, and money, rather than an array of isolated components. This leads to the breaking away from conventional techniques and approaches, both in machine and product design and in operating procedures.[3]

Advanced automation may be regarded as the phenomenon of machine controlling machines; i.e., a machine or device measures the output of the processing machine, makes sure that it is following programmed instructions, and corrects any mistakes which are made. Feedback is a

[1] John Diebold, *Automation: The Advent of the Automatic Factory,* D. Van Nostrand Company, Inc., Princeton, N.J., 1952, p. ix.

[2] Bernard Karsh, "Work and Automation," in Howard Boone Jacobson and Joseph S. Roucek (eds.), *Automation and Society,* Philosophical Library, Inc., New York, 1959, p. 387.

[3] Eugene M. Grabbe, "The Language of Automation" in *Automation in Business and Industry,* John Wiley & Sons, Inc., New York, 1957, pp. 21–22.

required element in this philosophy of automation; the output of the system is measured continually in terms of the item being controlled, and the input is modified to reduce any divergence or error to zero (Chapter 4). Advanced automation, therefore, is an example of a closed-sequence system where control is built into the system, and the system is operated without the need for any further external action. It is an illustration of a structured system with each component arranged in precise order; the output can be predicted and measured, and the operating efficiency of the system can be determined.

Rethinking for Automatic Systems

In a *Fortune* Round Table discussion an official of the automobile industry was asked if he thought the final assembly of automobiles could be automated. He replied that it would never happen during this century; applications of automation would be confined to the subassembly divisions of the plant. Another member of the Round Table pointed out, however, that the present automobile was designed to be hand-assembled, whereas future automobiles could just as well be designed to be assembled by machine.[4]

Automation involves a process of complete *rethinking*. Rethinking means the attitude of mind which enables one to get outside of a problem that seems insolvable and approach it in a new and perhaps entirely different way. This approach should be practiced in every systems-design program. Diebold has stressed this need for rethinking: "In many cases we must redesign our products, our processing methods, and our machines in order to take advantage of automation. This involves rethinking."[5]

Rethinking in relation to the product resulted in the printed circuit for the electronics industry. This made it possible to mass-produce radios and television sets by a semiautomatic process. A second and more complete example was Project Tinkertoy, sponsored by the Navy's Bureau of Aeronautics. This project incorporated the principle of standardization with flexibility. The process, known as modular construction, standardized the basic wafers and made them the common denominator for machine-made modular resistors, capacitors, and tube mounts.[6] This principle helped solve the problem of the manufacturers who had found it difficult to standardize the many sizes and shapes of resistors and condensers so that these units could be adapted to the printed circuit.

[4] "Automatic Factories," *Fortune,* October, 1953, p. 168.

[5] John Diebold, "Automation: The New Technology," *Harvard Business Review,* November–December, 1953, p. 63.

[6] Edmund L. Van Deusen, "Electronics Goes Modern," *Fortune,* June, 1955, pp. 132–136.

Another example of product redesign deals with the manufacture of a cooking stove, a case of partial automation. Before installing the automatic machinery the manufacturer had been selling two price lines and offering eight different styles in each price category—sixteen product variations in all. It was not economical to make so many different styles with the new machinery, but by redesigning the product it was possible to reduce all sixteen varieties into one basic body. Different variations were created from this basic body by arranging the heating elements in various ways and adding special features to some models. Shortly after the installation of the automatic machinery, competition forced the introduction of another price line, but again, it was possible to vary the panel and a few accessories to achieve the necessary change.[7]

Often it is necessary to analyze how a product is being made, with the thought of developing new processes which would be easier to automate. The net result might be a plant-wide system of automation similar to an oil refinery.

In all types of automation it is necessary to rethink the entire operation as a system and integrate it as a whole. Of the numerous applications of the philosophy of automation, three broad applications stand out: Detroit-style automation, process-control automation, and office automation. These are discussed briefly in the following sections. A more comprehensive discussion is presented on a specific type of automation (numerical-control machines) later in the chapter.

Detroit-style Automation

Detroit style describes that type of automation which typically has been applied in the mass production of standardized parts or components. It was suggested earlier that automation had its origin in Detroit. When the term was first published in a report on the pioneering work at Ford, it was defined as "the art of applying mechanical devices to manipulate work pieces into and out of equipment, turn parts between operations, remove scraps, and to perform these tasks in time sequence with production equipment so that the line can be wholly or partially under pushbutton control at strategic stations." [8]

Detroit-style automation of plant operations may range from a single line of automatic equipment (e.g., milling machines which are fed and cycled continuously with automatic handling) to complete production facilities where components are fed, positioned, adjusted, sorted, assembled,

---

[7] Diebold, *Automation: The Advent of the Automatic Factory,* p. 44.

[8] Ruppert LaGrande, "Ford Handles by Automation," *American Machinist,* Oct. 21, 1948, pp. 107–122.

and tested automatically. Detroit-style automation has been introduced in the metal-working, component-manufacturing, and assembling types of industries, e.g., automotive, primary metals, fabricated metal products, machinery, transportation equipment, paper manufacturing, and electrical- and electronic-equipment industries.

Detroit-style automation applies the systems concept. Groups or sequences of operations, automatic mechanisms or machines, and control and handling devices are brought into a single man-machine system in a continuous operation. In the electrical field, for example, General Electric produces motors ranging from 7½ to 30 horsepower on two automated lines in its Schenectady plant. More than a hundred standard models are produced in batches, each model being turned out once in two weeks. The equipment for this plant took over two years to design, build, and get into operation. The cost was in excess of $7 million.

Another significant example of automation is the Bucyrus plant of the Timken Roller Bearing Company, where all the complex operations involved in the manufacture of roller bearings are performed automatically. In this plant there are 11 automatic lines with a combined capacity of 30 million tapered roller bearings a year. The production rate of 192 bearings per man per eight-hour shift is about four times the rate produced by more conventional production systems.

Most radio and television manufacturers are using printed circuit boards and assembling components to these boards automatically. This has required the redesign of most of the components in order that they may be integrated into the printed circuit. In certain instances the components are inserted into the printed-circuit boards automatically, and the connections are soldered as the board moves through a molten solder bath and are tested automatically as the board proceeds along the production line.

Basically, Detroit-style automation has been utilized for items produced in large quantities. It has been geared to the concept of high-volume production with few variables. Although it is not as glamorous as those examples of automation which incorporate feedback control with a closed-loop system, Detroit-style automation is a more rudimentary example of the application of the systems concept and is of fundamental importance in the mass-producing industries.

Automation in the Process Industries

Automation has been applied in its most complete form in the process industries. The process industries are those that handle bulk solids, liquids, or gases in some form and modify these materials either by physical or chemical means to produce a finished product with the desired properties.

Many of these processes are strictly physical in nature. Some are chemical, and some are combinations of the two.[9]

The implementation of the systems concept and automation in the processing-type industry has been made possible by the development of process-control computers which receive information, perform mathematical computations, make comparisons and evaluations resulting in decisions, and provide output information signals for process control. By the use of computers it has been possible to automate the many process industries under the closed-loop concept, with feedback.

One of the earliest applications of the computer to process industry was at the Texaco Refinery at Port Arthur, Tex., where a computer has been operating in the catalytic polymerization unit since 1959. In the system the computer receives a vast number of inputs, including 26 flow rates, 72 temperatures, 3 pressures, and 3 gas compositions. The computer performs calculations and initiates several independent control actions and optimizes performance of the total system, given the various inputs and the required outputs. The computer (1) determines the maximum reactor-inlet pressure; (2) distributes the available feed materials to five parallel pairs of reactors to take advantage of any differences in catalyst activity; (3) determines the amount of water to be injected into the catalyst activation; and (4) when needed, determines the amount of unreacted material which should be returned to the reactor inlet.[10]

Many other examples of automation in the process-control industry exist. Within the past six years these applications have advanced from theory to practice in petroleum refining, electrical power, cement and paper, gas transmission, and many other industries.

Office Automation

The third example of automation is the application of the systems concept to information-handling and decision-making problems in the office. Mechanization in the office once was limited to man-machine systems, such as the typewriter, adding machine, and so forth. Later machines performing several operations appeared, such as the typewriter combined with the adding machine, complex bookkeeping machines, and finally punched-card accounting machines. The recent development of electronic-data-processing machines has provided business managers an opportunity to engineer better systems of information processing, data recording, and decision making.

[9] C. G. Laspe, "Process Control in the Petroleum and Chemical Industries," in Eugene M. Grabbe (ed.), *Automation in Business and Industry,* John Wiley & Sons, Inc., New York, 1957, p. 420.

[10] Thomas N. Stout, "Process Control: Past, Present and Future," *Annals of the American Academy of Political and Social Sciences,* March, 1962, pp. 32–33.

These applications are discussed more completely in Chapter 10, Data-processing Systems.

In the future the difference between the factory and the office operation will become less distinct, for there is a trend toward integrating the information processing of the office and automatic factory. This is another example of the development of increasingly complex, total systems.

Automation and Versatility

The question of designing machines for automation centers around the need for versatility. Applications of the general systems concept must be applied to the unique characteristics of the industry under consideration. Production of single continuum items such as oil, wire, and sugar present different problems in automatic production from discrete objects such as radiator castings, automobile engines, or a complex electric motor. The problems of automation vary with the characteristics of the end product, the materials used, and the nature of the components. When the output volume is small or uncertain and/or the chance of product-design changes are great, the risk of introducing Detroit-style automation may be substantial. One approach is to construct special-purpose systems and write off the cost of such a system quickly. Another approach is to use a more flexible automated system. Numerical control is an example of automation which may be applied to a single task. Flexibility is achieved by automating the basic functions of production. Currently, numerical-control programs may be created as a *facilitating system* (Chapter 6) to service the various *project systems* by processing material through specific stages. It may be possible in the future to link these basic machines into a processing line and manufacture an entire product automatically. If a different output were required, it would be necessary only to change the instructions and sequence of operations. Such an arrangement of machines would become a project system in an automated factory.

NUMERICAL CONTROL DEFINED

Numerical control is a closed-sequence system with feedback. Moreover, it is a structured system and, to a large degree, predictable. Inputs of technical information flow to the processor (the producing machine) in the form of a numerical code which describes a complete work cycle.

The instructions are coded on media such as punched cards, punched tape, or magnetic tape. Machine operations may be controlled as a point-to-point positioning or by controlling the machine tool in a continuous path for two or more axes of coordinated motion.

A "positioning" system sequentially locates the tool at specified points of the work. At these points the machine tool performs an operation. The locus or path of the tool between the points of operation is relatively unimportant and unspecified, because machine operations are not conducted during these intervals. *Continuous-path* machining is accomplished when the location points become closer and closer together, until the machine operations are continuous with the movement of the tool rather than only at specified points.

The instructions command the movements of the machine through electronic impulses to servomotors which control the movement of the

Fig. 18. Giddings & Lewis spar and skin milling machine. Photograph Courtesy of Giddings & Lewis Machine Tool Company, Fond du Lac, Wis.

tools. Each instruction is followed in sequence until the task has been completed. This system makes it possible to process a single part or to repeat the cycle over and over until the desired number of parts are produced.

In contrast to conventional processing systems, numerical control can reduce or eliminate the need for complicated jigs, fixtures, and templates; reduce setup time, machine time, and operator decision time; increase accuracy; and prolong tool life.

Figure 18 is a photograph of the world's first machine tool to be automated and controlled by the medium of magnetic tape—the Giddings & Lewis spar and skin milling machine. Shown on the machine's table is an integrally ribbed skin for the North American F-100D Super Sabre. Seen at the right are the system's magnetic-tape playback and machine-control units which operate all machine movements.

The majority of applications of numerical control have been in the machine-tool field. The concept of numerical control, however, is not limited to machine tools. Any process may be controlled numerically if its operating characteristics can be planned and measured. Schaller states:

> Operating items of speed, feed, length, flow, temperature, and pressure, for example, are amenable to control. These elements can be translated by electrical or electronic signals or mechanical devices to control the basic operation.[11]

HISTORICAL DEVELOPMENT

Joseph Jacquard used punched cards to control his textile looms. The perforations in the cards activated mechanical devices and controlled the operation of the looms. These remarkable machines were exhibited in Paris in 1801. Since that time many other machines have been built to operate on the same principle, e.g., the player piano. Even the numerical-control machines of today use the same idea developed by Jacquard, but now electronic devices transfer information and activate the machines.

The numerical-control concept originated as a result of a study sponsored jointly by the Parsons Corporation of Traverse City, Mich., and the United States Air Force. The Parsons Corporation had experienced difficulty in the manufacture of propeller-blade inspection templates, and it was hoped that some form of automatic machine control could provide a solution to this problem.[12]

A report describing design and performance specifications of the proposed system was submitted in June, 1950. The first phase of the program involved an investigation of possible applications of automatic control to a wide range of machine-tool systems. A milling machine was chosen as the most convenient tool which could be adapted to three-axes control. Following the initial report, a program was started to construct an experimental machine-control system incorporating the principles of numerical control. When the construction of the prototype was approximately 30

[11] Gilbert S. Schaller, *Engineering Manufacturing Methods,* McGraw-Hill Book Company, Inc., New York, 1959, pp. 330–331.

[12] *Design, Development and Evaluation of a Numerically Controlled Milling Machine,* MIT, Servomechanism Laboratory, Final Report, D.I.C. 6873, Cambridge, Mass., 1956.

per cent complete, the Parsons Corporation terminated its sponsorship and the Air Materiel Command of the United States Air Force assumed full financial responsibility for the program. In March, 1952, the construction of the first numerical-control milling machine was completed. Later in the same year, this machine was demonstrated to representatives of the airframe industry and to a group of machine-tool builders.

During the next three years, the Servomechanisms Laboratory at MIT, under Air Force sponsorship, conducted an extensive program to test the performance of the machine. A number of reports were published detailing all phases of the machine development, as well as possible applications in industry.

The construction of a second machine was completed in May, 1955. The design of this machine incorporated a number of refinements which eliminated many of the difficulties experienced in the operation of the first model. This industrial prototype machine was built under the sponsorship of the Giddings and Lewis Machine Tool Company of Fond du Lac, Wis. (Figure 18).

The experiment at MIT was highly successful, but the feasibility of using this machine could not be judged in a nonindustrial environment. It was decided, therefore, to introduce the machines to manufacturers in the airframe industry, where close tolerances, complex manufacturing problems, short lead times, and increasing costs were prevailing characteristics. Although numerical control was a new concept, it was decided to install the machines without delay. In most instances the companies designated to receive the machines were not fully informed with regard to effective operations of the machines. However, the Air Force decided that sufficient insight had been gained from the MIT program to allow limited operation during a learning period. In 1957, the first numerical-control skin and profile mills were delivered to the airframe industry. The acquisition of additional numerical-control equipment has been steady since that time.

SYSTEM FLOW

The work flow in the production of parts generally goes through six stages: (1) engineering drawing, (2) production planning, (3) tool design, (4) tool fabrication, (5) machine setup, and (6) machine operation. Various systems of numerical control require different components, media, and arrangement of functions. It is very difficult, therefore, to relate the stages of numerical control to a conventional system of planning and manufacture.

The Boeing Company in Seattle has adopted a system of work flow which is standard in the Aero-Space Division and representative of many numerical-control systems. This flow is traced (see Figure 19 for graphic illustration) through sixteen steps as follows:

1. The source data are analyzed by the part programmer. Source data include the master dimension listing, part drawing, and tool drawing.

2. The programming of the part is completed. The instructions for the machine plan, machine commands, and the part geometry solutions are converted into numerical-control language.

3. The program is transferred from the data contained on the program sheet to a deck of punched cards.

4. The information punched on the cards is verified against the written program.

5. The information contained on the punched cards is printed out in a listing, one line of information for each card in the deck.

6. The printed data in the listing are checked against the information on the program sheet.

7. The data on the punched cards are transferred into the media of magnetic tape.

8. The part-programming data on tape and a tape of master dimensional data are input for the computer. The computer processes the data and computes the cutter center path and the time and distance required for each axis of machine motion. This information is stored on tape.

9. The computer output tapes are converted into numerical-control punched control tapes, intermediate tapes, card decks, and printouts.

10. The printout is checked against the original program sheet prepared in step 2.

11. The intermediate control media are maintained: punched cards for the Cincinnati; 1-inch, 7-channel punched tape for the Concord; and 1-inch, 8-channel punched tape for the ECS (electronic control system).

12. The IBM 80-column card deck is converted into a Remington Rand 90-column card deck for the Cincinnati system.

13. The data contained on the media described in steps 11 and 12 are processed further. The data on the Remington Rand deck are interpreted, verified, and listed. The 7-channel punched tape in the Concord system is converted into 1-inch, 14-channel magnetic tape. The 8-channel punched tape in the ECS system is converted into ½-inch, 8-channel magnetic tape.

14. The media, as described in Figure 3, are maintained for numerical-control-machine control.

15. The parts are machined by the numerical-control machines which are controlled by the tapes or cards.

16. The entire process is coordinated from the program development and tool and machine fabrication through final acceptance of the finished part by quality control.

Most of the steps listed in this example of numerical-control work flow involve the conversion of data into other media, the processing of the data, and the checking of the converted or processed data against the original program sheet. The usual methods planning, fixture design, tool design, and work scheduling must be done. Further, the path to be followed by the cutter must be determined, together with speeds, feeds, cutter sizes, checking points, and other machine functions which are to be accomplished during the processing cycle. It should be noted that there are two kinds of information generated, dimensional data defining the path geometry and information concerned with the processing aspects of the job, e.g., feed rates, sequence of cuts, and cutter size.

Programming Numerical Control

In the early stages of the development of a numerical-control programming system, the time required for computer-program debugging more than equaled the time required for manual programming. Consequently, an effort was made to minimize programming time by developing subroutines for carrying out the steps in the computation process.

Most complete programs were used less than ten times; therefore the approach was to set aside and reuse the appropriate portion of an old program whenever it could be adapted to a new program. The subroutine was given a number to which the programmer could refer when incorporating it in the system he was designing. Early experience indicated that a major portion of each new program could be created by referring to a library of subroutines from former programs.

The library of subroutines solved many of the problems encountered in program design but created others. Before long the library became large, and the difficulty of selecting the appropriate subroutine for a new program and of modifying it according to current needs increased.

Often the subroutines used were similar. This led to a different approach, that of using a single generalized program which could be adapted to fit each particular case. The first step in this approach is to determine the common factors so that a skeleton program can be devised. The computer then proceeds to make the necessary calculations. It is sufficient to say that the technical aspects of devising a systematized solution to the problems of programming data for the computer are extremely complicated.

Recently the Aerospace Industries Association of America, Inc., adopted a standardized system. This system is called APT (automatically programmed tools) and is a collection of computer programs designed to eliminate most of the tedious mathematical operations.

To produce a part using the APT system, the programmer analyzes each design in terms of its geometric forms, e.g., straight lines, circles, el-

NUMERICAL CONT

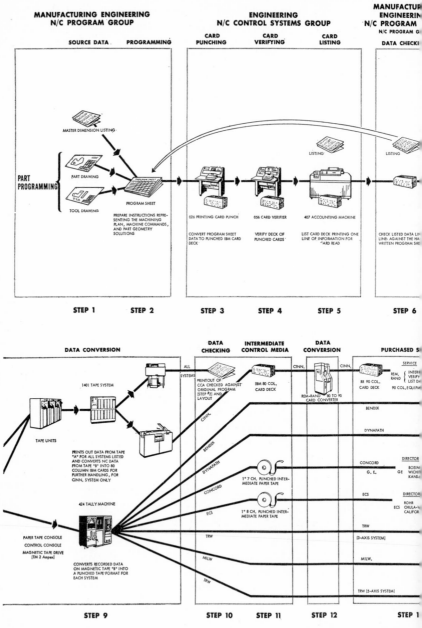

Fig. 19. Numerical-control w

?K FLOW

ENGINEERING
N/C CONTROL SYSTEMS GROUP

DATA CONVERSION   DATA PROCESSING

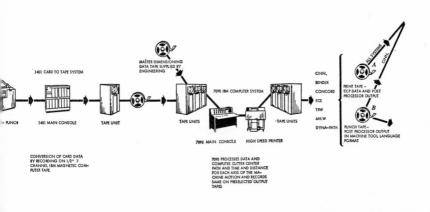

1401 CARD TO TAPE SYSTEM

MASTER DIMENSIONING DATA TAPE SUPPLIED BY ENGINEERING

7090 IBM COMPUTER SYSTEM

CINN.
BENDIX
CONCORD
ECS
TRW
MILW
DYNA-PATH

ALL SYSTEMS   CINN.

A

PRINT TAPE –
CCP DATA AND POST PROCESSOR OUTPUT

B

PUNCH TAPE –
POST PROCESSOR OUTPUT IN MACHINE TOOL LANGUAGE FORMAT

– PUNCH   1401 MAIN CONSOLE   TAPE UNIT   TAPE UNITS   • TAPE UNITS

7090 MAIN CONSOLE   HIGH SPEED PRINTER

CONVERSION OF CARD DATA BY RECORDING ON 1/2" 7 CHANNEL IBM MAGNETIC COMPUTER TAPE

7090 PROCESSES DATA AND COMPUTES CUTTER CENTER PATH AND TIME AND DISTANCE FOR EACH AXIS OF THE MACHINE MOTION AND RECORDS SAME ON PRESELECTED OUTPUT TAPES

STEP 7   **STEP 8**

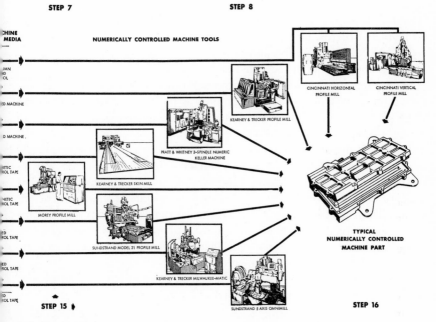

:HINE
MEDIA

NUMERICALLY CONTROLLED MACHINE TOOLS

CINCINNATI HORIZONTAL PROFILE MILL   CINCINNATI VERTICAL PROFILE MILL

KEARNEY & TRECKER PROFILE MILL

PRATT & WHITNEY 3-SPINDLE NUMERIC KELLER MACHINE

KEARNEY & TRECKER SKIN MILL

MOREY PROFILE MILL

SUNDSTRAND MODEL 21 PROFILE MILL

KEARNEY & TRECKER MILWAUKEE-MATIC

SUNDSTRAND 5 AXIS OMNIMILL

TYPICAL
NUMERICALLY CONTROLLED
MACHINE PART

STEP 15   **STEP 16**

y of the Boeing Company.

lipses, parabolas, etc. Then in the English-like APT language, the programmer describes the part geometry and motions to be accomplished by the numerically controlled equipment.[13]

The computer translates these instructions, makes the necessary mathematical calculations, and automatically produces the coded instructions for the machine-controlled equipment.

EVALUATION OF NUMERICAL CONTROL

Numerical control is being applied successfully within the airframe and missile industry, but not without some problems. Most of the problems can be traced to the rapid development of this concept. Some of the problems and criticisms which have been encountered can be summarized as follows:

1. There is a high capital investment required for the purchase of the machines and supporting equipment. This criticism applies more to continuous-path systems than to positioning operations.

2. The cost of establishing suitable computing and programming facilities is great. The programming requires a high level of skill, particularly in devising new routines.

3. There is a lack of compatibility among the various systems designed by competitive machine manufacturers. Even the media are not standardized (cards, tape, or magnetic tape). A National Aerospace Standard (NAS 943) does exist, however, for punched tape, and this form of machine input is generally accepted as the most desirable.

4. Preparation of magnetic tapes for the machine tools often has been a time-consuming process, inasmuch as there are only a limited number of directors within the United States to perform the process.

5. Machine-tool operators, programming errors, and machine malfunctions are the prime sources of parts rejections when they occur. This is usually due to a lack of adequate techniques for checking tapes and the inexperience of some programmers, operators, and maintenance personnel.

6. The numerically controlled machines operate at standard machine speeds. They must be utilized to a greater capacity than conventional machines, therefore, if an economic advantage is to be gained.

7. Maintenance of these machines is more complicated, and it requires special training and equipment.

8. Quality control has been a problem. An unusual amount of time has been required to check a finished part of irregular design.

[13] *Introduction to Part Programming,* Aerospace Industries Association of America, Inc., San Diego, Calif., 1961, p. 1.

9. Equipment is being developed so rapidly that the user may install machines where the development will continue after installation. This is time-consuming and expensive.

10. Many shop supervisors and workers are reluctant to accept numerical control.

Many of the problems or criticisms of numerical control which were stated relate to first-generation machine design, the difficulty of preparing machine instructions accurately, and the large initial capital investment. Machines are being designed, however, which will perform more accurately and with fewer breakdowns. Moreover, most machines will soon be controlled by compatible systems. Problems associated with information preparation are a function of the skill of the program-engineering group. These problems will decrease as that group gains experience and adopts improved techniques of programming. Numerical-control machines are expensive, but the costs must be reviewed relative to the cost of the entire system and relative to the capabilities and productivity of the system.

Numerical control has many advantages which are present in most applications and which tend to offset the high capital investment of this equipment. These examples may be summarized as follows:

1. Extreme accuracy is available on the more complicated shapes and larger parts. These are the kinds of parts which are the most difficult to manufacture with man-operated equipment.

2. The equipment is flexible. More than one machine of the same type can be operated from the same tape. The machines may be adjacent to each other or at different and remote locations.

3. Shorter lead times are required to get a part into production since some of the traditional operations are eliminated, e.g., tool fabrication.

4. There is less scrap due to the greater accuracy of the system and the reduction of machinists' errors.

5. It is not necessary to store large inventories of tools, jigs, and templates. Tapes can be stored outside of the factory area and require but a fraction of the space needed by templates.

6. It takes less time to prepare the machine for operation than the setup time required with the conventional machine.

7. Fewer skilled operators are required, even on close-tolerance jobs.

8. The machine can duplicate parts on succeeding runs within close tolerances. This is important in the production of interchangeable parts.

9. Normally, fewer inspections are required, and experience indicates that only the first part needs 100 per cent inspection.

10. The machine can operate continuously without interruption, except for maintenance.

These advantages may be summarized by pointing out that numerical-control machines can perform work which would be impossible to perform with conventional machines. Further, the productivity of these machines is greater than that of conventional machines in many applications. The real value of these automated systems, however, can be tested only in specific applications.

After the MIT machine was operating successfully, the people involved in the program were anxious to demonstrate its potential to save money. A study was organized to investigate the economic feasibility of the new system. Parts were selected for manufacture, and ten independent job shops were invited to submit estimates on the cost of manufacture. The plan was to compare these estimates with the cost of manufacturing the part on a numerical-control machine. Results of the study indicated that the different bidders used various methods in the manufacture of the part and different approaches in estimating the costs of manufacture. This discrepancy was apparent throughout the study, and it led to the conclusion that there are no prevailing prices in the market based on costs alone.[14] Therefore manufacturers with numerical-control equipment could be underbid on a job if the competitive firm needed business or used a different method of figuring costs. The bid price would not prove or disprove the economic feasibility of numerical control.

It is difficult to compare this system with a conventional system, for different kinds of planning and information preparation are involved. It is not sufficient to compare the operation of the machine unit alone, but instead the total system cost must be measured and compared.

IMPACT OF NUMERICAL CONTROL

As an advanced type of processing system, numerical control will have a definite impact in most areas of the industrial firm. Certainly the engineering department will be affected by this development.

Engineering

In the near future many companies using numerical control will change traditional drafting practices. It will be possible to discontinue drafting in many designs, for the tape will become the new form of record. Tape records will be supplemented by photographs of engineering sketches and pictures of oscilloscope images stored on microfilm.

Mathematics will gain in importance, for much of the actual testing of a new design will be accomplished mathematically. The engineer's job

---

[14] Robert H. Gregory and Thomas V. Atwater, *Economic Studies of Work Performed on a Numerically Controlled Milling Machine,* MIT, Servomechanisms Laboratory, Engineering Report 18, D.I.C. 6873, Cambridge, Mass., 1956.

will be to transfer the design and operating requirements into computer language as a mathematical function. The computer will do the rest.

Manufacturing

The production of parts will become highly technical because of more refined design techniques. Most shop managers will have an engineering background. The production shop will be backed by a group of engineers who will solve production problems. Minor design problems, tooling problems, cutter problems, machine application, and problems in manufacturing technique will all be a part of this group's work load.

Other manufacturing activities to be affected will include machine-maintenance scheduling of processing as lead time is reduced and machine utilization becomes critical; control of quality with new inspection devices; and change of product design to conform to the capabilities of the new equipment.

System Design

The effect of numerical control will be felt throughout the entire company. However, the principal effect will be reflected in systems design. This concept will change the traditional requirements of work and information flow. The language of data transmission, the components in the system, and the control features of the system can all be different, which will free the design from past limitations. For example, much of the processing and technical information will be combined as a single input of information, and these inputs will occur in a language compatible with machine usage. A different type of person will be planning the operation of a system which will be more structured and predictable. Further, it will be a system which is capable of adjusting to changing market demands without confusion or time lag.

APPLICATIONS

Numerical control has been applied in a limited way outside of the aircraft industry. Further, most companies considering numerical control are thinking of *positioning* applications, rather than continuous-path. This is understandable, since the positioning machines are moderately priced and easier to justify. In addition, these relatively simple systems rarely need computer service because they are based on linear motions and positioning can be accomplished by punched tape. The prime advantage is the inherent accuracy of numerical control. Drilling, punching, spot welding, riveting, boring, tapping, countersinking, etc., can be accomplished quickly and without error.

Continuous-path applications are typical in the aircraft industry. However, there have been a few in other industries. The Parsons Corporation was interested in numerical control because of the difficulties experienced in the manufacture of propeller templates. In the MIT economic study previously referred to, the templates were unquestionably the best application. The template studied was a testing device required in moderate quantities. In another example, Giddings and Lewis's bid on a series of templates for an Onsrud spar mill was 60 per cent lower than the closest competitive bid and they were produced at a profit.[15]

Another interesting application of numerical control occurred in the manufacture of warped surfaces. The capabilities of the concept were demonstrated at MIT early in 1956 when a General Electric turbine blade was produced on the laboratory milling machine.[16] The number of possible profiles was more than a hundred, and the designer had spent considerable time calculating the desired curvature for each new turbine blade. The advantage of numerical control in this situation was obvious; the computer could reduce the design time and even create new designs when necessary. General Electric proceeded to use numerical control in the manufacture of these blades.

The application of numerical control to die sinking was not economical at MIT because of high preparation costs. In an industrial application, however, it was proved that reductions in lead time and labor costs made tape control feasible. The first dies machined were produced on the DiMil developed by Giddings and Lewis, and the results were significant.

> On this job, in which a large hammer die was produced with a 43 per cent reduction in time as compared with the template method, manufacturing included complete programming and recording of the tape. Actual machining time was reduced 67 per cent.[17]

Application of numerical control in the production of dies is of major importance to such industries as the manufacture of automobiles. However, most applications make use of the traditional drawing, which must be converted to a system of coordinates and then fed into the computer to determine the tool path.

The application of numerical control in the aircraft industry has followed the trend of increased performance requirements of airplanes and

[15] J. R. Joerger and J. A. Downdelinger, *Machine Capabilities When Computer Controlled,* paper presented Jan. 23, 1958, at the Conference of Automation Systems sponsored by EIA, Arizona State College, Tempe, Ariz.

[16] George Bromfield, *Numerical Control for Machining Warped Surfaces,* MIT, Servomechanisms Laboratory, Engineering Report 14, D.I.C. 6873, Cambridge, Mass., 1956.

[17] "Die Sinking with Tape Control," *Western Machinery and Steel World,* Nov. 24, 1958, p. 86.

missiles. There is a need for high strength-weight ratios in craft operating in and beyond the thermal barrier. This has brought about the development of new alloys and metal combinations. This in turn has exerted greater demands on manufacturing facilities. Machining, welding, and forming these new materials to tolerance requirements are not possible with man-

PART NO. & DESCRIPTION			Guide Plate, Entry Door		
MATERIAL 4130 Steel	HEAT TREAT	- - - - - -	FINISH ROMTS	125 & 250 RMS	
CUTTER TYPE	CUTTER SIZE	TEETH OR FLUTES	SPINDLE SPEED	FEED RATE	
H.S.S. CENTER DRILL	60*		640 RPM	3.8 IPM	
H.S.S. METRIC DRILL	.253	2	468 RPM	4.6 IPM	
H.S.S. END DRILL	.499	2	640 RPM	3.8 IPM	

REMARKS   Close tolerance part: N/C machining is accomplished by using the same type for both dash numbers and revising the "X"-Axis.   K & T Profile Mill (2–3710)

	CONVENTIONAL METHOD TIME	NUMERICAL CONTROL METHOD TIME
PLANNING	* 20.0 hrs.	- - - - -
PROGRAMMING	- - - - -	25.0 hrs.
COMPUTING	- - - - -	0.1 hrs.
TOOL DESIGN	* 40.0 hrs.	3.0 hrs.
TOOL FABRICATION	* 80.0 hrs.	4.0 hrs.
DIRECTOR	- - - - -	- - - - -
TOTAL LEAD TIMES	140.0 hrs.	32.1 hrs.
MACHINE TIME/PART	* 1.0 hrs.	0.16 hrs.

* ESTIMATED OR STANDARD DATA

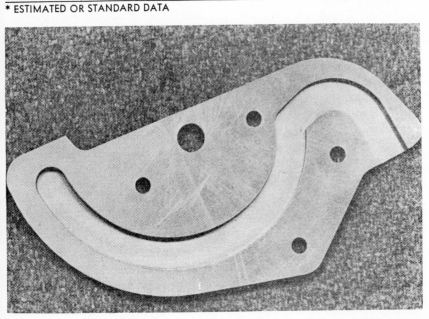

Fig. 20. Numerical-control manufacturing analysis. Courtesy of the Boeing Company.

operated machines. In addition, the economy of producing parts with numerical-control machines in recent application indicates the gradual improvement in numerical-control machines and their operation. Figure 20 shows the cutter and machining requirements for producing a guide plate for an entry door and a comparison of the lead and machine time required to manufacture by conventional methods and numerical control. In this instance, the application of numerical control reduced the lead time from 140 to 32.1 hours, and the machine time per part from 1.0 to 0.16 hour.

SUMMARY

Automation is a term which describes the control of machines by machines—a closed-sequence system where control is built into the system, and the system is operated without the need for further human action. Automation may be applied to a single task, or it may be an integrated, company-wide system. It involves a complete process of rethinking, i.e., the attitude of mind which enables one to get outside of a problem that seems insolvable and approach it in a new and perhaps wholly different way.

Numerical control may be defined as a specific kind of automatic system which controls the movements of an operating mechanism by means of previously programmed instructions coded on media such as punched cards, punched tape, or magnetic tape.

The numerical-control concept was developed as a result of a study at the Massachusetts Institute of Technology, sponsored jointly by the Parsons Corporation of Traverse City, Mich., and the United States Air Force. After the feasibility of numerical control had been established, it was decided to install this type of equipment in the aircraft industry, where close tolerances, complex manufacturing problems, short lead times, and increasing costs were prevailing characteristics.

The work flow of the system includes engineering drawing, program engineering, process-tape preparation, control-tape preparation, and machine operation. Various systems of numerical control, however, require different media, components, and arrangement of functions.

There is some question whether or not numerical control is economically feasible. Each application must be reviewed and evaluated on its own merits, but numerical control can provide better quality at reduced cost in many instances. Further, it has a degree of flexibility impossible in the typical man-operated machines.

Numerical control will make a significant impact on current engineering and manufacturing practices. However, the greatest impact will be reflected in terms of systems design. It will free the traditional processing system from outdated concepts and illustrate principles of system design useful in other business applications.

Chapter Ten

DATA-PROCESSING SYSTEMS

Systems concepts have been applied extensively in data processing; indeed the term *data-processing system* has widespread usage. In this chapter we shall explore in some detail the development of data processing and its implementation via systems concepts. We shall structure this discussion around the following topics:

Automating Information Systems
Data Processing
Evolution of Equipment
Electronic Computers
Electronic Data Processing (EDP)
Integrated Data Processing (IDP)
Real-time Data Processing
Future Data-processing Systems

AUTOMATING INFORMATION SYSTEMS

Throughout history man has sought to replace his own efforts with mechanical devices. His efforts have led to devices such as the lever, the wheel, the windmill, steam power, electricity, and other forms of harnessed energy. The industrial revolution saw the focusing of harnessed energy on the productive process. The concept of mass production was added, utiliz-

179

ing interchangeability of parts. The relentless trend, increasingly sophisticated mechanization, has involved using machines to replace human effort. The net result has been a continuing increase in productivity or output per man-hour.

Sophisticated mechanization, particularly mass-production-oriented production processes, has utilized systems concepts in order to coordinate and control the movement of raw materials and component parts through manufacturing facilities. Managerial decision making in such an environment has necessarily been geared to an over-all systems concept. Automation is an additional step in the long line of technological innovations. As pointed out in earlier chapters, automation has different shades of meaning to different people. However, a common element includes the concept of energy harnessed to a mechanical process which is carried out without human intervention. It implies self-adjusting control, which is maintained by continually measuring desired or planned results with actual performance, adjustments being made according to the determined differences. As pointed out in Chapter 9, numerical control is an example of the application of automated systems to the production process.

The term automation has also been applied to the flow of information necessary to guide the production process. Thus automation can be applied in two different ways: (1) the processing of the product and (2) the processing of information necessary to produce the product. This latter function sometimes has been referred to as *office automation*. The activity to which automation is applied, in this case, is that of data processing. The ultimate, from the standpoint of automated systems, would entail a production process controlled completely from start to finish on the basis of pre-established criteria and by means of an information-decision system which can be implemented without human intervention. We shall consider some examples which have such goals, later in this chapter. However, before looking at specific applications, it will be useful to discuss the concept of data processing in general and the evolution of equipment which has facilitated advancement in data-processing systems.

DATA PROCESSING

Data are facts used as a basis for reckoning, and processing involves a series of actions or operations definitely leading toward an end. Thus facts are the raw material for the function of data processing. In the modern business enterprise the number of relevant facts for decision making at various levels is quite staggering. They are so voluminous that only the most pertinent facts can be reported in the normal course of operations. One of the prime purposes of the data-processing function is that of screening, collating, arranging, and relating the various facts that are collected in day-to-day operations in order to develop meaningful information for managerial decision making.

Facts and Information

Many facts are generated daily both inside and outside the business enterprise. Only a few of these are of interest to management. The information-decision system must be designed to garner pertinent facts and screen unwanted or unusable data. Screened data may become information for managerial decision making. However, it is more likely that additional processing is necessary before meaningful information is available. Translating absolute sales dollars by territory into percentage figures provides useful information. Ratio analysis may be important in other cases, or sophisticated manipulations such as correlation analysis might be applied

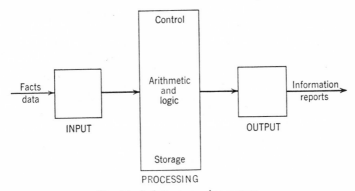

Fig. 21. A data-processing system.

to source data. The exception principle (referring only nonroutine cases to a superior for decisions) is an example of the use of small amounts of pertinent information rather than massive amounts of factual data.

The concept of a data-processing system serving to translate facts into information is illustrated in Figure 21. Three basic elements are involved: input, processing, and output. The input is represented by facts or data. The processing includes the element of control in order to guide the manipulations, some means of storage of data or facts, and a way of applying arithmetic and/or logical operations to the data. The output is represented by information which might come in a variety of forms, including management reports. This representation of a data-processing system is appropriate, regardless of the elaborateness of equipment utilized in the various stages. We shall discuss this aspect in more detail in a later section. First, however, it would be useful to distinguish scientific- and business-data processing.

Data Reduction

Since our definition of data processing was general, referring to the translation of facts into information for every purpose, the term data processing obviously applies in both business applications and scientific computations. However, other terms can be used to provide a clearer picture of the various types of data processing. Normally, *computing* applies to typical mathematical calculations which are carried out by a computer. In the precomputer era this was called *calculating*. The age of computers also ushered in the term *data reduction*. It stems from the processing of voluminous facts, often generated in experimental situations, into a meaningful form. In a sense, the data are "reduced" to manageable proportions and information is gleaned which is used in subsequent calculations or to make decisions.

Problems of mammoth proportions in the scientific fields actually fostered the development of large-scale electronic computing equipment. Today there are computers of all sizes used in scientific computations and data reduction. In terms of numbers of applications such usage outnumbers those in the business-data-processing area. However, the number of hours involved in business-data processing exceeds that spent on scientific computations and data reduction.

Business-data Processing

In order to control operations, management needs facts translated into meaningful information—this is the function of data processing. Most data processing can be viewed as a file-maintenance job. For example, companies maintain a file of employee records which are updated periodically in payroll processing. Current information is collected and translated into a form suitable for input into the data-processing system. It is processed in conjunction with the perpetual file, and both an updated file and current-output information (in this case payroll checks) are generated. During the processing other exceptions may be uncovered and noted for management's attention during the output phase.

Inventory processing may also be considered a file-maintenance operation. In this case, the "file of people" is replaced by a file of part numbers or numbers for finished inventory. Similarly, an accounts-payable data-processing application can be considered as a file of suppliers, while accounts receivable can be thought of as a file of customers. For labor-cost distribution the file might be job numbers. In all these cases an updated file is maintained summarizing transactions connected to either a part number, an employee, a customer, or a supplier. Current activities are processed in conjunction with the file, a new file is generated, and current output also is developed. Simultaneously, any exceptional situations can be noted and signaled for managerial attention.

A number of steps normally are involved in any business-data-processing application, but all these steps can be summarized in four basic categories as follows:

Collect
Process
Compare
Decide

The collection of data can be relatively straightforward, or it can be complicated, depending on the sources involved. Collection of data may involve verbal communication, hand-written notes, formal source documents, or machine-sensible media. Depending on the complexity of the data-processing system and its equipment, the data collected may require translation into a proper form for input. The processing phase includes such functions as sorting, collating, calculating, and summarizing. These tasks may be carried out in various ways.

Although both the compare and decide phases might be considered as part of processing, they are sufficiently distinct to be discussed separately. The end result of processing facts or data is information which can be used in making decisions. Normally, information is used in comparisons with expected values, past performance, competition, or other yardsticks in order to present a meaningful picture for management. These comparisons provide a basis for managerial decision making, the fourth phase in the data-processing cycle. Decisions lead to actions and also provide guidelines which serve as inputs in subsequent cycles.

In order better to understand the concept of degrees of complexity in data-processing systems, we shall look at two extreme examples. On the one hand, visualize a small, family-owned delicatessen. At the beginning of the month cash on hand amounts to X dollars. During the month purchases of supplies are made out of this fund and sales are made to customers, with the proceeds being added to the fund. At the end of the month the fund is tallied and is found to amount to Y dollars. The collection of facts in this situation is represented by the series of expenditures and receipts over the month. However, in this case it is conceivable that none of the individual transactions are recorded and that the only observable facts are the starting and the ending amounts.

Notice that the processing phase in this data-processing system can be handled with a stubby pencil and the back of an old envelope. The facts for input include the figure recorded as the amount in the till at the beginning of the month (X) and the current amount in the till (Y). These facts are entered into the processing operation. The figure for X has been stored on a piece of paper in the drawer throughout the month. The figure Y has been accumulating as a file of cash throughout the month. Both facts are then entered into storage on the piece of paper being used to process the data. The control element in the processing phase is the human mind of the delicatessen's proprietor. He carries out the steps of deciding which is the larger, X or Y, and writing that one down near the top of the paper. He then writes the smaller of the two below and performs a subtraction operation to get the net difference. A combination of the paper, the pencil, and the proprietor's hand provides the setting and tools for the arithmetic operations. The output of the processing operation would include a figure for net profit or loss, which might be written on a separate sheet of paper and filed. Also, a new figure would be output, representing the level of cash in the till; this figure becomes the X for the subsequent month.

A comparison might be made of the current month's results as against previous months, as against expected performance, or as against the performance of the delicatessen across the street. Such comparisons might lead to a decision to maintain the *status quo,* or it could lead to alternative courses of action. Normally, the compare and decide phases of this data-processing operation would be implicit; that is, a manager probably would not consciously consider the comparisons indicated above nor would he consciously "decide" on the alternative courses of action. Rather, he most likely would continue his normal procedures unless something quite drastic happened during the month.

Many refinements could be considered if the size of the operation warranted it. A larger business might keep more detailed records of purchases and/or sales. Also, it might employ some mechanization in the processing phase such as an adding machine or possibly a desk calculator. With such equipment we see the addition of storage capacity in the mechanical equipment and the arithmetic ability which such equipment obviously provides. On the other hand, control in such a data-processing system would still rest with the human being involved in the processing. However, a set of control procedures might be established at a higher level and handed down to a machine operator, who would refer to such instructions in the processing phase. Regardless of the mechanization involved in the processing phase or of the form of input or output data, the data-processing system always involves the collection, processing, comparison, and decision phases. Furthermore, its primary function is one of translating facts into meaningful information for managerial decision making.

Modern large-scale enterprises obviously employ data-processing systems which are much more elaborate and sophisticated than that described above. The development of such systems has depended to a considerable extent on the equipment available. Thus, before discussing some of the typical applications of data-processing systems, it will be helpful to trace the evolution of data-processing equipment.

EVOLUTION OF EQUIPMENT

Going back in history, an extremely important invention for facilitating information flow and data processing was paper. Such "equipment" permitted the maintenance of records. Records of facts could be filed and updated periodically when the need arose. The written record increased the size and reliability of data storage, thus transcending human memory and vocalizing ability. Even with records, however, the human element remained responsible for data input, control, and output in business-data processing.

The invention of the typewriter allowed even more elaborate record keeping by increasing legibility and providing a means for multiple copies. The invention of calculating devices to add, subtract, multiply, and divide was also an important step in facilitating data processing. Such devices provide a faster, more accurate approach to arithmetical operations.

Combination calculator-typewriter machines were developed for bookkeeping and accounting operations. Such machines facilitate performance of multiple operations: the preparation of statements, ledgers, and journals. Another giant step in the evolution of equipment facilitating data processing was the development of electromechanical punched-card equipment. The use of punched-hole patterns as a control device was conceived as early as 1801 for a loom in which weaving of textiles was performed according to punched-hole patterns. The player piano is operated on the same principle. When it took nine years for the Bureau of the Census to compute the 1880 census, it was evident that a radically new approach was urgently needed. It was estimated that by using traditional methods the computations on the 1890 census would not be completed until the 1900 census had been taken. Herman Hollerith, an employee of the Census Bureau, devised a code and applied the punched hole to cards which could be sorted mechanically. Holes punched in various positions on a card represented individual items of data. The control of sorting and other operations was obtained by means of electrical contacts through the punched holes.

Referring to Figure 21, the facts or data would be represented in punched cards as input to the processing phase. Such input would be keypunched from numerous sources in the data-collection phase of the cycle. The cards themselves provide a storage medium for data. Also, there are storage elements in the tabulating equipment in order to facilitate the accumulation of totals, subtotals, and other similar bits of information. The control element is a wired board with instructions which are triggered by control punches in the cards themselves. The electromechanical equipment provides limited arithmetic and logic operations. The output in such a process is usually in the form of a printed report which can be expanded or contracted according to the needs and wishes of management.

During World War II electronic digital computers were developed for scientific and military computation problems. In the postwar period efforts continued toward adaptation of such equipment to business-data processing. In the early 1950s this objective was attained with the first strictly business application by General Electric at Louisville, Ky. Since that time, thousands of small-, medium-, and large-scale computers have been installed to facilitate more elaborate data-processing systems. Before discussing some of these applications in detail it will be helpful to describe the electronic digital computer in some detail in order to appreciate its impact on data-processing systems.

ELECTRONIC COMPUTERS

A computer is "a machine that manipulates symbols in accordance with given rules in a predetermined and self-directed manner. Speaking more technically, an automatic computer is a high-speed, automatic, electronic, digital data-processing machine." [1] A discussion of the adjectives involved in the above quotation is helpful in understanding the equipment, or "hardware," involved in electronic data processing. As mentioned previously, the electronic computer was developed primarily to provide a faster means of computation in scientific problems, particularly in the World War II period. Earlier calculators had been able to supplant human effort and improve productivity manyfold. However, the speed of computation was limited by movement of mechanical parts, thus imposing a relatively low upper limit on ultimate speeds of calculation. A significant principle for electronic computers is that the flow of electrons, acting as signals in the circuitry of the equipment, is susceptible to direction and control. Numbers and alphabetic characters are symbolized by electronic pulses or other manifestations. The controlled movement, or flow, of these symbolic signals provides the basic framework for electronic computers.

Another important adjective is "high-speed," since speed of computation was one of the prime goals sought. The speeds obtained to date by electronic computers are fantastic and promise to increase ever more in the future. Increasing computational speed plus larger and larger storage, or memory, devices makes the electronic computer an extremely versatile tool for use in any data-processing system.

[1] Ned Chapin, *An Introduction to Automatic Computers,* D. Van Nostrand Company, Inc., Princeton, N.J., 1957, p. 4.

The term digital is used in contrast to the term analogue, which describes an important group of computing machines which use a physical analogy as an approach to the problem being studied. The physical analogy is constructed electronically within the computer's work area. The digital computer, on the other hand, is based on symbol manipulation and counting (the binary number system).

The term automatic refers to the self-controlling aspects of electronic computers, which have internally stored programs, or lists of instructions, that determine the sequence of operation in a processing or computational routine. These instructions are predetermined in the sense that human effort is required to plan and set forth in minute detail all the steps involved in any processing job. Once the program is designed, it acts as the control element in the data-processing system. During processing, the program itself can be modified, again according to predetermined rules, and hence provide directions according to the situation which input data represent. It is this quality which parallels the feedback-control concept of production automation and that has led to describing electronic data processing as office automation. The concept of internally stored, self-adjusting programs for controlling operations sets the electronic computer completely apart from predecessor equipment. In this sense it is not just an additional step in the long line of increased mechanization. It provides a new dimension for data processing and allows much more sophisticated and imaginative systems of information flow.

Implementing Systems of Information Flow

The electronic computer offers tremendous potential as a management tool. It can do work (suited to its talent) faster and more economically than any other equipment. It is more accurate than people or other machines in use. It can easily perform operations previously considered impractical, if not impossible, in an area of operations research and analysis. But most important, the electronic computer offers a rare opportunity to expand the scope of current mechanized information flow.

It is a potent tool which might well be used for expanding the scope of current systems; this is the most significant contribution of the electronic computer to business-data processing. Because it is such a potent tool and represents such an advance over its forerunners (electromechanical equipment), it provides analysts with a real opportunity for redesigning systems of information flow. Yet it is in this area that relatively little progress has been made. Why?

There are many reasons why the full potential of electronic computers has not been realized in the majority of present installations. The following list is only representative. It could be extended or modified for any particular case.

1. Too much emphasis was placed on immediate cost savings.

2. This led to adaptation of existing systems and procedures to electronics, the result being faster processing of the same old system of information flow.

3. The emphasis on immediate results and substantial cost savings also led to the predominance of a piecemeal approach, with little regard for the over-all picture. Integrated data processing was often considered a "cloud nine" concept, something to be discussed at conferences, but for the other fellow to install. "Our operation is different!"

4. Management has not been convinced of the merit of electronic computers in all instances, as might have been hoped for by those in the field. This attitude has, of course, fostered the situations outlined above. In addition, the lack of staunch support from top management has made the job of "selling" the departments affected very difficult.

In general, the problem in most data-processing installations has been the preoccupation with "brush fires" at the expense of time which should be devoted to long-range planning. It is not a new problem; administrators in other functional areas are similarly plagued. For example, one manager in charge of an operations-planning and control staff stated that his job had been created eighteen months before to deal with four functions: long-range planning, program planning, systems, and controls. Zero per cent of his effort had been put into long-range planning. And more important for this discussion, of the time spent on systems, very little attention was given to the over-all system of information flow and none of the effort had been spent on long-range aspects of the system. This approach is typical and indicates why the full potential of electronic computers has not been attained. Concerted effort must be focused on the long-range aspects of the data-processing function in order that optimum results may be obtained from such a potent tool. A complete reevaluation of a company's system of information flow must be undertaken in order to provide a proper frame of reference for the applications put on the computer. If each such application is related to the over-all plan (or communication model), the ultimate result actually should be a completely integrated data-processing system.

But the starting point for the necessary reevaluation must not be the present system; the analysis should start from scratch without reference to present systems or machines. Yet this approach is not feasible until top management is convinced that it is necessary in order to ensure the greatest long-run benefits. The importance of top-management support and involvement is reflected in the following remarks by E. D. Dwyer, Chief, Navy Management Office:

> Whenever and wherever a computer installation has failed to achieve any truly astounding or significant improvements in management, I am utterly convinced that the responsibility for the failure must be assumed by top management. . . . The desire on management's part for immediate results in realizing marginal economic benefits . . . reflects management myopia in its most chronic, advanced stage.
>
> If we agree that a computer can do anything we instruct it to do, then why isn't it obvious that the failure of a computer to deliver the hoped-for output is the fault of the one issuing the instructions? . . . If we wish to improve management, we should study management rather than the computers. That is, the Board of Directors and the officers of the company and those who are responsible for expending company funds should study themselves, their attitudes, objectives, techniques, and limitations—foremost of which may well be a lack of vision or atrophied imagination.[2]

There is a great need for creative thinking on the part of systems analysts. Such thinking can come only in an atmosphere conducive to research on information flows, an atmosphere that must be fostered by top management. Those involved must have time to reflect on the long-run future. According to Dwyer:

> In contrast to the usual procedure for correcting something wrong by finding a "practical man" to do the job, what is really needed is an "impractical man"—a theorist. When a thing will not work, then you need a "thinker," a man with some doctrine as to why things work at all. Management cannot expect computer programmers to initiate revolutionary new applications nor can they expect management analysts or systems surveyors to initiate startling new management concepts. If any of these people could do these things—then certainly they wouldn't need top management at all.

He concludes by saying:

> I see no point in congratulating ourselves on a small job well done, when the big job remains undone. It's not that I'm *against* computers being used on small or *conventional* work to *save* money. Rather, it's more a case of my being *for* computers being used on big or *unconventional* work to *make* money.[3]

How can this desired transition from conventional to unconventional work be promoted? How can long-range planning in the area of electronic

---

[2] E. D. Dwyer, Chief, Navy Management Office, an address before the Life Office Management Association, Apr. 15, 1959.

[3] *Ibid.*

data processing be encouraged? Can top management reap the full benefit of the potential offered by the impact of the electronic computer on systems of information flow? Can systems be designed that are neither application- nor hardware-oriented? These are questions which we shall attempt to answer later in this chapter. We shall look at some typical applications of electronic computers in data-processing systems, some advanced integrated- data-processing systems, and some proposed real-time, or on-line, processing systems. Before looking at specific applications, however, let us develop a general framework for the state of the art in electronic data processing.

State of the Art

Automatic data processing may be expected to advance in three stages:

1. Visible source material will be prepared by the same methods as heretofore (handwritten, typed, etc.) and converted to machine-sensible information (punched cards, magnetic tape, etc.) prior to processing.

2. Original source material both visible and machine-sensible will be prepared simultaneously; for example, the perforated tape produced as a by-product of a typewriter operation.

3. The source data will be machine-sensible only; for example, the use of employees' keys to punch a time clock, no visible time card being pro- duced.[4]

This framework will be used extensively throughout the remainder of the chapter; the reader should keep it clearly in mind.

It is interesting to note that the three stages of data-processing develop- ments for the future do not mention the electronic computer itself. The preoccupation here seems to be with the collection and preparation of data for input to the computer. Referring to the four-phase cycle of data proc- essing—collect, process, compare, and decide—implementation of this data-processing cycle on a wide-scale systems basis hinges primarily on the collection phase. Processing, primarily in terms of computer capabilities, seems to be no problem. Indeed, we have equipment today which is more than adequate in terms of computational speeds, storage capacity, and speed and flexibility of input-output devices. Sophisticated computer pro- grams are being developed continually to include more and more compari- son and decision-making functions. The real stumbling block to imple- mentation of information flow remains the collection, transcription, and transmission of data suitable for input to central processing units. The collection phase needs equipment for source recording and suitable high-

---

[4] International Business Machines Corporation, *The Auditor Encounters Elec- tronic Data Processing*, p. 13.

speed transmission facilities. It also involves all the organizational and administrative problems involved in designating sources of data which should be introduced into the system in order to provide information for managerial decision making.

The first stage of the above three-step schedule has been most prevalent in electronic-data-processing installations. Most companies have progressed from punched-card accounting to electronic data processing. In some cases the existing applications were transferred "as is" to the new media. In the case of medium-scale computing equipment, punched cards have remained, in many installations, as the only input-output media. Often the existing systems and procedures are utilized with only minor improvements and refinements. Obviously, this approach is the most straightforward and probably the easiest. On the other hand, it might not lead to as much improvement as might be obtained through systems analysis which starts from scratch, ignoring existing procedures and practices.

For many years IBM has focused attention on the word *think* as the key to success in business, particularly systems analysis. In the field of electronic data processing a stronger case might be made for emphasizing the word *rethink*. The concept involves the substitution of *entirely new* systems or methods rather than the improvement of existing systems.

Some computer people assert that the most successful electronic-data-processing installations seem to develop from operations that were originally entirely manual. This is reasonable because the computer performs the various steps of a program essentially the same as a person does. Each record or item is processed completely as a unit (in the file-maintenance approach), rather than bit by bit, as is the case of punched-card systems. Similarity to the human approach allows a great deal of imagination in systems analysis connected with electronic data processing. High-speed computers should force analysts to rethink the entire flow of paper work and reporting in order to utilize an expensive piece of equipment. At the same time, more detailed step-by-step procedures must be provided for the computer than for people because the machine must consider *every* possibility before making a logical decision.[5]

All in all, the state of the art in *utilizing* electronic computers in data processing has fallen behind the technological innovations of the sixties. The gap may widen in the future unless more attention is given to the design of systems of information flow. The next several sections trace the development of electronic-data-processing systems.

[5] "The thing that distinguishes humans from machines is the ability to arrive at a conclusion without all the facts; an important attribute because some facts are always unknown." H. R. Huntley, American Telephone and Telegraph Company, in a speech to the Association of American Railroads.

ELECTRONIC DATA PROCESSING (EDP)

An electronic-data-processing system is depicted in abstract fashion in Figure 22. Note the obvious similarity between this representation and that of a data-processing system in general; that is, there are five basic elements, including input, output, operations, storage, and control. The larger circle represents the total system with connection to the environment via input and output media. The media could include punched cards, punched paper tape, magnetic tape, typewriters, or console instructions on the input side and the same elements for the output side, with the addition of high-speed printed output. The input phase is critical in the

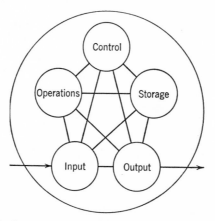

Fig. 22. An electronic-data-processing system. Source: Anthony Oettinger, "Principles of Electronic Data Processing," *Proceedings Automatic Data Processing Conference,* Harvard University, Graduate School of Business, Boston, 1956, p. 29.

sense that data must be presented in a form compatible with the electronic-data-processing system in use. Achieving this compatibility is no small task. As mentioned previously, the collection phase of the data-processing cycle continues to present formidable problems for systems designers.

The operations element of the electronic-data-processing system involves arithmetic and logical manipulations described earlier. Storage facilities include magnetic cores, magnetic drums, magnetic disks, and auxiliary storage via the use of magnetic tape. The control element includes the program which covers, in minute detail, the steps to be taken in the processing operation. Each element in the electronic-data-processing system is connected to every other element. It is this phenomenon that provides the significant advantages found in electronic systems over predecessor systems; these interrelationships allow the entire system to function as one unit.

Given this electronic-data-processing system, what are some of the typical applications that have been developed?

Payroll

For many large companies the initial application designated for electronic data processing has been payroll. In the first place, it is one of the major data-handling jobs and offers a fruitful area for cost reduction. Second, it is often the most "routinized" processing job, hence giving the impression that payroll would be the easiest application to convert to EDP. At first glance, paying people seems like a simple, straightforward task. However, the conversion never seems to go quite as smoothly as initially envisioned.

The sheer numbers involved in a typical payroll application often are quite staggering. Also, the processing job turns out to include more than just multiplying hours worked times rate per hour and writing a check for the resulting amount. For example, records must be kept of such items as year-to-date earnings, year-to-date withholding tax, year-to-date social-security payments, vacation, and sick leave. Numerous deductions must be taken into account: life, medical, and accident and health insurance; savings bonds; credit union; and others. Each day sees changes such as new hires, terminations, and transfers, or different rates, locations, names, and tax codes. In addition, requests for vacations and/or pay in lieu of time off must be processed, as well as sick-leave transactions. All in all, there is a seemingly infinite number of steps involved in what appears to the uninitiated as a relatively straightforward task. Since each and every possibility must be accounted for in programming the computer, the task becomes monumental. Whereas in a manual system the individual could act with only partial information, the computer must have *all* the facts. Without *all* the facts, the computer is either stymied or else it generates erroneous output at lightninglike speeds.

Payroll applications have been predominantly *stage 1* approaches. Traditional timekeeping methods are used whereby employees report on and off the job via a conventional timeclock which records (prints) the time on a punched card. Cards with a considerable amount of prepunched information are furnished by the timekeeper, weekly to salaried employees, daily to hourly employees. The typical clock card would have, for each individual, space for prepunched identification data, attendance time, and elapsed job time. Elapsed job time is checked manually, and labor-distribution cards are key-punched from this information. Before input to the computer the amount of time in the labor-distribution cards is reconciled with the total attendance time. The next step is a card to tape conversion immediately preceding the computer processing.

The employee master record tape, including all the various items of information mentioned above, current changes, and labor-hours information, serves as input for payroll processing. Output from the processing includes payroll checks, reports on earnings and deductions, termination checks, an updated master record, and information for processing labor-cost distribution. Electronic data processing provides a real contribution of increased speed, better information, and reduced costs to payroll processing. The activities required to prepare computer input consist of manual and electromechanical operations. This phase of the operation is handled essentially as in the precomputer era. Moreover, it is this phase of the data-processing cycle that is wide open to human error—manual checking and key punching, for example.

Inventory Control

Inventory applications involve keeping records of all material issued in manufacturing operations. The precomputer approach might have been one of keeping inventory on Kardex visible-tip records. Such records are replaced by magnetic tapes in electronic-data-processing applications. Information from a material requisition is key-punched and eventually fed into the computer, where the transaction is carried out and a list of the activity is produced. The list is designed to be filed behind the item ledger card to show the up-to-date information concerning usage and current balance. After sufficient activity (a predetermined number of transactions), a new-item ledger card is produced which replaces the old card plus the interim lists of activity. This application is obviously in stage 1 since the initial records are hand-created and eventually translated into a medium suitable for input through an electronic computer. Advancement to *stage 2* would require something like a perforated tape created simultaneously with the initial material requisition. Such a tape could be used to produce the major portion of subsequent records required for input to the computer and for other purposes. To arrive at *stage 3,* a direct hookup between stores and inventory would be required. Information punched in the manufacturing record could be transmitted via data-transmission equipment and lines to the magnetic-tape storage of the central installation. The ultimate in this approach would be the use of some type of file computer,[6] on line at all times, in order that random access to the status of each and every item may be available immediately.

---

[6] A file computer is distinguished by a vast amount of storage capacity, usually allowing random access to any item stored. It is so named because complete "files" of information can be stored internally and transferred from storage to arithmetic and logic units with great speed.

Accounts Payable

For an accounts-payable application, a combination of stages 1 and 2 can be found. The goal in the over-all material-records system involves the integration of the processing of requisitions, purchase orders, etc., with the processing for accounting distribution and the inventory control. Purchase orders are usually made up from a requisition. A control file (ledger card) can be established with a perforated tape punched as a by-product. The tape can be converted to cards, and the cards to magnetic tape. With the master file on magnetic tape, the processing is done via a combination of magnetic tapes and punched cards. Basically, visible records are produced as previously, with conversion to machine-sensible media for input to the computer (stage 1). However, the intermediate steps include elements of stage 2, simultaneous production of perforated tapes and hard copy. The outlook for stage 3 operations, similar in concept to the ultimate in control applications, is long-range but certainly not impossible.

INTEGRATED DATA PROCESSING (IDP)

One of the evident problems in most stage 1 installations is the extensive duplication of effort necessary to convert visible source material to machine-sensible language prior to processing. Normally, the justification for electronic-data-processing equipment is the elimination of clerical-work stations and electrical accounting machines. More often than not, however, installations of supporting EAM (electrical accounting machines) equipment have increased with the addition of EDPM (electronic-data-processing machines) equipment. Pressure to perfect the cards and/or tape for input to the computer has resulted in increased pressure on supporting equipment. Often, there is human intervention between the initial source document and input to the computer. If so, the chance for errors is obvious. Since impure input may generate compound errors at extreme speeds, it is highly advisable to strive for error-free input. In order to enhance this development, integrated data processing seems to be a worthwhile goal.

IDP coincides to a considerable degree with stage 2 of the three-stage trend outlined above, namely, "original source material both visible and machine sensible are prepared simultaneously." According to P. B. Garrott:

> Integrated data processing is not an entirely new creation, but rather is one of those highly valuable innovations combining elements of several existing ideas into a new, more effective pattern. It might be described fairly as a plan for mechanizing the recording, transmitting and reuse of necessary business information. Integrated data processing, in other words, is a plan for mechanizing business paper work. One of its prime purposes is to reduce the danger of human failures by reducing the degree of direct

human participation in the processing of vital business information. Another is to provide that information wherever it is needed, and in the form it is needed—more quickly.[7]

A wide variety of machines have been developed which provide, for example, both a hard copy and a perforated tape. Or more commonly, a punched card is developed initially and used to produce subsequent documents or information with a minimum of human intervention, thus cutting time, effort, and errors. At present the perforated tape is used most often as the common-language element of an integrated-data-processing system, and it can be produced by cash registers, typewriters, bookkeeping machines, desk calculators, teletype setters, and others. It can actuate some of these same pieces of equipment plus punched-card machines and computers. Therefore the means exist for integrating data processing for a given installation. Garrott sums it up as follows:

> Keeping in mind the general characteristics of common language machines and the interchangeability of information through the use of common language tapes, here are two simple rules:
> 1. Record data at the point of origin on office machines which create punched tapes or cards as the automatic by-product of the recording operation.
> 2. Process original and subsequent data on office machines which read and punch tapes or cards, so that all data are self-perpetuating.
> Thoughtful analysis of these rules . . . provides a hint of the powerful potential of integrated data processing to speed, simplify, and reduce paperwork burdens by practical mechanization.[8]

Integrated data processing (as pictured today), with all its evident advantages, still does not encompass stage 3 of the advancement schedule set forth previously. In the ultimate system (completely integrated data processing) the source data will be machine-sensible only, for example, the use of employee keys to punch a time clock, no visible time card being produced. In this case there will be no human intervention similar to even the handling of perforated tapes or punched cards. For large-scale computer installations the initial recording would be made on magnetic tape. Such information could be transferred, sorted, etc., from tape to tape.

In order to eliminate the handling of cards and paper tapes between initial recording and input to the computer system, some type of direct data-transmission system must be utilized. This phase of the problem is now receiving much attention on the part of equipment manufacturers and potential users. Many present and potential users of such devices are evi-

[7] P. B. Garrott, "Integrated Data Processing Brings Automation in Paperwork," *Automation,* December, 1954, pp. 33–34.

[8] *Ibid.,* p. 39.

dent, such as multiplant companies with central data processing, companies with widespread sales offices, and companies with widely scattered, in-plant recording stations. In the latter case the recording of time for payroll purposes usually takes place in numerous, widely dispersed areas. It has been suggested that much time and many man-hours could be saved by linking time clocks directly to the central computing installation and recording in and out times directly on magnetic tape. Although the elimination of timekeepers seems to be a radical step, it is an obvious goal when the analyst starts from scratch to rethink the entire problem. This step has already been taken by several companies.[9]

Source Recording and Data Transmission

The point of origin of valuable information and the point where it is needed often are widely dispersed. Some way must be devised to facilitate the accumulation, processing, and distribution of required information. Most often this task has been accomplished by physically carrying the data from place to place. Modern communications equipment, however, indicates the possibility of transmitting the required data from point of origin to point of processing and subsequently to wherever the results are required as information for decisions. Long-range transmission over hundreds of miles is possible but costly. Short-range data transmission is more promising in the immediate future.

Large-scale telephone wires can be used to transmit data between the sender and the receiver. In such cases adequate checking must be employed to ensure that data transmitted and data received are identical. Whenever an error is discovered by the receiver, it signals the sender to that effect. The sender must then back up and retransmit what, *in all probability,* will be the correct data. Several manufacturers are working on "black boxes" necessary at either end of the data-transmission line. There is real need for a versatile instrument which is easily adaptable to a wide variety of data-producing equipment and identification devices.

We are not interested in the details of equipment and design. Our main consideration is, how can electronic-data-processing applications be improved in the light of present and foreseeable developments in source recording and data-transmission equipment? Given the ultimate in equipment, what can be done to utilize it? Considering the payroll application described earlier in terms of a stage 3 approach, "source data will be machine-sensible only," what would be the requirements? Keeping the ultimate in equipment in mind, the following might be representative objectives:

[9] See "Oral Timekeeping Plan Replaces Clock Punching," *American Business,* May, 1957, p. 42, and "New Look in Timekeeping," *Factory Management and Maintenance,* June, 1957, p. 139.

1. To provide management with information it must have in order to take action before status becomes history

2. To reduce over-all company costs by using a mechanical system to provide timely man-hour and scheduling information that can be obtained currently only through manual means

3. To provide a means of more effective man-hour control

4. To provide a means of reducing the flow time of schedule status and man-hour reports through a mechanical system

5. To record a transaction immediately in a form directly usable by the computer program

6. To reduce the manual transcription and mechanical conversion of the data used as input to the computer

These objectives focus attention on the data collection and preparation phase of the management information system shown in Figure 23.[10] The

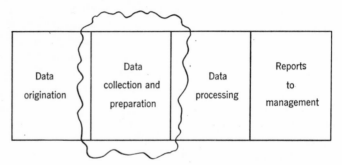

Fig. 23. A management information system.

potential applications of the proposed innovations include job and man time, job status, shop load, inventory, and labor standards. The benefits which would accrue from automating the data collection and preparation phase are obvious. Such a trend would push all the listed possible applications into stage 3. In each case the source data are machine-sensible only with the original information recorded directly on magnetic tape.

With regard to job and man time for payroll purposes, the employee clocks in and out by using his badge and some coded information contained in a work order. The first requirement is a machine to prepare a unique badge for each employee. Likewise, a corner of the work authorization must be prepared by a similar machine. Insertion of both the badge and the work order into the point-of-activity recorder provides the information necessary to account for what the employee does during the time

[10] This scheme is an adaptation of the basic phases of a data-processing system: collect, process, compare, and decide.

he is in attendance. Flexibility can be achieved by allowing additional information to be inserted by a keyboard. Data-transmission lines are necessary to connect the point-of-activity recorder with a magnetic tape. The magnetic-tape reader will receive the badge identification, the job work-order number, variable data, and location code from the point-of-activity recorder. It will record these data on tape with the time recording of the activity in language acceptable to a data-processing system. Also, all data recorded on tape will be verified with the original input data to assure positive recording of the data.

The resulting tape is similar to a typical payroll input tape. It can be prepared automatically by the computing system from data received over the transmission lines directly from the work areas. This means the elimination of the time and effort now spent in physically transporting the data to the payroll department plus the time and effort spent at the point in preauditing, key-punching, verifying, balancing, and converting cards to tape. After the payroll input tape is developed, the processing is the same as previously, pay checks and labor-cost distribution being the most important goals. Additional reports for factory use are available on an immediately current basis, thus fulfilling, in part, the objectives set forth above.

Source recording for payroll and labor-cost applications is a first step toward a complete system of integrated data processing. Before long payroll, labor-cost distribution, accounts payable, material records, production control, and many other applications will all be processed electronically, using data collected and prepared for input to the computer via source recording and data transmission. As interdependent applications are tied together, duplication will be eliminated. The success of some companies in implementing the first phases of such an approach lends credence to the long-run goal of a total system of information flow utilizing electronic data processing as the core.[11]

REAL-TIME DATA PROCESSING

In spite of the advanced appearance of some of the electronic-data-processing systems described above, there is still another level of attainment which we have not mentioned previously, real-time processing. All the applications outlined previously are examples of batch processing; that is, facts or data are collected, manually or electronically, over a period of time and then merged with a master file in a processing run. Such processing might take place biweekly, weekly, daily, or even at shorter intervals. However, batch processing implies that the system is not completely up to

[11] The Boeing Company has implemented a payroll and labor-cost-distribution application along the lines described in the foregoing paragraphs. Other companies are progressing in the same direction.

date at every possible moment. Real-time processing, on the other hand, involves updating the master file or description of the current situation with every transaction, regardlesss of how frequent. For example, a wholesaler's inventory might be kept entirely in the magnetic storage of a file computer. As orders are received and processed, the inventory status is updated immediately. Thus a perpetual inventory record is maintained which is current in terms of transactions at any given point in time. Information on stockouts is obtained as an exception printout at the first possible moment. Also, a purchase order is printed the minute the reorder point is reached. If transactions were collected for a week and then processed, serious gaps could be present in the information necessary for managerial decision making.

Real-time Control

The material in this section draws on Donald G. Malcolm's article "Exploring the Military Analogy: Real-time Management Control." [12] By way of definition Malcolm states:

> In using a computer as an integral on-line controlling device, the term "real-time control, communication, and information system" has evolved as a system design concept. By this is meant that the information is transmitted instantaneously, without conversion, into a centralized computer, which processes it, compares it with predetermined decision criteria and issues instructions to men and/or machines for corrective or purposeful action. This may be thought of as "real-time control." Further, the computer by means of direct outputs informs affected parties of this information as it is developed. This is "real-time communication." Lastly, suitable condensations of the above information are prepared, transmitted and displayed to higher levels of management for broader system decisions. This is "real-time management information."
>
> The meaning of the word "real-time" lies in the fact that information is used as it develops and that elements in the system are controlled by the processed information immediately, not after the fact or by making periodic forecasts of the expected future state of the system.[13]

Operational examples of real-time management control systems are presently in the design stage only. In the military area, however, several examples are available which indicate the general concept involved and the feasibility of ultimate systems in civilian management applications. The most familiar application is that of the SAGE (Semi-Automatic Ground Environment) system.

[12] In Donald G. Malcolm, Alan J. Rowe, and Lorimer F. McConnell (eds.), *Management Control Systems,* John Wiley & Sons, Inc., New York, 1960, pp. 187–208.

[13] *Ibid.,* pp. 190–191.

SAGE is a continental air command and warning system designed to maintain a complete, up-to-date picture of the air and ground situation in the continental United States and other parts of North America. It was designed to control modern air-defense weapons rapidly and accurately and to present appropriately filtered pictures of the air and weapon situations to Air Force personnel who conduct the air battle. The SAGE system includes numerous radar installations, and a widespread interconnected network of air-defense direction centers which receive information from numerous sources and process the information rapidly on electronic-data-processing equipment. Elaborate means are available for displaying pertinent information to human decision makers stationed at the direction centers in order to issue battle orders controlling interceptor aircraft and other weapons in the air-defense system. In general, an air-defense control system must be able to do the following:

Provide positive recognition of an air attack
Provide up-to-the-minute status of defense capabilities
Issue immediate defense instructions
Operate immediately at high efficiency
Operate on a continuous basis with high reliability
Adapt to a growing air-defense capability

In order to meet the requirements listed above, provision had to be made for the automation or semiautomation of the following:

1. Collection of information and data and elimination of noise therefrom

2. Sorting, correlating, and further processing of the information

3. Generation of displays to permit human monitoring, decision making, and intervention

4. Displays to include a presentation of the air situation and kept current

5. Means for identifying individual aircraft in the air situation

6. Filtered and summarized displays to permit high echelons to make general decisions about the situation

7. Transmission of information and data to all points where they are needed

8. Means for deciding about the use of weapons and for directing them against the attack

9. Means for computing control information and transmitting it to the various weapons

10. Means for systems training

A block diagram of the SAGE system is shown in Figure 24. It illustrates the manner in which human and automated decision making takes place, the closed-loop feedback of control and monitoring of infor-

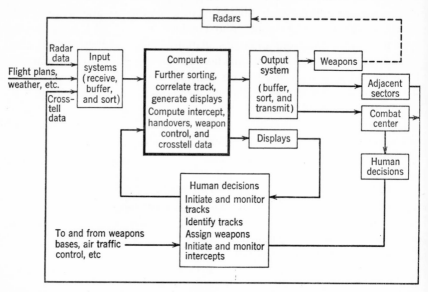

Fig. 24. Conceptual system design of SAGE. Source: Donald G. Malcolm, "Exploring the Military Analogy: Real-time Management Control," in Donald G. Malcolm, Alan J. Rowe, and Lorimer F. McConnel (eds.), *Management Control Systems*, John Wiley & Sons, Inc., New York, 1960, p. 200.

mation, and the central role of the computer. Malcolm summarizes the data-processing features of the SAGE system as follows:

> 1. Use of a general-purpose information processing and computing device with large and readily available information storage capacity and with very-high-speed computing capability.
>
> 2. Automatic real-time transmittal of control and other operational information in digital form through a versatile output system that sorts information according to destination and acts as a buffer between computing cycles and transmitting equipment.
>
> 3. Use of a large integrated computer program of some 100,000 instructions which includes and ties together 100 subprograms and handles thousands of types and varieties of information, controls the sequence of operations of all subsystems, performs all information handling and computing tasks, and assists in evaluation of alternatives and in decision making.[14]

[14] *Ibid.*, p. 201.

Several objectives for information-decision systems are brought to mind by the SAGE example. Management by exception is a must in large-scale systems where voluminous facts are generated continuously. Only a few of these facts are pertinent for managerial decision making; hence the bulk of the data generated within the system must be screened before it is reported to decision makers at key points.

The use of a complete model of the information-decision system for a given firm would allow top management to check the repercussions of alternative policies. Such interrogation, or *fast simulation,* of the company's operations would provide a valuable tool for decision makers, allowing some insight into the impact of alternative decisions without committing resources in an experimental situation.

The fact that the SAGE system has proved feasible indicates the possibility for similar real-time management control systems in the civilian sector. It points up the need for broad-gauge thinking on the part of systems analysts and the necessity for starting from scratch with questions such as, "What information do we need for decisions?" The best possible system design must be the goal in the initial stages. While an optimal system may not be feasible, it still provides the objective for efforts on the part of system designers.

FUTURE DATA-PROCESSING SYSTEMS

Electronic-data-processing systems of the future will depend primarily upon progress in two areas: (1) computer technology and (2) innovations in information-decision systems. There seems to be no question concerning technological progress. Although the transaction speed in most electronic computers is already fantastic, product-research people assert that machines many times faster will be available within the next five to ten years. With proper programming and clean input data, the electronic computer leaves little to be desired in the way of accuracy. Memory sizes undoubtedly will be increased manyfold in order to provide space for storing entire files of information. This would facilitate real-time processing, depending upon improvements in the input-output phases. Thus the technological aspects of the electronic-data-processing system of the future will probably leave little to be desired.

Our ability to capitalize on the potential capabilities is another question. According to Kami:

> But I also said that while *technological* progress itself can be revolutionary and make all these possible, *methodological* progress is by its very nature evolutionary. We cannot expect to achieve the rosy picture of the integrated data processing applications, the "fast time" business simulation,

"optimum" production scheduling and automatic "decision making" functions by an explosive and revolutionary breakthrough. It is going to take a long, evolutionary process, involving hard and persistent work on the part of all of us, before we shall be able to use computers for all the tasks they are technically capable of performing.[15]

Unfortunately, methodological progress involves human beings, who are typically resistant to change. New concepts of systems of information flow require organizational adjustments and realigned concepts of authority and responsibility. Integrated data processing and/or real-time processing for an entire system will require centralization of the processing phase of the complete data-processing cycle. However, it does not necessarily mean centralization of decision making since data may originate at distant points, be processed, and returned in terms of pertinent information for managerial decision making in diverse locations within the business enterprise. Kami cites some of the changes that are likely to occur in the future in order to implement progress in methodology commensurate with technological progress.

As we progress, gradual changes and improvements necessary to the exploitation of computer potential will become apparent. Among them will be certain changes in company structure and in methods studies:

1. Methods studies of over-all company operations and objectives, as a whole, rather than of individual applications or departments, will become far more common.

2. Methods departments will not only be upgraded and organized on a higher management level, but will also be given authority as well as responsibility for performance.

3. Part of their work will be devoted to long-range plans and operational changes, rather than merely to immediate and pressing fire-alarm situations.

4. Department structures will be reorganized according to operating functions and the most direct information flow. This may necessitate consolidation of departments previously reporting to separate managements.

5. Procedures will be formalized and spelled out in greater detail; exceptions will be particularly well defined in strict and quantitative terms.

6. Personnel will be trained gradually to accept the principle of pooling and sharing common data and file information, whether mechanized or not, until the concept of "individual" and "separate" departmental records becomes a legend of the past.

7. Accounting, bookkeeping, and record-keeping departments will become more understanding of operating departments and more closely

[15] Michael J. Kami, "Electronic Data Processing: Promise and Problems," *California Management Review*, Fall, 1958, p. 77.

integrated with them, so that common raw data can be processed to serve both operating and accounting purposes.[16]

Each business enterprise must be cognizant of the above trends and make an attempt to facilitate its development rather than provide road blocks. Systems analysts for individual companies must determine the best channels of information flow and determine the needs and requirements for information at various management levels and at different points in the flow of material and information through the organization. Once the system has been designed, then the question of equipment available to implement it becomes important. So far this has not been a major problem in electronic-data-processing installations. In fact, most installations have adapted their systems to fit available hardware. In a growing number of instances, however, manufacturers have developed special equipment for customers who have seen fit to outline their needs and requirements without reference to existing hardware.

Special-purpose Equipment

Special-purpose data-processing systems that can be found in the military and in industry today attest to the fact that systems design can precede the development of necessary equipment. For example, the SAGE data-processing system described previously is the solution for an extremely complex military problem, that of providing all the information necessary for decision making in an air-defense system. The various reservation systems of the airlines (Reservisor, Resitron, etc.) are good examples of data-processing equipment designed to fulfill an established need. The banking industry is another good example. The Bank of America perceived the need, the Stanford Research Institute carried out the research and development of the design, and General Electric produced the equipment for installation in various branches of the Bank of America. This system (ERMA) was developed for one company, but it and similar approaches are finding widespread acceptance throughout the industry. Some of the telephone companies have developed their own special-purpose equipment for automatic message accounting.

Other examples of special-purpose equipment could be cited, and they are steps in the right direction. However, these examples rarely deal with the over-all system of information flow for an entire company. Rather, they deal with one segment which has been completely automated. But importantly, they have established the principle of perception of need (in system design) preceding equipment design. Naturally, equipment manufacturers might shy away from special-purpose computers because of the

[16] *Ibid.*, pp. 77–78.

smaller market for each model. However, if the old adage "the customer is always right" still has meaning, there is likely to be a trend toward computer installations that are at least special for a given industry. For example, the insurance field might require one type of equipment, and metal-fabrication companies another. In the future it should become feasible to produce a sufficient volume of both models.[17] The purpose of such a team approach is to get the viewpoints of users and other outside observers in order that the manufacturers may better tailor their research, development, and production to the needs of ultimate users. There obviously must be some compromise; each company probably cannot have an individually designed computer, at least not at present or in the foreseeable future. However, this still should not deter systems analysts from designing the optimum system of information flow for their particular operation. The fact that individually designed computers will not be available does not diminish the feasibility of an individually designed data-processing system. This approach may require an impractical man, a theorist, who is not hamstrung by existing systems or installed equipment. The result may be a "cloud nine" concept that appears to be an impossible goal. Nevertheless it is a goal, and once a long-range plan is set up for reaching that goal, management has a frame of reference for evaluating the impact of short-range or current decisions on the over-all system of information flow.

SUMMARY

Automated information systems represent the office counterpart to production automation in the factory. Data processing provides good examples of the application of systems concepts in industry.

In describing data processing several significant points were stressed. First, data must be screened by the processing system in order to develop pertinent information for managerial decision making. Thus we recognize a significant difference between *data* and *information*. Second, the concept of data reduction was defined as the processing of vast amounts of scientific data usually gathered from experimental or test situations. In a sense, unwieldy amounts of data are "reduced" to manageable proportions in scientific computation and analysis. Third, business-data processing involves the flow of information for decisions within an organization. It was emphasized that data processing is involved regardless of the tools of implementation, whether paper and pencils or large-scale electronic digital computers.

The evolution of data-processing equipment was traced to show how

---

[17] At least some equipment manufacturers are currently engaging in joint studies of system requirements with both using companies and consulting firms (public-accounting firms with experience in systems analysis).

newer, more elaborate equipment facilities the design of sophisticated systems. Technological progress is needed in all phases of the data-processing cycle—collect, process, compare, decide—in order that an entire system of information flow may be developed. To date, processing equipment has outstripped the ability of systems designers to use it to the fullest. However, technological progress is needed in other phases; for example, source-recording and data-transmission facilities are needed to implement the collection phase of sophisticated data-processing systems.

Some examples were presented of typical electronic-data-processing applications: payroll, inventory, and accounts payable. Examples of integrated data processing—tying all the separate applications together into an over-all system for the entire company—were also presented. Integrated data processing implies stage 3 of the following three-stage advancement schedule for data processing:

1. Visible source material will be prepared as usual and converted to machine-sensible information prior to processing.

2. Original source material, both visible and machine-sensible, will be prepared simultaneously.

3. The source data will be machine-sensible only. It will provide a means for tying all information about current activities and transactions into an over-all, integrated system of information flow.

The most sophisticated data-processing systems are represented by real-time, or on-line, systems. In these cases, the computer is an integral part of an information-decision system and it is used to provide information during the actual decision process. Whereas typical applications call for collection of data over some period of time to be processed as a batch, real-time, or on-line, processing requires up-to-the-minute processing and current information for decision making. The SAGE system for continental air defense was described as an example of a real-time data-processing system. So far this approach has not been evident in industry. However, such systems are bound to evolve in the future.

Special-purpose equipment has been developed to implement systems of information flow for particular companies or particular industries. This trend is likely to continue and should allow systems analysts a free hand in designing the information-decision system best suited for the particular operation under study. After the system is designed, the equipment necessary to implement it can be developed. Currently, combination user-consultant-manufacturer research teams are studying future needs for information-decision systems and, on the basis of their findings, are recommending the most appropriate direction for equipment manufacturers in terms of research, development, and production.

Each day a hundred thousand rout
Followed this zigzag calf about
And o'er his crooked journey went
The traffic of a continent.
A hundred thousand men were led
By one calf near three centuries dead.
They followed still his crooked way,
And lost one hundred years a day;
For thus such reverence is lent
To well-established precedent.

A moral lesson this might teach
Were I ordained and called to preach;
For men are prone to go it blind
Along the calf-path of the mind,
And work away from sun to sun
To do what other men have done.
They follow in the beaten track,
And out and in, and forth and back,
And still their devious course pursue,
To keep the path that others do.
They keep the path a sacred groove,
Along which all their lives they move;
But how the wise old wood-gods laugh,
Who saw the first primeval calf.
Ah, many things this tale might teach—
But I am not ordained to preach.
        Sam Walter Foss, *The Calf Path*

Part Three
IMPLEMENTATION
Introduction

The theoretical underpinnings of management via the systems concept were set forth in Part One. That the systems approach can be useful to practitioners was demonstrated by current examples in Part Two. Now the reader asks, and logically, "How do I apply this concept?" Therefore Part Three is concerned with the implementation of the systems concept in the management process.

209

Chapter 11 considers the present and potential contributions of management science to the implementation of systems concepts. We have chosen the term management science in order to convey a broader connotation than operations research or quantitative methods inasmuch as a wide spectrum of techniques or approaches is discussed. While an emphasis on "whole" systems is apparent in much of the operations-research literature, successful applications of such large-scale analysis are relatively few. Simulation, particularly symbolic system description, is presented as a tool with considerable potential in implementing systems design.

One particular type of simulation, network analysis, or critical-path scheduling, is the subject of Chapter 12. Timing the integration of parts, components, minor subsystems, and major subsystems for projects is usually a key management responsibility. Critical-path scheduling, the design of production and information flows on the basis of explicit networks of relationships, helps management plan, organize, and control complex operations. PERT (performance evaluation and review technique) is discussed as a specific example of implementing systems concepts through network analysis.

Chapter 13 covers systems design, an activity which we contend is one of management's most vital functions. Systems design requires recognition of the economic, political, and competitive environment plus perception of the niche occupied by the organization in larger systems. The design activity also includes identification of the critical decision and processing points involved in a proposed operation. It requires connection of these points to meaningful flows of materials and/or information. The design phase involves planning and organizing both the job-task system and the information-decision system to develop an integrated whole.

The impact of systems concepts on people is covered in Chapter 14. The discussion includes such points as the human need for systematic relationships, the need for systems change, human resistance to change, and how people resist change. Major areas of impact resulting from the implementation of systems concepts are also delineated. Finally, some steps are outlined for management to consider in meeting the human and social problems which may arise.

Chapter Eleven
MANAGEMENT SCIENCE

The systems concept provides a framework for integrated decision making. Within the framework a number of tools of analysis have been developed over the years, including the latest, most sophisticated techniques of operations research. One of the objectives of this chapter will be to place all these tools in perspective as they relate to the science and art of managing. In order to do this we shall trace the common elements of problem solving, decision making, and management, with particular emphasis on the scientific method.

In surveying the field of *management science,* no attempt will be made to cover the techniques exhaustively; each warrants book-length treatment to ensure some degree of expertise or even understanding. Rather, we shall describe the techniques from the manager's point of view, emphasizing those aspects which are important in assessing applicability. In particular, we are interested in their usefulness in implementing the systems concept—either in analysis and decision making or in systems design. Emphasis in this chapter will fall on the former; the latter will be covered in more detail in Chapter 13.

The following topics will be considered:

Problem Solving
Scientific Method
Mathematical Analysis
    Models

Computers
Large-scale Complex Problems
Problem Solving under Uncertainty
Simulation
Gaming
System Simulation

PROBLEM SOLVING

Throughout history man has approached problem solving in a number of ways. At least six reasonably distinct methods can be identified:

1. Appeal to the supernatural
2. Appeal to worldly authority—the older the better
3. Intuition
4. Common sense
5. Pure logic
6. The scientific method [1]

No chronology is implied by the list since all the approaches are being employed currently in problem-solving situations throughout the world. The list does imply, however, a gradation leading toward more careful, searching, and rational approaches. Combinations of several of these are involved in many problem-solving efforts. Intuition can be helpful in the laboratory, as can common sense and logic. Disciplined imagination, a vital ingredient for researchers, may depend on both intuition and common sense.

In business organizations the problem-solving activity often is termed decision making. In this context decision making sometimes is considered synonymous with managing. The process of managing or decision making has been described as follows:

> The first phase of the decision making process—searching the environment for conditions calling for decision—I shall call *intelligence* activity (borrowing the military meaning of intelligence).
>
> The second phase—inventing, developing, and analysing possible courses of action—I shall call *design* activity
>
> The third phase—selecting a particular course of action from those available—I shall call *choice* activity.[2]

These phases of the decision-making process coincide closely with the related stages of problem-solving activity described by Dewey:

---

[1] Stuart Chase, *The Proper Study of Mankind,* Harper & Brothers, New York, 1956, p. 3.

[2] Herbert A. Simon, *The New Science of Management Decision,* Harper & Brothers, New York, 1960, p. 2.

What is the problem?
What are the alternatives?
Which alternative is best? [3]

In a sense, these listings are simplifications of the problem-solving or decision process; yet it is useful to spell out the process explicitly in order to understand it better. Obviously, the stages overlap in any particular case. And there are normally a number of simultaneous problems "in the wind." Thus the manager is involved simultaneously in intelligence, design, and choice activity. Attempts at designing alternative courses of action may turn up additional problems, thus setting off new intelligence activities. An over-all problem-solving cycle or decision process might contain subcycles, which in turn involve subcycles.

Such a description brings us back to the systems concept and emphasizes the concept of an organization as an integrated decision system. As the system becomes more complex it is obvious that refined tools of analysis must be developed in order to facilitate the decision process. The fundamental framework of management science, as for any science, is the scientific method.

SCIENTIFIC METHOD

The term scientific method means many things to many people. Quite often, however, it involves taking the following steps:

1. Define the problem.
2. State objectives.
3. Formulate hypotheses.
4. Collect data (empirical verification).
5. Classify, analyze, and interpret.
6. Draw conclusions, generalize, restate or develop new hypotheses.

Such a list of actions seems more appropriate to formal research activity than problem solving or decision making in general. They refer primarily to Simon's "intelligence activity." The development of alternative courses of action, "design activity," would follow the steps listed above, as would the actual decision with regard to the alternatives.

A similar set of steps is described as the creative process. It is said to include some or all of the following phases:

1. *Orientation:* Pointing up the problem
2. *Preparation:* Gathering pertinent data
3. *Analysis:* Breaking down the relevant material

[3] John Dewey, *How We Think,* D. C. Heath and Company, Boston, 1910, pp. 101–115.

4. *Hypothesis:* Piling up alternatives by way of ideas
5. *Incubation:* Letting up, to invite illumination
6. *Synthesis:* Putting the pieces together
7. *Verification:* Judging the resultant ideas [4]

This sequence suggests decision making by use of the term judging. It seems to imply that some explicit action is taken with respect to the alternatives facing the problem solver.

The specific steps involved in the scientific method are not particularly important for our purposes. We are interested, however, in certain fundamentals implied by the term scientific method. It suggests the use of generally recognized procedures and techniques. We shall discuss such techniques of analysis later in the chapter. Another important ingredient of the scientific method is the attitude of the researcher or decision maker. A relatively formal, systematic, and thorough approach to problem solving implies rationality and reasoning rather than emotion. It applies logical solutions to problems with as little bias as possible. Using the scientific method, either explicitly or implicitly, one reserves judgment until all the facts are in. For many centuries man sought final, definitive answers to problems; more recent approaches have pointed toward a spectrum of possibilities and show a tendency to express knowledge in terms of probability rather than certainty. The scientific method suggests a mind which constantly is challenging, weighing, and explaining—one which continually asks "why." The scientific method implies objectivity rather than subjectivity; it implies selectivity and discrimination; and it implies creativity. According to Brown:

> The scientist is primarily *creative* in his efforts. The thrill of discovery is his great reward. After he has taken things apart, he sees new ways to put them together, new arrangements to make. This is the mark of creative thinking. Without the creative thinking, which carries analysis into the synthesis which produces an integrated result, there can be no true scientific method.[5]

This comment points up the similarity in typical descriptions of the scientific method, problem-solving or decision-making processes, and creativity. Emphasis in all cases is on both the methods and techniques used and the attitude of the researcher, decision maker, or innovator.

On the business scene, managers are confronted with complex situations involving both men and machines. When problems arise which deal with the inanimate aspects of the business environment, "finding a pattern

---

[4] Alex F. Osborn, *Applied Imagination,* Charles Scribner's Sons, New York, 1953, p. 115.

[5] Lyndon O. Brown, *Marketing and Distribution Research,* The Ronald Press Company, New York, 1949, p. 275.

in a set of phenomena" can be relatively straightforward. When dealing with the human aspects, such a task becomes more difficult. When the analysis must include large-scale, man-machine systems, the problem becomes even more complex. If social science involves the use of the scientific method to answer questions about human behavior, then management science can be defined as the use of the scientific method to answer questions of concern to managers. Scientific management represents one approach to development of a science of managing.

Scientific Management

Frederick Taylor in his book *The Principles of Scientific Management* had the following purpose:

> 1. To point out, through a series of simple illustrations, the great loss which the whole country suffers through inefficiency in most all of our daily acts.
> 2. To try to convince the reader that the remedy for this inefficiency lies in systematic management, rather than in searching for some unusual or extraordinary man.
> 3. To prove that the best management is a true science, resting upon clearly defined laws, rules, and principles, as a foundation.[5a]

He wanted to show that the fundamental principles of scientific management are applicable to all kinds of human activities, from our simplest individual acts to the work of our great corporations, which call for the most elaborate cooperation. A prime goal in scientific management was the substitution of science for rule-of-thumb approaches to problem solving. Taylor's efforts were focused on relatively simple tasks, as indicated by the "science of shoveling" and the "pig-iron-handling experiment."

The term scientific in the phrase scientific management is justified primarily in terms of the approach used in problem solving. The scientific method was employed to provide a logical, systematic, thorough analysis of the problems arising in the course of business operations. Efforts toward increased efficiency which would result in both increased profits and higher wages fostered the development of "patterns in a set of phenomena" within individual companies. Thus the findings in some cases could be generalized to similar operations. However, Taylor himself emphasized the fact that each situation must be analyzed separately in order to ensure success. He continually stressed that the findings in any specific study were only narrowly applicable and that the important factor was the approach used, the scientific method. He was convinced that the greatest problem involved in the change to scientific management was the need for a complete revolu-

---

[5a] Frederick W. Taylor, *The Principles of Scientific Management*, Harper & Brothers, New York, 1947, p. 7.

tion in the mental attitudes and habits of all those engaged in management. He called attention to the interrelationship of the following four points: [5b]

1. Science, not rule of thumb
2. Harmony, not discord
3. Cooperation, not individualism
4. Maximum output, in place of restricted output; the development of each man to his greatest efficiency and prosperity

Out of the early beginnings of scientific management a number of tools of analysis and groups of practitioners have developed. The whole field of industrial engineering stemmed from the early scientific-management movement. The field of statistical quality control has grown substantially over the past decades. As the problems have become more complex, additional tools and techniques have been developed, including systems analysis. In many cases they represent fairly straightforward approaches which can be related directly to the scientific method. However, other more sophisticated techniques (fostered by the development of electronic computers) have evolved, almost as fields in themselves. The term operations research developed during World War II, and it encompasses a substantial number of specific techniques for use in problem solving. As we explore some of these more sophisticated techniques in greater detail, let us bear in mind that the over-all umbrella for these tools of analysis is still the scientific method, the primary justification for the term management science.

MATHEMATICAL ANALYSIS

We have now introduced under the general heading of management science several terms: scientific management, operations research, and now mathematical analysis. It might be well to attempt some reconciliation of terminology before proceeding with the more detailed discussion of specific mathematical techniques.

In terms of its philosophy, operations research fundamentally is *not* different from general approaches to problem solving, particularly the scientific method. From the standpoint of methodology, there is nothing that differentiates operations research from many other types of business or economic analysis. The method involved is still the scientific method: the analyst must examine a problem and pick out the dominant variables, then hypothesize specific relationships between these chosen variables, and finally test his model in the real world. The acid test is the ability to make improved forecasts of future behavior.

Such definitions imply that operations research is the application of scientific method to business problems. The scientific-management prac-

[5b] *Ibid.,* pp. 36–37.

titioners and/or the industrial engineers would insist that they have been using this approach for years. The interdisciplinary-team approach distinguished operations research in its early days. In many cases, however, the research team now includes industrial engineers. Thus "no meaningful line can be drawn any more to demarcate operations research from scientific management or scientific management from management science." [6]

Although there is no clear-cut line of demarcation between operations research and other applications of the scientific method to management decision making, the term mathematics is stressed somewhat more in its definitions. For example:

> O.R. [operations research] is the application of scientific methods, techniques, and tools to problems involving the operations of a system so as to provide those in control of the system with optimum solutions to the problems. . . . Its procedures can be broken into the following steps:
>   1. Formulating the problem
>   2. Constructing a mathematical model to represent the system under study
>   3. Deriving a solution from the model
>   4. Testing the model and the solution derived from it
>   5. Establishing controls over the solution
>   6. Putting the solution to work [7]

The use of mathematical models is stressed in operations-research problems, and the definition implies treatment of larger-scale problems—the operation of a system—than was practicable with earlier techniques. The team approach which draws members from various disciplines has been an integral part of many operations-research studies. Again, the team concept implies the ability to handle larger-scale problems than were feasible with other approaches.

The systems concepts embodied in the definitions of operations research are particularly important. As stated previously, the systems concept provides no cookbook approach to problem solving; rather, it involves a frame of mind which can serve to orient the application of specific techniques.

> Along with some mathematical tools, . . . operations research brought into management decision making a point of view called the systems approach. The systems approach is no easier to define than operations research for it is a set of attitudes and a frame of mind rather than a definite and explicit theory. At its vaguest, it means looking at the whole problem— again, hardly a novel idea, and not always a very helpful one. Somewhat more concretely, it means designing the components of a system and mak-

[6] Simon, *op. cit.,* p. 15.

[7] C. West Churchman, Russell L. Ackoff, and E. Leonard Arnoff, *Introduction to Operations Research,* John Wiley & Sons, Inc., New York, 1957, p. 18.

ing individual decisions within it in light of the implication of these decisions for the system as a whole.[8]

The reader should evaluate the various techniques described throughout the remainder of this chapter in terms of their contribution to implementation of a systems approach. Before discussing specific techniques, it will be helpful to set the stage by describing two general aspects of the mathematical-analysis phase of management science—mathematical models and computers.

Models

Construction of a model is a common technique for studying the characteristics or behavioral aspects of objects or systems under varying conditions. The model itself is usually a representation of objects, events, processes, or systems and is used for prediction and control. Models may be descriptive or explanatory. Manipulation of the model is used to test the impact of changes in one or more components of the model on the entity as a whole. In this way tests can be carried out without disturbing the subject of the model. The various types of models have been classified into three general groups.

> We shall distinguish three types of model: iconic, analogue, and symbolic. Roughly, we can say that (1) an iconic model pictorially or visually represents certain aspects of a system (as does a photograph or model airplane); (2) an analogue model employs one set of properties to represent some other set of properties which the system being studied possesses (e.g., for certain purposes, the flow of water through pipes may be taken as an analogue of the "flow" of electricity in wires); and (3) a symbolic model is one which employs symbols to *designate* properties of the system under study (by means of a mathematical equation or set of such equations).[9]

Scale models and wind tunnels represent an iconic model used to simulate actual flight conditions. In operations research, the word model is used to mean a mathematical description of an activity which expresses the relationships among various elements with sufficient accuracy so that it can be used to predict the actual outcome under any expected set of circumstances. Mathematical models are of many types, depending upon the real-life situations they are designed to represent. They have both advantages and disadvantages as analytical tools. The model, rather than the system it represents, can be manipulated in a variety of ways until a relatively good solution is found. On the basis of such experimentation, the actual system can be adjusted with a minimum of disruption. An obvious disadvantage

---

[8] Simon, *op. cit.*, p. 15.
[9] Churchman, Ackoff, and Arnoff, *op. cit.*, p. 158.

of model building is the difficulty in duplicating reality completely. Also, the process, while extremely beneficial, can be time-consuming and costly.

Model building provides a tool for extending the researcher's judgment in handling large-scale, complex systems.

> In a sense, the use of a model frees the intuition and permits it to concentrate on those problems to which it is particularly suited. It permits the creative manager to test rigorously the implications of new plans, new schemes, and new ideas.[10]

Although the model is often thought of as simulating a large organization or process, any set of equations designed to represent a particular problem area, no matter how narrow, can be thought of as a model. Various assumptions are made about the number of factors which must be included in order to represent the situation accurately. Then numerical values must be assigned to the parameters in the problem in order to develop a workable model. Once the system has been described and numerical values have been assigned to all parameters involved, the problem can be solved with whatever technique seems appropriate. Implementation of mathematical models to represent complex systems has been facilitated by the use of electronic computers.

Computers

Electronic computers have fostered much of the advance in management science over the past several decades. Trivial problems, often used as textbook examples, can be solved quite readily with hand calculations or, at most, the use of a desk calculator. However, real-life problems in complex industrial settings often are not amenable to such approaches. Numerical solutions to such problems often require thousands of individual steps, which may require endless hours of clerical work. A computer allows solution of typical problems in a matter of minutes rather than weeks or months. Moreover, the computer is not subject to fatigue and hence is more likely to provide error-free solutions than is the typical statistical clerk. While the programming of solutions to typical problems can be both challenging and time-consuming, the results of such effort can be applied over and over again to similar problems as they arise. The trend toward modular programs, which can be put together in a variety of forms, facilitates the solution of new problems with existing computer programs.

It is dangerous to assume that all mathematical analysis must be done via electronic computers. The problems in question must be analyzed in light of the most likely techniques and the most efficient processing of data required for solution. As techniques are developed for automating

[10] Franklin A. Lindsey, *New Techniques for Management Decision Making*, McGraw-Hill Book Company, Inc., New York, 1958, p. 6.

management decisions in areas such as inventory, quality, and production control, the mathematical analysis involved can be integrated into the general data-processing system. In such cases the mathematical analysis required for automatic decisions is imbedded in an over-all information-decision system programmed to handle all but the exceptional situations involved in day-to-day operations. Larger-scale mathematical analysis may be required for management decisions in areas such as long-range planning. In this case a computer serves primarily as a calculator in the solution phase rather than as a data processor in the information-decision system.

The importance of electronic computers to management science will be increasingly evident as we explore the various tools and techniques in the following pages.

Large-scale Complex Problems

For purposes of discussion the techniques of mathematical analysis will be discussed separately. However, the reader should not assume that industrial problems fall into neat categories which lend themselves to solution via algorithmic, or cookbook, approaches. Combinations of several techniques may be appropriate in given instances. The analyst must define the problem carefully and then fit the most appropriate technique into the problem-solving process. Tailoring the techniques to the problems, plus the use of good judgment, will lead to the best possible solution.

Some of the techniques to be described have proved worthwhile in management decision making over a period of years. Some have not been applied fruitfully in real situations as yet. Still others fall in between these extremes, having had limited application in practical situations. It will be important to ascertain the usefulness of particular techniques in implementing the systems concept.

Linear Programming. One of the most useful of the operations-research techniques is linear programming. It is both an approach to the formulation and statement of the problems for which it is suited and a set of mathematical procedures for making the calculations leading to selection of the best course of action. It has been defined as:

> . . . a technique for specifying how to use limited resources or capacities of a business to obtain a particular objective, such as least cost, highest margin, or least time, when those resources have alternate uses. It is a technique that systematizes for certain conditions the process of selecting the most desirable course of action from a number of available courses of action, thereby giving management information for making a more effective decision about the resources under its control.[11]

[11] Robert O. Ferguson and Lauren F. Sargent, *Linear Programming,* McGraw-Hill Book Company, Inc., New York, 1958, p. 3.

Linear programming has been applied with good results in the determination of:

1. The most profitable manufacturing program
2. The best inventory strategy
3. The effect of changes in purchasing and selling price
4. Whether to make or buy certain components
5. The best location of plants
6. The lowest-cost manufacturing schedule
7. The best location of warehouses and distribution outlets
8. The most profitable product mix

This is only a partial list of applications, but it does point out the type of problem for which linear programming is most useful. There are some common characteristics in each one of these problems, including the fact that complex systems are involved. First, various processes are in competition for the allocation of a given and fixed number of units of resources. Second, the cost of allocating a given number of units of a resource to a given process is proportional to the number of units allocated. Such a situation will have a solution in which the total cost of the over-all process is a minimum, or conversely, the profit is a maximum. In addition to these similarities, in each instance the manager must consider a large number of factors affecting his decision. Also, these factors are interdependent, so that the manager must consider them individually and in relation to each other. Finally, the choice must be made of one solution or course of action from among many obvious alternatives and, perhaps, some others which are not so obvious. Without linear-programming techniques, these decisions must be based on experience, feel, intuition, and hope.

Application of linear-programming techniques forces a clear-cut statement of the aims of the system involved in the analysis. To the extent that the system under analysis involves one or more areas of managerial responsibility, it will allow a closer approach to the stated goal by forcing on all participants an awareness of the basic purpose and structure of the system. As stated earlier, different departments often pursue divergent purposes because each follows its own objectives, whether reduced costs, higher production, greater utilization of capacity, or greater profit. Within the linear-programming framework, such diversity will not work. The analytical procedure makes painfully clear that to push for one goal is to do so at the expense of another. From the viewpoint of the larger system, only one of these purposes can be the correct one for the system under the set of conditions which exist. Thus linear programming provides a rationale for the homogeneous operation of those systems to which it can be, and is, applied.

Once a linear-programming problem has been set up, slight modifications can be made with little additional work. Thus, once large-scale complex problems have been defined and variables specified, relationships can be developed which allow reasonably quick assessment of the impact of changes in pertinent variables.

One of the limitations of linear programming is apparent in the name itself. The fact that it treats all relationships as linear limits the realism of the analysis. In many cases linear approximations are entirely appropriate. In others, they may be less appropriate, to the point of rendering the application of results to a real system meaningless. Linear programming cannot deal effectively with more than one set of conditions at a time. Optimal solutions to real problems involving simultaneous changes in several variables are extremely difficult to compute. Even with large-scale computers, computational problems for real situations do develop. Thus problems often must be simplified in order to reduce them to a form that can be handled by analytical techniques and available computational facilities. When this is done the application of the results to the over-all system may not be appropriate.

Quadratic and Dynamic Programming. These two techniques have been developed in order to offset some of the disadvantages inherent in linear programming. For example, quadratic programming, like linear programming, is an algebraic technique, but one that can handle problems with nonlinear relationships. This allows development of a mathematical model yielding a more complete description of the system under study.

The objective of dynamic programming is that of facilitating solution of sequential problems. It is a method of solving multistage problems in which the decisions at one stage become the conditions governing the succeeding stages. The pervasiveness of multistage decision processes in real business problems is evident. Management of business organizations calls for a sequence of decisions in order to keep the system in control.[12]

Dynamic programming is still in a state of development and has not been applied widely to real problems. However, it does have considerable potential and may allow implementation of systems concepts which are vital in providing a frame of reference for analysis of large-scale, complex operations. According to Lindsey:

> Dynamic programming is therefore of considerable potential value in a large class of critical management problems. But whether or not a given problem can be solved today, even by approximative techniques, can only be determined by detailed examination of that specific problem. Some of the types of problems which may be solvable include:

[12] Richard Bellman, *Dynamic Programming,* Princeton University Press, Princeton, N.J., 1957, pp. vii–viii.

1. Long-range capital budgeting
2. Timing of equipment replacement
3. Machine-loading in job shops
4. Transportation scheduling to meet shifting demands
5. Smoothing of production levels to meet variable demands
6. Allocation of limited resources between current consumption and reinvestment to increase future output

Since dynamic programming is clearly in the developmental stage, its applications should be limited to situations of high potential payoff and situations where management is prepared to regard the necessary expense in the same light as it would research-and-development expenses. Because of the complexity of most management problems of a dynamic character, it may be that simulation will provide a more practical approach to most problems than will formal dynamic programming. The essential difference is that the dynamic programming attempts to provide the exact optimum by the solution of a set of mathematical statements or equations. Simulation, instead, is a controlled trial-and-error process in which successively better numerical answers are obtained by repeated trial solutions. The process is repeated until an answer is found which approximates the true solution sufficiently closely to be acceptable.[13]

The appropriateness of simulation techniques is discussed in considerable detail later in this chapter.

Input-Output Analysis. Input-output analysis, originally developed by Wassily Leontief as a means of studying an over-all economy, provides an approach to analyzing interrelationships in large, complex systems. To date input-output analysis has been used to relate production and distribution of products throughout the economy. The output of each industry is traced in detail through intermediate stages to final destinations. Similarly, the source of raw materials and components as inputs to a given industry is also traced in considerable detail. When arrayed in a large matrix format and given the coefficients which relate the industries directly and indirectly, a change of demand for finished goods of a particular industry can be traced throughout the system. Lindsey describes the technique as follows:

Mathematically, it is a variation of linear programming and provides a quantitative framework for the description of an entire economy. Basic to input-output analysis is a unique set of input-output ratios for each production and distribution process. For example, the inputs of coal, ore, limestone, electrical power, etc., all enter in the production of pig iron in fixed ratios. Thus, if the ratios of inputs per unit of output are known for all production processes, and if the total production of each end product of the economy—or of that section being studied—is known, it is possible to compute precisely the production levels required at every intermediate

[13] Lindsey, *op. cit.,* pp. 42–43.

stage to supply the total sum of end products. Further, it is possible to determine the effect at every point in the production process of a specified change in the volume and mix of end products.[14]

Given the input-output matrix, detailed analysis could be made of such changes as an increase in residential construction or increases (or decreases) in military spending (including additions to or cancellations of specific weapon-system procurement programs). Tracing the impact of such changes throughout the economy by hand would be impossible. The input-output matrix and the computer make such analysis feasible.

Even the largest of the input-output matrices involves aggregation in order to make computation feasible. Such aggregation may limit the usefulness of this type of analysis for particular industries or products. The development of useful matrices is necessarily a laborious, time-consuming task. However, as is often the case in developing models of large, complex systems, the process itself can be extremely valuable in understanding the over-all system and the interrelationships among its parts.

Problem Solving under Uncertainty

Another class of problems confronting management involves decision making under conditions of uncertainty. The question of probability arises, a factor which management must consider in the decision-making process. For purposes of discussion, the concept of uncertainty or probability will be developed under four separate headings: statistics and probability, queuing, or waiting-line theory, game theory, and Monte Carlo techniques.

Statistics and Probability. One of the most firmly established analytical techniques for management revolves around the use of statistical inference. Quite often the term statistics is considered primarily in terms of data, or at most in terms of descriptive statistics. However, modern statistical techniques provide a useful tool for the decision-making process, primarily in the realms of estimation and hypothesis testing. A broad connotation is represented in the following:

> It is the purpose of statistical analysis to provide methods of treating data so that the maximum information can be obtained with a predetermined risk of drawing false conclusions. No method of analysis can extract more information from a set of data than is contained therein, and no method, statistical or otherwise, can draw conclusions from experimental data with zero risk of error. The use of statistical methods is based on a reasonable assumption that accepted principles of logic and probability should produce correct answers more often than guessing.[15]

[14] *Ibid.,* p. 43.

[15] E. Bright Wilson, Jr., *An Introduction to Scientific Research,* McGraw-Hill Book Company, Inc., New York, 1952, p. 57.

The use of sampling is widespread; in some cases it is the only approach to obtaining data for decision making, and in other cases it is the only feasible approach in terms of time and/or money. Many managerial decisions involve assumptions concerning the probability of future events, particularly those which are not controllable. Therefore it is important to understand the nature of probability theory and its application in decision making. For example, the probability of certain outcomes must be related to the importance of those outcomes in order to provide meaningful information. The probabilities which must be attached to particular events may be obtained from past experience (a probability distribution is available), and/or it may require informed judgment on the part of the decision maker. When a sequence of events is involved, each with a probability distribution for various outcomes, the problem becomes extremely complex. In such cases it is imperative that a systematic approach be employed which takes into account every pertinent facet of the problem.

A subcategory in the area of statistics is that of factorial analysis, a technique designed to study complex interactions of many variables. It provides a means of relating a number of variables and assessing the relative impact of independent variables on a dependent variable. Factorial analysis provides a maximum amount of information for minimum effort. It is an efficient way of isolating the effects of individual variables, even though numerous variables are interacting with one another and also acting simultaneously on a given outcome.

Statistics and probability provide valuable techniques for decision making. However, statisticians and managers must be constantly on the alert to check results against logic. Raw answers sometimes can be misleading, as in the case of spurious correlation. Results of statistical analysis which are to be used for estimation or prediction must be scrutinized for reasonableness.

Queuing Theory. Queuing theory, sometimes referred to as waiting-line theory, applies to those decisions which arise when service must be provided to meet some demand which is in any way irregular (neither controllable nor precisely predictable by management). Queuing theory is not a single set of mathematical formulas, but an expanding collection of methods and techniques based on a variety of assumptions. Some of the basic characteristics which may vary from problem to problem include:

1. The size of the group being serviced, i.e., whether it is finite or infinite
2. Whether the elements requiring service are "patient" or not
3. The distribution of holding or servicing times (the two most com-

mon assumptions being the constant and exponential servicing-time assumptions)

4. The characteristics of arrival, i.e., their time pattern

5. The number of servicing units

The general approach involved in this type of analysis can be described
as follows:

> There are costs connected with the length of the waiting line and the time
> lost in waiting. There are also costs associated with increasing the capacity
> of the servicing unit, both capital costs and labor costs. Since arrivals are
> random, there may be times when there are waiting lines and other times
> when there is idle servicing capacity. As the mean arrival rate approaches
> capacity, it can be shown that, if that rate is maintained, the waiting line
> will tend to approach infinity as an ultimate limit. Clearly, then, capacity
> must be at least a little greater than the mean arrival rate. The optimum
> solution to this class of problems will provide a processing capacity just
> sufficiently in excess of the mean arrival rate to minimize the total of the
> cost of the added processing capacity plus the costs of waiting. It is also
> possible to determine the probable waiting time to be expected for each
> arrival for any given mean arrival rate and processing capacity.[16]

The optimal balance between excess capacity and time lost in waiting is
an important consideration in many types of problems. The appropriate
number of toll booths, bank tellers, and maintenance men can be determined with these techniques. The level of airport facilities or the capacity
of job shops can be approached in similar fashion.

Even in the simpler cases, the computations tend to get quite lengthy.
In most cases practical results come from (1) the use of tables which gives
general solutions to various waiting-line situations or (2) the use of Monte
Carlo techniques.

Game Theory. Game theory involves analysis of the choice of
strategies in competitive situations. It had a major impact on the development of linear programming, as well as starting a new way of thinking
about competitive decisions.[17] Aside from its contribution made through
linear programming, game theory to date is still primarily a field of pure
theory. Applications have been few in number and limited in scope because
of the unmanageable complexities that arise once the number of con-
testants exceeds two and the rules allow more than trivial freedom of
action.

While game theory is not applicable as yet to real management problems, the approaches used in applying the technique can provide insights

[16] Lindsey, *op. cit.,* p. 20.

[17] Churchman, Ackoff, and Arnoff, *op. cit.,* p. 519.

for managers contemplating competitive situations. Again, the formal process of analysis, forcing management to consider all possible alternatives for both their own and their competitors' strategy, can be extremely beneficial. The formal thinking process ensures consideration of the total problem.

Monte Carlo Techniques. When problems facing management involve uncertainty, a formal analytical solution may be difficult or impossible to obtain. Some expressions within a model, because of mathematical or practical considerations, may not be susceptible to a satisfactorily accurate numerical evaluation. Also, the problem may involve events which can be stated only in terms of probabilities. If probabilities can be represented by standard statistical distributions, a solution may be possible. On the other hand, most problems involve variables which cannot be represented by standard probability-distribution curves. Moreover, many problems involve the interactions of a number of probabilistic events, and some representation must be made of the combinations.

In cases such as those outlined above, a particular application of random sampling called the Monte Carlo technique can serve to obtain a satisfactory solution. Basically, the technique is a process for developing data through the use of some random-number generator. For variables which are difficult to evaluate, the Monte Carlo technique can be used to generate their respective values from the proper distribution. In other words, a sample of values can be generated and used to represent observations in the real world.

Examples of such approaches might include the generation of arrival times at some servicing station. Actual data from operations might not provide enough information unless collected over a long period of time. In order to facilitate analysis, the real world is simulated in the form of arrivals. Other problem areas such as transportation, production, inventory, and distribution usually have random factors which are too complicated for mathematical treatment. In such cases Monte Carlo techniques can be used to simulate activity, and hence develop approximations which suffice in the decision-making process. The use of Monte Carlo techniques to simulate certain aspects of problems which cannot be approached via rigorous mathematical analysis points up the need for techniques which allow more flexibility in the analytical process. In the next section we shall discuss one of the most important of such tools, simulation.

SIMULATION

Simulation means "to obtain the essence of, without reality." In the narrow sense, simulation can be used in the application of operations-research techniques to specific problems. When applying Monte Carlo techniques, the method involves setting up a stochastic[18] model of a real situation and then performing sampling experiments upon the model. The stochastic model is the feature that distinguishes a simulation from a mere sampling experiment in the classical sense.[19] This approach allows the generation of a large amount of data which otherwise might take years or months to accumulate. Following the generation of data via simulation, analytical computations can be made and the problem solved in a straightforward manner. While simulation of a single event or narrow process is beneficial from the standpoint of applying operations-research techniques to problem solving, by far the greatest potential benefit lies in simulation of larger-scale systems.

Two basic types of large-scale-system simulation have been developed. In one case, the decision-making process is programmed into the simulation in order that the entire system may be run automatically without involvement of human decision makers. A second type requires recurrent decisions on the part of outside decision makers, the results of those decisions being generated by a simulated system which ordinarily is programmed for an electronic computer. The former approach is called system simulation; it will be discussed in a later section. The latter approach has been described as competitive simulation, or simply gaming.

Gaming

In business, many of the most significant problems are those where managers must not only contend with a complex environment but must also make decisions in competition with other managers seeking the same or similar goals. Simulation of these competitive situations has been called business gaming. This approach evolved from the traditional war games practiced by the armed forces.

The American Management Association wondered if a similar approach could be used to give businessmen the same practice in decision making. A research team was formed, headed by Franc M. Ricciardi, AMA Vice-President.[20] The top-management-decision game was designed as a mathematical model of business. It consists of a large number of cause-

---

[18] Variable quantities with a definite range of values, each one of which, depending on chance, can be attained with a definite probability. A stochastic variable is defined (1) if the set of its possible values is given and (2) if the probability of attaining each particular value is also given.

[19] John Harling, "Simulation Techniques in Operations Research: A Review," *Operations Research*, May–June, 1958, pp. 307–319.

[20] Following these initial efforts, other games were developed around the country, for example, by Albert N. Schrieber, University of Washington, James R. Jackson, University of California at Los Angeles, and a group at Carnegie Institute of Technology.

and-effect formulas which determine the results of each move made by the decision makers. In effect, the gaming model is a simulation of an entire industry. In most cases, play is designed for two to six teams representing a group of companies in a particular industry. While some games have been developed which can be scored by hand, the typical approach utilizes a computer in order to accommodate a large number of equations and hence helps provide the realism which stimulates those "playing" the game.

A number of basic equations must be programmed which depict the total industry performance based partly on external environmental influences and partly on the combined actions of the "companies" in the industry. Individual company decisions have less effect on this total market picture than on their own performance as it relates to other companies.

The other large set of equations which must be programmed in a gaming simulation relates to a performance of a particular company in the industry environment. As the executives of each company make decisions, the effects must be analyzed and results determined. In order to evaluate performance, the game must be entirely quantitative, with performance measured in terms of such factors as market share, dollar sales, per cent profit, or return on investment.

So far, simulations of the gaming variety where an entire industry is involved have been used primarily as training devices, with little effort focused on research and analysis that might be feasible. Some research has been done with regard to the decision process itself, and attention has also been focused on the human relations aspects of forming small groups (in this case, the top executive committee of a company). The subsequent interaction of these team members and their attempts to organize for playing the game is a fruitful area for research.

Other gaming-type simulations have been developed which deal with only a part of the business enterprise. In most of these, however, there is not the same competitive atmosphere that develops in the industry-simulation setting. When simulating a part of the company operation such as the production scheduling or the distribution of finished goods, the interaction involves only the decision maker and the environment as modeled. For example, a job shop might be simulated—given machine capacities and labor availability—the problem being one of scheduling a certain number of orders through the plant in the most efficient manner. Individuals or teams might play this type of game, the objective being one of producing the items requested at the lowest cost. The production environment might be relatively straightforward, or it might be extremely complex, with random variations and unforeseen hazards such as machine breakdowns, labor difficulties, or other similarly haphazard events. The only competitive element of such a gaming approach would be that of allowing several individuals or teams to play the same game and declaring a winner according to the ability of the individual or team to program the production operation at the least cost.

A similar approach might be used for the distribution process. For example, the American Management Association developed a "physical distribution simulation model" involving three products, *lanks, torps,* and *dossets.* Each product had different characteristics in terms of size, shape, weight, and value. The assumed distribution system is shown on the map in Figure 25. The products are manufactured in three plants: lanks in

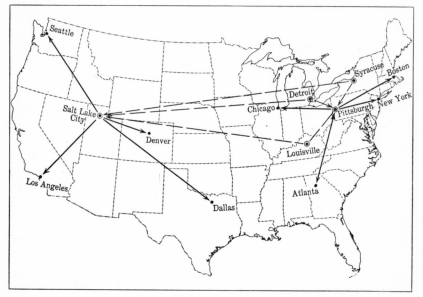

Fig. 25. Assumed distribution used for the "physical-distribution simulation model."

plant A in Syracuse, torps in plant B in Louisville, and dossets in plant C in Detroit. Distribution centers for all three products are located in Pittsburgh for the East and Salt Lake City for the West. Regional warehouses are located in eight sales regions: Seattle, Los Angeles, Denver, and Dallas in the West; Atlanta, Chicago, New York, and Boston in the East.

Modes of shipping include truck, rail, and airplane, with delivery times and transportation costs varying accordingly. Shipments can be made from the plants to either of the two distribution centers and/or directly to the eight sales-region field warehouses. The schedule of shipping rates is based upon the nature of the product, mode of transportation, and the loading capacity of that particular mode of transport.

Detailed costs are outlined for storage and handling of the various products at either a regional warehouse, a distribution center, or the plant itself. Storage capacity is represented in cubic feet, and penalties are assessed for operating at less than capacity in terms of space availability and requirements. Additional costs are charged for demurrage when the inventory at any point exceeds available space.

The problem in this case is one of balancing the production of three plants with the demand on the part of consumers in the various regions. Demand is a stochastic variable where average consumption by quarters is known but actual consumption per week is allowed to vary widely. Therefore there is a problem of smoothing the flow of material through the distribution pipeline by shipping proper amounts via the most economical modes of transportation in order to have the goods on hand when needed at each regional warehouse. This smoothing of the distribution flow must be done without unduly affecting the production process (an opportunity to apply rhochrematics).

The decisions required must be made by a distribution manager and his staff. This group is trying to find an optimum approach to a particular distribution problem. In this case, they are dealing with decisions in a simulated environment. As in other functionally oriented simulation exercises, the competitive element is present only in the comparison of relative success in optimizing the physical distribution system on the part of several groups of players. This type of simulation does not describe a specific problem, but is generalized to provide an exercise in decision making and allow for training of individuals involved in the problem of physical distribution systems.

Other functional simulation exercises could be established in areas such as finance or sales management. For example, a sales-management game could include an exercise in attaining the optimal routing for salesmen, or a more complex simulation could be developed which would include routing, scheduling, compensation plans, and other pertinent factors in the sales-management environment. The measure of effectiveness in such a gaming situation would probably be net dollars returned from territories under the sales manager's jurisdiction. Here again, the competitive element would come by comparing the performance of several individuals or teams who had gone through the same exercise of playing the game.

While operational gaming, or competitive simulation, is an interesting and worthwhile exercise, it does not describe a concrete, particular situation with the realism necessary for research work. The other broad field within simulation, symbolic system simulation, appears to be a powerful tool for both training and research.

System Simulation

Computer simulation can be used as a problem-solving technique and is valuable as a part of research methods directed toward obtaining a better understanding and improved control of complex business operations. Large-scale computers have facilitated total-system simulation, which has in turn allowed problem-solving efforts in the areas of designing better systems, understanding the workings of operative systems, and studying decision-making processes in man-machine operations.

We quote a summary report on the Eighth Annual American Institute of Industrial Engineering symposium on system simulation.

Now, we may well ask the crucial question. "Why should business men, management scientists, or anyone as far as that is concerned, be interested in simulating a system?" Well, there are some pretty important reasons, and they are as follows:

1. *For purpose of experimentation or evaluation;* in other words, to try and predict the consequences of changes in policy, conditions, methods, etc., without having to spend the money or taking the risk to actually make the change in real life.

2. *To learn more about the system* in order to redesign or refine it. The very complexity of most of our business and industrial systems makes necessary a means to provide understanding of both the system as a whole and of its parts.

3. *To familiarize personnel* with a system or a situation, which may not exist as yet in real life.

4. *To verify or demonstrate* a new idea, a new system or approach; in other words, quantify the risks and benefits, and demonstrate the chances of success.

Now, let's take a look a little deeper behind this question, *"Why simulate?"* What are some of the specific advantages which are not so apparent when one tries to generalize? Well, first of all, simulating a system enables one to compress or expand real time. In other words, a business man can simulate a year of his operation in a matter of minutes or he can slow down the process so that he can, like a slow motion film, analyze just what is going on in his problem areas. We are trying to alert the manager to the fact that here, for the first time, he is going to have a laboratory which enables him to analyze his business and look at it either in slow motion or in high speed. The second advantage is a tremendous one, because it's at the heart of the business man's need to plan and forecast. He can, with system simulation, look before he leaps and test his ideas and changes in advance. The results of a year's operation under different assumptions can be his in a matter of hours. Tied in with this is the fact that in many cases it is impossible, impractical or uneconomical to try many management ideas today because of the disruption or cost involved in changing a going operation.[21]

Any reference to optimal results or best solutions is noticeably lacking in the foregoing summary. In contrast to the application of operations-research techniques, the application of system simulation is not undertaken with the idea of optimizing the total system or even a segment of it. In any reasonably large system or subsystem, conditions such as interdependence, immeasurability, incompleteness, ineffectiveness of practical working rules, and imperfect coordination make it impossible to derive and set forth an organization and set of decision rules which will optimize the operation of the system. Simulation of complex business-enterprise behavior allows one to analyze the dynamic behavior of the system as it exists and also allows for testing new and different organizational arrangements or policies. In order to get a clearer view of the application and benefits of system simulation, it will be useful to look at some specific examples. The following list of large-scale simulation models, described at the simulation symposium previously referred to, will provide some idea of the scope and content of this approach to analysis of business problems:

Arthur D. Little	A General Purpose Inventory Control Simulation
Rand Corporation	Simulation for the Training of Air Force Personnel
	Simulation of the Air Defense System
	Simulation of the Air Force Logistics System
Cornell University	Evaluation of Alternatives on Profits
United Air Lines	Operational Model of a Waiting Line Problem
Stanford Research Institute	Selection among Alternative Models
Massachusetts Institute of Technology	Monte Carlo Methods
California Texas Oil Company	Model of the Entire Enterprise
Port of New York Authority	Computer Simulation of a Bus Terminal Operation
Council for Economic & Industry Research, Inc.	Establishing Deviation Limits for a Complex System

[21] Warren E. Alberts, "Report to the Eighth AIIE National Conference on the System Simulation Symposium," *Journal of Industrial Engineering,* November–December, 1957, pp. 368–369.

IBM Corporation	Simulating the Shop Scheduling Process
American Management Association	Top Management Decision Game
Imperial Oil Company, Ltd.	A Distribution Network
General Electric Company	Machine Shop Scheduling Problem
	Simulation of the Strategic Air War
Air Materiel Command	USAF Aircraft Engine Management Model
Remington Rand Corp.	A Review of Early Simulation Efforts
Johns Hopkins University	Simulation of the Quartermaster Supply Problem
Ramo-Wooldridge Corporation	Inventory Control Solution by Simulation

United Airlines has set up and operated a simulation of the activities involved in operating a large airport such as New York's La Guardia Field. This simulation is referred to as the station model. Using a large-scale computer, months of actual operation at an air terminal can be simulated in a matter of minutes. Essential elements in the model include (1) time of day, year, week, (2) weather conditions, (3) need for maintenance for type and length of repair job, (4) availability of spare aircraft, (5) delays in landing or take-offs, (6) absenteeism of personnel, and (7) required number of maintenance personnel.

All these uncertainties, as well as company policies and practices, are built into the station model. Policy changes can be programmed and their effect tested by simulating operations under the new conditions. According to those involved in the exercise, perhaps the greatest gain from the simulation has been to instill the *concept of systems thinking* in management and to provide a format for reasoning and decision making in the broader problems of system performance.

The distribution and inventory-control model was an approach used by Imperial Oil Limited of Canada in attempting to develop the best system of warehousing their products. The problem involved determining requirements and meeting difficulties arising from severe overcrowding at many field plants. Those involved in the analysis worked with management in the manufacturing operation to develop a detailed flow diagram which represented the system and the decisions which would have to be made. Working with the computation-center personnel, a program was devised for instructing the computer in order to provide all basic information, control points, and other pertinent data, including various practical constraints. With this basic information in the machine, the computer could be given an initial set of inventory levels for the many hundreds of items being stocked, and a detailed daily recapitulation of orders from field plants could also be fed into the process. Data for a number of critical months were particularly useful in testing this system for possible shortages. The computer was programmed to put out periodic stock reports to indicate the inventory levels in addition to providing information on all unusual conditions such as shortages or waiting lines for facilities. These were then analyzed so that refinements could be introduced into the actual operation.

The Operations Research Office of the Johns Hopkins University studied the problem of maintenance of equipment in an army battalion. The basic question was one of how many mechanics to include in the organization and how many and what parts to carry under varying conditions of desired mobility of operations. This presented a difficult problem, particularly when required data were not available. In addition, there are measures to keep the number of nonfighting soldiers to a minimum while requiring that equipment be maintained in a state of readiness. A complex flow diagram indicating the variety of considerations involved was developed as a preliminary step toward simulation. A great deal of data had to be collected and stored in the computer. Numerous policies had to be set forth, and the entire package integrated in the computer program designed to simulate the maintenance operation. Operation of the simulation model permitted estimation of the effect on the system of various basic loads of repair parts that are carried, the resupply rate contemplated, and the number of mechanics assigned to the unit. Such analysis should give insight into the best balance of maintenance manpower, parts, and mission-performing ability.

Other examples from the above list could be described; however, they are all designed to do somewhat the same type of job for the analyst. Some of the examples listed are relatively broad-scale simulation projects involving an entire firm, while others are more narrowly oriented toward specific functions such as production or distribution.

Maffei and Shycon have described their work in simulating the distribution system for the H. J. Heinz Company.[22] In this case, a large number of products are involved with complex problems of assembling raw materials, producing the products, and then marketing them through a pipeline that includes accumulation at certain points, with distribution fanning out from such central points. The complexity of a distribution system for stable items such as Heinz products can easily be imagined. Deriving an optimum solution for the number and location of warehouses

---

[22] Harvey N. Shycon and Richard B. Maffei, "Simulation: Tool for Better Distribution," *Harvard Business Review*, November–December, 1960, pp. 65–75.

throughout the continental United States would be an utterly impossible task. On the other hand, simulation of this distribution system could be accomplished, and on the basis of various "runs," better arrangements and numbers of warehouses could be programmed.

Establishing flow diagrams and programming the operation of the system for a large-scale computer involved nearly three years of calendar time and many man-years of effort. Once accomplished, however, the simulation model allowed researchers to vary parameters involved and hence to make decisions concerning the appropriateness of policy changes and possible benefits to be derived from them.

An extremely important by-product of an exercise such as programming the description of an entire system is the benefit that occurs from merely tracing explicitly the system itself. Most businessmen or decision makers are not fully aware of all the factors involved in the operations under their control. When these operations have to be described quantitatively and explicitly, it forces those persons involved to describe the process in complete detail and thereby gain new insight into what they might have considered an entirely familiar operation. While the Heinz study and other simulation exercises are extremely large scale and complex, they deal primarily with only one or a few functions. In this case, the simulation dealt with the distribution problem and did not treat the accumulation of raw materials or the production function.

Some work is being done in isolated instances on simulation of an entire firm. An example of this approach is the work being done by a research group at MIT under the direction of Jay W. Forrester.

Industrial Dynamics. In a series of memoranda, and later in a book, Forrester and his colleagues in the School of Industrial Management at MIT have presented the philosophy, nature, structure, and use of industrial dynamics.[23] The following material on industrial dynamics has been taken from these sources.

The tool of analysis is a dynamic model of the behavior of an industrial organization. A typical industrial-dynamics model is a mathematical model for analyzing stability and fluctuation of an industrial system. It has closed-loop, information-feedback characteristics and also incorporates decision-making procedures. Five interacting subsystems are developed—material flow, order flow, money flow, capital-equipment generation and usage, and manpower employment and mobility—all interconnected by information flow or a decision-making network. Preliminary studies have dealt primarily

[23] Jay W. Forrester et al., various memoranda concerning industrial-dynamics research (unpublished materials), MIT, School of Industrial Management, Cambridge, Mass. Also included in Jay W. Forrester, *Industrial Dynamics,* John Wiley & Sons, Inc., New York, and the MIT Press, Cambridge, Mass., 1961.

with material and information flow.[24] Although these studies in themselves have been extremely complex, continuing efforts are being devoted toward incorporation of all the subsystems into one all-encompassing system. Since the situations to be studied can be represented realistically only by nonlinear mathematical systems, they are so formulated. Likewise, if the real-life situation is unstable, then the system-simulation program must accommodate this phenomenon. To describe accurately a total system, it is often necessary to incorporate hundreds or even thousands of variables in order to be sufficiently realistic and useful. The immediate goal is to find *improved* but *not optimum* system design; there is no meaningful definition of an optimum system nor any method of proving that the designated system behavior is the best achievable.

The industrial-dynamics philosophy claims that there is a general misunderstanding to the effect that a mathematical model cannot be undertaken until every constant and functional relationship is known to high accuracy. This often leads to the omission of admittedly highly significant factors (most of the "intangible" influences on decisions) because they are unmeasured or unmeasurable.

A model must start with a "structure," meaning the general nature of the interrelationships within it. Assumptions about structure must be made before one can collect data from the real system. The structure is developed by obtaining a verbal account of the decision-making process at each critical point in the system. This verbalization and structuring can be accomplished only through the tedious task of asking questions and probing for answers on the part of the decision makers. Having a reasonable structure that fits descriptive knowledge of the system, one can take the next step and assign plausible numerical values to coefficients, since the coefficient should represent identifiable and describable characteristics of the real system. The analyst can then proceed to alter the model and the real system to eliminate disagreement and move both toward a more desirable level of performance. Mathematical models for representing industrial and economic activity adequately for top-management purposes are probably no larger (in terms of hundreds of variables) than some which have already been simulated in military operations. But they will be more subtle and more complex (higher degrees of interdependence between the variables).

The general concepts of information-feedback systems are essential in industrial-dynamics model building, because such systems exhibit behavior as a whole which is not evident from examination of the parts separately. The pattern of systems interconnection, the amplification caused by

[24] The relationship of industrial dynamics and rhochrematics was discussed in Chapter 8.

decision and policy, the delays in actions, and the distortion of information flows combine to determine stability and growth. The interconnection of entirely ordinary corporate action can lead to production fluctuations, unemployment, and excess plant capacity. As one action feeds into another and eventually back to the first, it causes instability, which is the counterpart of "hunting" in mechanical servomechanisms. Careful attention must be given to representing properly time delays and information distortion.

Decision making in an information-feedback system couples the information and the action channels. In the model structure the decision functions receive information and thereby control the rates of flow that interconnect the various levels (inventories, stocks, reservoirs) of the system. Representing dynamic system behavior requires formal expressions to indicate how decisions are made. The flow of information is continuously converted into decisions and thence into action. No plea about inadequacy of understanding of the decision-making process can excuse the analyst from estimating the decision-making criteria. To omit decision making is to deny its presence, a mistake of far greater magnitude than any errors in the best estimate of the process.

The decision functions are statements of *policy*. One of the principal uses of the dynamic models is to study the influences of policy on system behavior. In formulating a model, one must extend the concept of policy beyond its usual meaning. All decisions in the system come under the complete control of policy; in this sense a policy is a statement of the basis for reaching decisions at a point in the system. *Decision functions* are therefore the statements of policy that control flows in all points in the system. These decision functions (or policy) may be complex and nonlinear; they may incorporate "superpolicy" that tells us how the decision functions themselves evolve with time and how they change in accordance with the history of system variables. The decision function can incorporate a random event variable of specified statistical characteristics to simulate some of the residual uncertainties that will remain after the principal direct variables have been incorporated.

In general, the industrial-dynamics approach seeks to develop a very simple system in terms of the fundamental nature of its equations. Simple algebraic difference equations are utilized to describe the entire system. The only complexity that does arise stems from the sheer size of the model; that is, it may take many hundreds of variables and equations in order to describe adequately the system under analysis.

The objective which is sought when designing a simulation model should fulfill the following requirements: (1) it should allow any statement of cause-effect relationships that we may wish to include; (2) it should be simple in mathematical nature; (3) it should be closely synonymous in nomenclature to industrial, economic, and social terminology; (4) it should be extendible to large numbers of variables (thousands) without exceeding the practical limits of available digital computers; and (5) it should be able to handle continuous interaction in the sense that any artificial discontinuity introduced by solution time intervals will not affect the results.

If simulation models of the entire system can be developed with the above-mentioned characteristics, it seems obvious that this approach would be useful as an analytical tool from the standpoint of top management's application of the systems concept.

Critical-path Scheduling. Another application of the general approach of simulation can be found in critical-path scheduling, or network analysis. The use of this technique has become increasingly widespread, particularly for planning and controlling large-scale weapon-system projects. We shall devote the next chapter to this topic.

SUMMARY

One of man's most pervasive activities is problem solving. His approaches include appeals to the supernatural, appeals to a worldly authority, intuition, common sense, logic, and the scientific method. The scientific method can be described as a systematic, orderly approach to problem solving which includes defining the problem, formulating hypotheses, collecting relevant information, analyzing the information, and drawing conclusions.

Parallels are evident between decision making and problem solving. While the scientific method is normally considered a fundamental part of good research, it can also be considered an integral part of good managerial decision making. In fact, the terms decision making and management have been considered synonymous by some writers. A systematic, orderly, exhaustive approach to decision making includes defining the problem, setting forth the available alternatives, analyzing them in light of environmental, competitive, and internal aspects, and choosing the most appropriate course of action.

Scientific management was described as the application of the scientific method to management problems. Stressing science, rather than rule of thumb, the early scientific-management practitioners applied the scientific method to the planning of activities at the operational level.

The terms operations research and management science have followed in the wake of scientific management. While these more current approaches stress quantification, model building, and mathematical analysis, they still fit under the over-all umbrella of the application of scientific method to business or management problems. Thus our definition of management science must be broad—the application of scientific method to managerial decision making. Within this broad framework are many tools and techniques. One of the most important of these is the concept of a model, used to represent the operational system under study. The development of models requires explicit treatment of system variables and forces an integrated approach. The introduction of electronic computers to management science has allowed analysts to attack large-scale problems heretofore not feasible.

Techniques such as linear programming, quadratic and dynamic programming, and input-output analysis afford management scientists an opportunity to deal with large-scale, complex problems. Although complex, this class of problems can be well defined and a state of certainty is assumed. Other classes of problems involving uncertainty require somewhat different techniques of analysis. Statistics and probability are appropriate tools in this area. One large class of problems is that of queuing, or waiting-line, theory; much work has been done in this area, and many applications are evident. Game theory provides an approach to managerial strategy, but the theory has not proved applicable in many real situations. Monte Carlo techniques can be useful in problems of uncertainty to simulate stochastic processes that are a part of the system model under study.

Because applications of typical mathematical analysis require explicit determination of all relevant variables in the system, simplifying assumptions often must be made in order to carry out analytical solutions. Such simplifications cut down the usefulness of the techniques since the results may not be applicable in real life. To offset this problem, simulation techniques have been developed with the goal of describing systems and developing workable solutions on the basis of trial-and-error methods. Rather than striving for an optimal solution which may not be applicable because of simplifying assumptions made in structuring the problem, simulation focuses on describing the system as it exists in order to model it realistically. Policy changes can be evaluated in terms of their impact on the simulated system, thus allowing a laboratory for testing managerial decision making without committing the resources of the organization.

Management science in general, and simulation in particular, can be useful in implementing the systems concept. Model building forces decision makers to structure the operation under analysis as an integrated system tied together by a series of equations. The use of computers in symbolic system simulation allows treatment of large-scale, complex systems. Thus the analyst can develop a model of a group of subsystems, their interrelationships, and the total system. Such an approach provides a framework for more detailed analytical examination of various segments of the system.

Chapter Twelve

PERT/PEP TECHNIQUES
OF NETWORK ANALYSIS

Network analysis is a managerial technique used to recognize and identify all the interconnecting links in a single system or in a series or network of systems. This technique can be used as a tool of analysis to predict or identify the performance of any subsystem for the purpose of design, coordination, and/or control.

Critical-path scheduling is an example of network analysis which has been used in construction and engineering projects; in research and development activities associated with the design, testing, and manufacture of complex operational systems for defense; and in other applications which impose exacting requirements of time and performance. The technique has broad application and can be used in almost any situation involving scheduling.

The material in this chapter is intended to familiarize the reader with network analysis, and particularly with a sophisticated variation of the technique, PERT (program evaluation and review technique) or PEP (program evaluation procedure). Techniques of analysis will be described as follows:

Network Analysis
Examples of Critical-path Scheduling

241

PERT/PEP Defined
Creating the Network
Developing the Critical Path
Evaluation of PERT

NETWORK ANALYSIS

A network may be defined as a system, with subsystems, where the various segments interconnect and interact at one or more points. The performance of a company-wide system will depend upon how effectively each subsystem is operated *and* integrated into the activities of the whole.

Network analysis is a useful tool in systems design and assists the analyst in recognizing and identifying the relationships which exist among the subsystems. First, each separate segment, or link, of the system is described in terms of other components or activities of the system. This makes explicit the total system and the interrelationships among the parts. The network may be illustrated by a flow chart or diagram. The flow of materials and/or information is measured as volume, specifications, or time. The visual representation of the system achieves a comprehensive description and therefore outlines the task to be accomplished. This technique allows the manager to reappraise existing systems and identify examples of duplication and overlapping which may detract from the effectiveness of the systems design. Further, it helps management to evaluate the subsystems and their interconnecting networks continuously, consistent with the over-all objectives of the system.

Continuous reevaluation of the system is necessary and feasible through network analysis. The purpose of a system changes; different outputs are specified, and different inputs are required. It is important that subsystems are adjusted to these changes and that the total system is revised accordingly. Network analysis fosters this type of approach by representing the entire system visually. It also allows an evaluation of the impact of various subsystem changes on other subsystems and/or the total system. A change in type of output or a change in scheduling in a particular subsystem can affect operations in other areas. The effect can be determined in units of time, money, facilities, or other resources.

Network analysis is a valuable technique because it encourages introspection of an existing system or provides the framework for visualizing the make-up of a proposed system. Predesign auditing may identify variations in performance which could occur. However, network analysis provides no guarantee of effective systems design. There is always the danger of assuming relationships among segments which do not exist, ignoring important relationships which should be considered, or weighing existing relationships improperly. Moreover, a system is dynamic, and every analysis needs to be followed up as the system continues to function, for the relationships among the segments may change with time.

There are many forms of network analysis: some are simple, and others are complex; some are generalized, and others have been designed for specific types of projects. In general, critical-path scheduling can be considered an over-all concept into which specific techniques (e.g., PERT, PEP, and others) may be included.

EXAMPLES OF CRITICAL-PATH SCHEDULING

One example of critical-path scheduling has been called critical-path method, a technique which has been used by construction management for planning, scheduling, estimating, and controlling engineering or construction projects. Critical-path method was used by Du Pont in 1959 to schedule plant-maintenance shutdowns during change-overs. Subsequently, it was used to plan building construction and other large construction projects.

The key tool in this technique of planning, scheduling, and controlling complex construction jobs is a diagram using arrows to represent specific jobs (Figure 26). The diagram may be complex, as is evident from the example which illustrates the construction requirements for building one floor of a multistory building. However, large projects are not simple either. Therefore it requires a comprehensive illustration to show all the required relationships of the project.

The important contribution of line diagrams showing all the key events or activities is that it clarifies the relationships of every task to every other task—something that the bar chart cannot do. In this way it also can show which jobs on a project are critical, the ones which can affect the completion of the project.

> Only the jobs, from start to finish of a project, that relate to one another, each depending upon completion of the one before it, can be critical jobs. It is the sum of the time the critical job will take that will be the total project time. It is a path that the lines representing these jobs take through the project's diagram that is the critical path from start to finish of a project. Thus the name: Critical Path Method.[1]

The diagram is the model which illustrates the jobs to be performed to finish a project. The simplest form of diagram gives you the sequencing required; other additional requirements may involve timing and costs. Once these elements are specified, both the total time and total cost of the project can be determined by adding the different subelements.

[1] "New Tool for Job Management," *Engineering News-Record*, Jan. 26, 1962, p. 26.

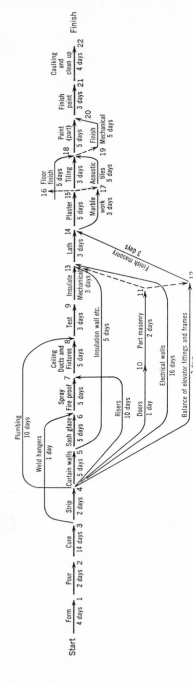

Fig. 26. A critical-path-method network. Source: "New Tool for Job Management," *Engineering News-Record*, Jan. 26, 1962, p. 26.

The consequence of various managerial decisions can be predicted by simulating their impact. It is obvious that total project time can be reduced only if the time required to perform the tasks on the critical path are reduced. It would be important to determine the cost involved in reducing the flow time in the critical path and whether additional effort or resources are warranted. A computer can be used to test and select the alternative most likely to succeed.

Critical-path method has been used as an aid in estimating and assessing the indirect costs which accompany the project throughout its life. According to one construction industry executive:

> It's given us a finer appreciation of what's in a building. Due to all manufactured components, building construction is a massive coordination job. Expediting goes way back into manufacturing. Experience in building work pays off, but new buildings involve new building products with which we have limited experience. Bar charts don't show us these things. Neither does construction know-how.[2]

Critical-path method is an example of network analysis which has been used in the construction industry. Similar developments have taken place in other industries, particularly in those areas relating to the planning, scheduling, and control of research and development activities. As technology advances, the complexity of intellectual and physical activity supporting such growth must increase correspondingly. In the field of research and development, activities tend to be more intellectual and less physical (i.e., more engineering creation and less manufacturing), although the complexity of each tends to increase. Often the task is divided among several companies, which magnifies the problem of coordinating the total program.

> Today, a weapon system requires many parallel subsystem developments, each usually carried on by a different contractor, all of which must closely mesh at various stages in the program if it is to meet its timetable.[3]

The vast quantity of significant and/or finite events required in the development of these complex systems is breath-taking; however, even more overwhelming is the task of planning, scheduling, and measuring the interrelationships and progress of a great number of events over several years of activity. Of particular significance is the fact that the planning activity must be accomplished today to identify all activity necessary to meet the end objective, perhaps five years in advance. The difficulty of this task is pointed out in the Navy's report on PERT:

[2] *Ibid.*, p. 27.
[3] Philip J. Klass, "PERT/PEP Management Tool Use Grows," *Aviation Week,* Nov. 28, 1960, p. 88.

First, we are attempting to schedule intellectual activity as well as the more easily measurable physical activity. Second, by definition, research and development projects are of a pioneering nature. Therefore, previous parallel experience upon which to base schedules of a new project is relatively unavailable. Third, the unpredictability of specific research results inevitably requires frequent change in program detail.[4]

Faced with these problems, management continually has sought more effective methods of fulfilling its responsibilities. In the development of complex systems, management has, in many instances, looked to system-engineering techniques to assist in facilitating its operations.

The timely success of any complex research and development task depends not only on the technical skills of the organization, but also on its ability to plan and control all development activities effectively. The essential elements of planning include an accurate knowledge of the forecast covering the scope of that which is to be planned, full understanding of the activity for which the plan is designed, and an accurate knowledge of how the process can be controlled according to plan.[5]

If we apply these elements to complex research and development activities, it is clear that top management will not have the detailed knowledge of the activities to be able to develop cogent and complete plans. Therefore, while management should perform the integration of detailed planning, it must look to the many individuals responsible for the subactivities for detailed plans.

It is important to develop a complex and integrated plan, but it also is necessary to control the progress of the system designed to implement that plan.

> The effectiveness of planning for technological activity is directly proportional to the extent to which the energies and components, of that which is being planned, can be controlled.[6]

Since planning and control are for all practical purposes inseparable activities, planning must be viewed as part of the research-development system. This is particularly true when the feedback-control system reports that progress does not, or appears that it will not, meet the requirements of the plan. When this occurs, replanning to meet objectives is necessary. In anything as complex as research and development, replanning must be reviewed thoroughly. In most cases, revised plans will provide alternative

---

[4] *PERT Summary Report, Phase 1,* Department of the Navy, Bureau of Ordnance, Special Project Office, 1958, p. 1.

[5] John G. Glover, *Fundamentals of Professional Management,* Simmons-Boardman Publishing Corporation, New York, 1954, p. 70.

[6] *Ibid.,* p. 71.

methods of recovery, and here management decision must determine what trades feasibly can be made between time, resources, and the performance specifications (that which is being developed).

To overcome the inherent disadvantages of existing management planning and control techniques, the Special Projects Office of the Navy, charged with the responsibility for system management of the Polaris design and production program, developed, in conjunction with the management consultant firm of Booz, Allen, and Hamilton and the Lockheed Aircraft Corporation, a new management planning and control tool. The tool was designed to determine and integrate all activity required to accomplish program objectives on time. This tool is known as PERT (program evaluation and review technique). The Air Force has adopted a similar technique, but calls it PEP (program evaluation procedure).

Undoubtedly, the PERT/PEP technique is based on critical-path scheduling. However, there is a fundamental difference between PERT/PEP and critical-path scheduling. The PERT/PEP technique is applicable where there is no established system for doing the task and therefore no exact basis for estimating the required time to complete each task. Critical-path scheduling, on the other hand, usually is applied to jobs which are established or have been done before and where it is possible to predict performance accurately. Consequently, more sophisticated mathematical models must be used in the PERT/PEP technique.

PERT/PEP DEFINED

The PERT/PEP technique (hereafter referred to as PERT) may be defined in the following manner:

> PERT is a statistical technique—diagnostic and prognostic—for quantifying knowledge about the uncertainties faced in completing intellectual and physical activities essential for timely achievement of program deadlines. It is a technique for focusing management attention on danger signals that require remedial decisions, and on areas of effort for which trade-offs in time, resources, or technical performance might improve capability to meet major deadlines.[7]

The PERT technique is based on the concept that in any program there are only three variables:

Time
Resources (personnel, facilities, funds)
Performance specifications

[7] Willard Fazar, "Progress Reporting in the Special Projects Office," *Navy Management Review,* April, 1959, p. 2.

Any one of these may vary within certain limits established for each program, while holding the other two constant. For example, holding time and performance constant, the requirements for resources may be determined. In its specific application to the Polaris program, the system held resources and performance specifications fixed while allowing the most critical element—time—to vary. However, time has a habit of becoming critical (reaching the maximum allowed by the customer), and at this point trades between resources or performance specifications are developed.

One facet of the PERT technique is that research and development work can be scheduled within a more or less predictable time frame. The procedure for accomplishing this is to break down a large complex research or development project into smaller, more easily accomplished subprojects. The second facet, that of scheduling and defining goals to be achieved and making the interrelationships and interdependencies of these goals explicit, will produce a gain in managerial control.

CREATING THE NETWORK

The PERT network is the working model of the technique. It illustrates, by diagram, the sequential relationships among the tasks which must be completed to accomplish the project. PERT treats planning and scheduling separately. First the plan is developed, and then the time limitations are added to the problem.

Gathering Preliminary Data

The first step in developing the PERT network is to gather a list of all the activities needed to complete the project. The people associated with the project activities have the best knowledge about the detailed tasks which need to be performed. Other activities will be added to this list as the total task is defined more comprehensively and the entire network develops. The activities listed should include every factor pertinent to the completion of the project. For example, customer approval and available resources would be considered and listed.

Mechanics of Network Building

Next, the network is constructed to show the sequential relationships among the activities. There are two elements shown on the network diagrams: activities and events.

Activities are defined as the time-consuming effort which is required to complete a specific segment of the total project. For example, activities might include the preparation of engineering drawings, the production of a specific forging, or the testing of the finished product. The activities in the graphic illustration of the network are shown as a solid line, with an arrow to depict the direction of sequential activities (———→).

All activities begin and end with an *event*. This is a "milestone" which indicates the completion of a distinct portion of a program and the signal for dependent succeeding activities to begin. An event is illustrated in the network as a circle, square, or other convenient geometric figure. Descriptions and symbols are written in the circle to identify each event.

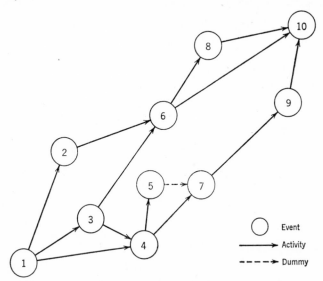

Fig. 27. Network example.

Figure 27 is an example of a simplified PERT network. Each event is numbered for the purpose of identification. Thus activity 1/2 is the activity which takes place between events numbered 1 and 2. It is possible to start the diagram from the completion of the project and work backward, or from the beginning and work toward completion.

The length of the arrow (the activity) is not indicative of the time it takes to complete the activity or to get from one event to the next. However, it does represent the logical sequence of activities and events. It illustrates, for example, which activities must be completed prior to the start of a particular activity, which activities can be worked in parallel, and which activities cannot start until a previous activity is completed. In Figure 27, activities 2/6 and 3/6 must be completed before activity 6/8 or 6/10 can begin. Event 6 signifies the completion of activities 2/6 and 3/6 and the starting point for the following related activities.

Dummy Constraints

A *dummy* constraint is a "dashed" arrow (— — — →) in the network which shows a relationship but does not require a time-consuming activity. The principal use for this symbol occurs when two separate activities both begin and end with the same event. In this instance the numbering system would not distinguish between the two events. In Figure 27, activities 4/7 and 4/5 begin at 4 and end at event 7. However, a dummy event is added (5), and the relationship between event 5 and 7 indicates zero time. Now it is possible to keep the two activities separate in the graphing and the computations.

DEVELOPING THE CRITICAL PATH

Once the flow network has been determined for the system, the next step is to obtain an estimate of the elapsed time (in weeks) required to accomplish each activity from the individual responsible for accomplishment of that element of work. This time forecast consists of three individual estimates:

The "most likely" estimate (m)
The optimistic estimate (a)
The pessimistic estimate (b)

The difference in these time estimates provides a measure of the relative uncertainty involved in accomplishing the activity in question, as shown in Figure 28.[8] From these estimates, the *expected time* t_e for each *activity* may be computed by applying appropriate statistical techniques developed

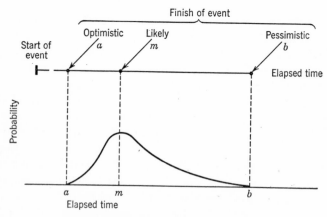

Fig. 28. Estimating the time distribution.

[8] Figures 28 to 31 are based on *PERT Summary Report, Phase I*.

for this purpose, as shown in Figure 29. The expected time is the average, or mean, time for the activity and may or may not be the most probable time (the estimator's most likely forecast). This discrepancy arises when the differences between the most likely estimate, the optimistic estimate, and the pessimistic estimate are not equal, thus tending to some degree to discredit the probability of the most likely estimate. The estimates (as well as the definitions of the events and activities) are outputs of the PERT planning technique, which have been based on a stipulated input of resources for the processing system. The estimate may change, however, if there is a change in resource allocation and/or a change in the task or product specifications.

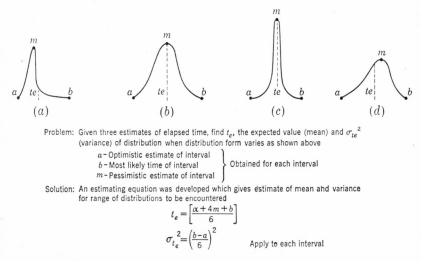

Problem: Given three estimates of elapsed time, find t_e, the expected value (mean) and $\sigma_{t_e}^2$ (variance) of distribution when distribution form varies as shown above

a - Optimistic estimate of interval ⎫
b - Most likely time of interval   ⎬ Obtained for each interval
m - Pessimistic estimate of interval ⎭

Solution: An estimating equation was developed which gives estimate of mean and variance for range of distributions to be encountered

$$t_e = \left[\frac{a + 4m + b}{6}\right]$$

$$\sigma_{t_e}^2 = \left(\frac{b-a}{6}\right)^2 \qquad \text{Apply to each interval}$$

Fig. 29. Determining "expected" value and variance of time intervals.

The flow network, with its coded events, can be programmed for a computer. The elapsed-time estimates can likewise be used as input to the computer processing. The computer solves the mathematical problems (calculation of each t_e) and, by adding the calculated expected times for each activity, computes the expected time for each event E, as illustrated in Figure 30. Next, the computer identifies those events which determine the longest sequence to meet the end objective—the critical path. Those events not on the critical path must therefore have some *slack* in their timing. Slack is computed by determining the latest time E_L that an event can take place without affecting the events on the critical path $E_x - t_e$, and then subtracting that from an event E not on the critical path ($E_L - E =$ slack). This relationship is illustrated graphically in Figure 31. Resources can be reallocated from the slack areas to the critical path.

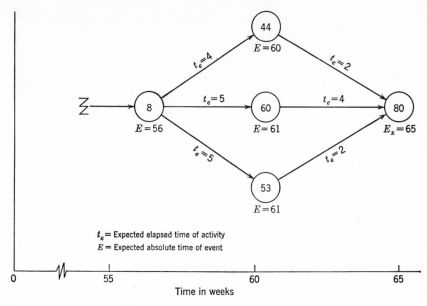

Fig. 30. Determination of expected time.

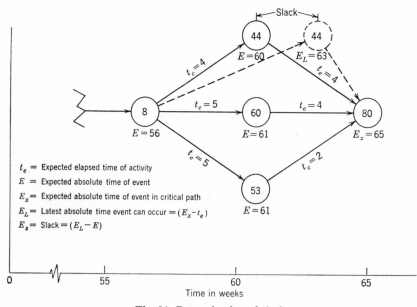

Fig. 31. Determination of slack.

One of the most useful outputs of this system (for management) is the determination of the possibility of meeting critical schedule dates. These schedule dates, determined or stipulated by the customer, usually represent contractual commitments and therefore will, at times, necessitate "trades" between resources and performance specifications as previously described.

EVALUATION OF PERT

PERT is useful in the analysis and design of systems. First, the technique can serve as an effective tool in analyzing the job to be accomplished and therefore provide insights in reference to the resources needed to do the job (system design); second, PERT can serve as an approach for input allocation in the operating system. Further, it provides the vehicle, the common language, for planning and controlling the system.

A GE spokesman said that in practically every instance where the Light Military Electronics Division has applied the PERT technique to programs already under way, it has discovered future schedule problem areas which were unknown to project managers.[9]

The PERT system has proved to be an excellent communications medium in the Polaris program, not only between the Navy and its contractors, but also within the various contractor organizations. This has been accomplished by basic adherence to communication theory, but also to organization, planning, and control theory. The specific facets of the PERT technique responsible for this success may be summarized as follows:

1. The flow network defines all activity to be accomplished. As the network is outlined and each activity is identified and planned, a distinct area of personal responsibility can be described. Thus unassigned areas, or areas of doubtful responsibility, can be identified and resolved as the network is developed.

2. Similarly, problems of coordination among organizations or operating elements within a large organization are quickly identified and resolved during the development of the flow network.

3. The development and biweekly revision of the time estimates for the activities in the PERT network, and the resultant computer outputs, serve as an excellent medium for providing progress information to all organizations and levels of management. Therefore the systems managers

[9] Klass, *op. cit.,* p. 88.

continually are notified of any problems which may be developing and are able to activate corrective input.

4. The flow networks, time estimates, and computer outputs serve as continuous stimuli for the program personnel to coordinate their efforts with other affected groups.

In any business organization the operating effectiveness of the system depends on the performance of people. The traits or characteristics of human behavior can influence the accuracy and thus affect the operational adequacy of the system. The PERT technique tends to minimize the effects of such behavior. For example, a worker may want to "pad" his work estimates. Under PERT, he knows that his activity may then appear on the critical path, and therefore under the closest scrutiny of management. If he overestimates the time required for the job, he may need additional personnel—again involving management review. Moreover, the fact that he must give optimistic and pessimistic estimates as well as his most likely estimate tends to make the latter more accurate. Further, with the system in operation and new time estimates being made every two weeks, management will soon discover repetitive overestimates of time required and may, without the knowledge of the individual, apply an "experience" factor to his future estimates. All these "checks and balances," when known throughout the organization, tend to encourage more realistic estimates.

One common objection to PERT pertains to the cost of using this technique. The nature of the logical requirements relating to network analysis does require a higher degree of planning skill. The amount of planning time spent, however, will depend on the complexity of the system, the skill of the planners, and the degree of sophistication built into the PERT program. In most instances the cost will be higher: "It is perhaps more appropriate to view the implementation of PERT as costing initially something in the order of twice that of a conventional planning system." [10] The advocates of PERT are quick to point out that the additional cost of planning will be more than offset by the gains achieved from avoiding critical problems and performing to schedule.

PERT has been adopted in many defense-oriented companies under the sponsorship and prodding of the armed services. It has been credited with making substantial reductions in research, development, and manufacturing flow time and with saving millions of defense dollars.

Both PERT and critical-path scheduling have been used in non-defense-oriented companies. The PERT technique was used in the construction of a student-faculty center at Stevens Institute in Hoboken, New

[10] Robert W. Miller, "How to Plan and Control with PERT," *Harvard Business Review,* March–April, 1962, p. 98.

Jersey. A network of 1,500 activities was constructed to describe this project.[11] Critical-path scheduling also is being used by a number of consulting firms and independent companies. "Dow is using it for expanding a power house. Catalytic Construction Company is using it on five projects at once. G.E., IBM, RCA, Procter and Gamble, and others are interested in it." [12]

Most applications of these techniques have proved to be effective and represent a pioneering effort toward developing even more sophisticated techniques of network analysis in the design, operation, and review of systems.

SUMMARY

Network analysis is a useful managerial technique which can be used to predict or identify the performance of any subsystem for the purpose of design, coordination, and/or control. Each separate segment, or link, of the system is described relative to other components or activities of the system. A visual representation outlines the task to be accomplished in terms of the resources allocated to do the job.

There are many forms of network analysis: some are simple, and others are complex; some are generalized, while others have been designed for specific types of projects. In general, critical-path scheduling can be considered an over-all concept into which specific techniques may be incorporated.

One specialized technique of network analysis is called PERT (program evaluation and review technique). It is applicable where there is no established system for doing the task, and therefore no exact basis for estimating the required time to complete each task. This technique of management planning and control provides industry with capabilities for program planning, evaluation, and control; program-status evaluation; and simulation techniques for decision-making assistance. The advantages of PERT techniques (which in themselves reflect a systems approach) in the management of complex research and development activities may be summarized as follows:

The sequence and relationship network of all significant events in planning how the end objective will be achieved is identified.

The relative uncertainty in meeting or accomplishing all activities in the plan is measured and identified.

[11] Herbert E. Klein, "Psychoanalysis on the Production Line," *Dun's Review and Modern Industry,* February, 1962, p. 58.

[12] J. S. Sayer, J. E. Kelly, Jr., and Morgan R. Walker, "Critical Path Scheduling," *Factory,* July, 1960, p. 74.

The relatively critical condition in areas of effort required to meet objectives is shown to management.

Also, slack areas are shown where some delay will not preclude the meeting of end objectives on time.

The current probability of meeting scheduled dates is provided management.

PERT has been adopted in both defense- and nondefense-oriented companies. Critical-path scheduling, a more straightforward technique of network analysis, also has been used extensively. Other results from the many applications indicate the value of describing and analyzing a system in this fashion.

Chapter Thirteen
SYSTEMS DESIGN

Systems design provides the over-all framework for implementing the systems concept. Specific techniques of management science are applicable in certain aspects of the implementation process, but it is vital to provide broad guidelines within which they can be employed advantageously. In this chapter we shall create such a framework by relating the systems-design function to the systems concept as set forth explicitly in Chapter 6. Once the conceptual foundation is established, we shall proceed to outline an approach to implementation. The discussion will focus on the following topics:

> Scope of the Design Function
> Flow Concepts
> Master Planning
> Resource Allocation
> Systems Review
> The Systems Approach in Design
> Constraints on the Design Function

SCOPE OF THE DESIGN FUNCTION

Design means to "mark out, designate, or indicate." It includes combining features or details and often calls for preparation of preliminary sketches or plans. A system is an array of components designed to accomplish a planned objective. Figure 6 (Chapter 6) depicted a basic system combining input, processor, and output, designed to operate according to a plan. The design function is important in establishing a relationship between the various stages or phases of a system, linking them together, and outlining the composite whole. For business systems the design function includes the arrangement of physical facilities for production and auxiliary activities. It also covers the arrangement of people and communication networks established to provide information concerning the process.

As the systems concept is accepted and as its various ramifications are applied throughout business and industry, the function of systems design will become increasingly vital in the future. For example:

> As automated subsystems take over minute-by-minute and day-by-day operation of the factory and office, the humans in the system will become increasingly occupied with preventive maintenance, with system breakdowns and malfunctions, and—perhaps most important of all—with the design and modification of systems.[1]

When establishing a new business operation, the design function seems fairly straightforward. However, the scope of systems design also covers the function of "redesign," assessing existing systems with an eye toward change. This activity has received considerable attention over the years under headings such as systems and procedures, work simplification, systems analysis, or systems engineering. Of these terms, *work simplification* seems to have the narrowest connotation in that it applies primarily to simple man-machine operations or clerical activity. However, as with most tools and techniques, its practitioners have proclaimed its applicability to a wide range of problems. In any case, it applies to existing systems rather than to the establishment of new systems.

Systems and procedures work also has been pointed up as an all-encompassing activity, covering many facets of the business operation. However, implicitly it seems limited to office work, the flow of paper work, and the design of forms. Since the advent of electromechanical equipment, systems and procedures activity has included the designing and programming of data-processing systems. Unfortunately, EDP has been overemphasized in recent years to the exclusion of broader concepts of systems design. The specific aspects of programming, form design, and routing of paper work—as a part of the information-decision system—should be fitted into the over-all systems design.

Another term used in describing this general sphere of activity is

---

[1] Herbert A. Simon, "The Corporation: Will It Be Managed by Machines?" in Melvin Anshen and G. L. Bach (eds.), *Management and Corporations 1985*, McGraw-Hill Book Company, Inc., New York, 1960, p. 50.

systems analysis. It also is focused on existing systems rather than on the design of new systems. Systems analysis often has a connotation of application primarily to information flow in the office and does not seem as applicable to a production or processing environment. This is not to say that it is not feasible; rather, most of the literature on the subject deals with information-processing problems.

Systems engineering implies the creation of systems as well as the analysis of existing systems. Systems engineering sometimes is assumed to deal only with physical components; that is, it deals with the integration of components and subcomponents into a total product such as a computer or missile. Using the definition of engineering as "the art and science by which the properties of matter and the sources of power in nature are made useful to man in structures, machines, and manufactured products," there is some systems implication. Moreover, systems engineering can be defined as "making useful an array of components designed to accomplish a particular objective according to plan." This approach implies the interaction of more than equipment. It suggests the development of a man-machine system which could function as a task-oriented assemblage. Systems engineering comes closest to implying design activity. In many cases the systems-engineering function involves "starting from scratch" to develop subsystems, larger systems, and a composite whole.

Both concepts, systems design and redesign, will be discussed in the remainder of the chapter. For the first half of the chapter we shall be concerned primarily with initial design of systems based on implementing the systems concept. Even here, however, some attention will be devoted to the function of *systems review,* which is primarily a redesign process. In the latter part of the chapter both design and redesign will be discussed but the emphasis will be on working with existing systems.

FLOW CONCEPTS

One general approach to systems design involves identification of material, energy, and information flow. These three elements are part of every system and subsystem. Consideration of them plus the use of flow concepts facilitates thinking about systems of systems.

Material

The material aspects of any system include both the facilities involved and the raw material, if any, which flows through the process. A system must be designed to ensure the *acquisition* of raw materials and/or components necessary for processing into finished products. The systems design would include identification of transportation means required to move the material to the processing location.

The *processing* operation needs to be designed in terms of constructing new facilities or realigning existing facilities. Questions of plant layout and materials-handling equipment would be a vital part of the systems-design function for in-plant processing and in-plant material flows. Industrial engineers have considered problems of this nature for many years and have developed detailed methods and techniques for optimizing layout and materials handling. The trend toward automation has been evident in many material-processing operations. We shall not consider techniques in detail in this chapter. Rather, we shall emphasize the conceptual problems in systems design and point up the areas where specific tools and techniques can be useful.

Much attention also has been focused on *distribution* of finished goods. Where items become raw material or components in additional processing operations, the distribution problem is often straightforward. In such cases the material flow would be considered part of the flow of raw materials for a subsequent processing operation. Physical-distribution management, for items moving from producer to ultimate consumer, can be a much more difficult problem. In this case, channels of distribution vary from direct producer to consumer to a myriad of combinations of middlemen. Inventory management, at various points along the distribution channel, must be considered, as well as modes of transportation. In many cases transportation costs have been isolated for analysis without reference to the impact of such decisions on stocks of material in the pipeline. Systems design, in this sphere, would concern itself with identifying the flow of materials and with the development of an explicit network of distribution, recognizing *all* the costs involved—handling, inventory, and transportation costs. Increasing effort is being devoted to the design of explicit material-flow systems from a raw-material stage through the production process and to the final consumer—the rhochrematics approach considered previously.

Whenever the operation in question involves the flow and processing of material, appropriate systems can be designed. For business operations such as insurance companies or other commercial institutions, there may be no flow of material per se. Rather, the material in these systems is represented by the facilities and equipment involved. Regardless of whether there is any material flow, all business operations, whether processing a product or service, contain elements of energy and information.

Energy

Some source of energy is present in any operating system. It may be electricity obtained from available sources or generated by a firm's own power plant. The process may require natural gas, petroleum, coal, or other fuel for production. A business usually requires electrical energy for operating facilitating systems, if not for the main processing operation itself.

Another obvious source of energy is people. Both physical and mental energy are required to operate business systems. People represent a renewable source of energy, at least for the short run. As an energy source, people are quite variable as individuals. However, *in toto,* the group represents a reasonably stable source of energy for the system.

Electricity, natural gas, or petroleum can be described in terms of flow concepts. Energy flows are under continual inspection by systems designers. However, they are concerned primarily with the energy or power system itself, not the integration of the energy system with other subsystems and the whole. It is somewhat more difficult to visualize people, or the work force, in terms of flow concepts. However, in a very real sense, this is entirely appropriate. There may be a continual flow of workers in terms of shifts where 24-hour, 7-day weeks are scheduled. Even for 5-day, 40-hour weeks there is a systematic flow of worker energy into the operation. In a larger sense, a business operation maintains a flow of worker energy throughout its life—from the recruiting, hiring, and orientation stages, all the way to retirement. Thus all energy can be considered as a flow process both in and of itself and as a part of other systems.

Information

Another basic element in any system is information. It facilitates interrelationships among subsystems and provides the linkage necessary to develop systems of systems. Information flow may be developed to flow along with the routing of material. Requisitions, orders, bills of lading, packing slips, receiving information, inspection reports, accounts payable, and checks might represent the information flow connected with the acquisition of raw material. The information flow appropriate to production control is another example. In this case production instructions, material requirements, processing information, inspection requirements, routing, and scheduling would be developed from engineering drawings and/or other specifications. The information would flow through the system along with the material necessary to accomplish the planned objectives.

The accounting system requires a flow of information toward the development of income statements and balance sheets for tax purposes or stockholder reports or both. While many data-processing systems have developed on the basis of periodic batch processing, more and more systems are being developed which call for flow concepts approximating real-time activity; that is, the action or activity to be considered is recorded at the time it happens and action is taken at that time.

Information flow is the primary focus of attention for systems designers in many cases. If manufacturing facilities are fixed and if layout requirements are rigid, then the only variables remaining are raw materials (which may also be uniform), energy (in the form of power and/or people), and information (in the form of plans and instructions). Systems design in such cases must concentrate on the arrangement of people and the use of information flow to optimize decision making within the system under observation. For many other systems where manufacturing and material flow are not present—service, commercial, and many governmental organizations—the flow of information is the critical element. Information must flow to key decision points where action is taken with regard to a service to be performed by the organization in question. In such cases the system can be defined primarily on the basis of the flow of information to appropriate decision points. Subsystems can be identified on this basis, and they in turn can be interrelated to define the total system.

Unfortunately, most present-day systems of this nature have been established on the basis of people relationships and organization charts without regard for project systems or task-oriented groups. In many cases these organizations function primarily on the basis of informal relationships and informal communications systems. One of the main points in systems design is the necessity of recognizing the natural relationships of subsystems in developing a total system. In this chapter, attention will be focused on the fundamental elements of material, energy, and information as they relate to each subsystem and as they provide insight to flow concepts. It is by means of these flow concepts that the total system can be conceptualized as a system of systems. Particular emphasis will be placed on the design of information-decision systems. Such systems are integral parts of any operating system, whether it is designed to yield a product or service. With these basic elements and flow concepts as a foundation, we turn now to the question of systems design as it can be visualized at various levels in organizations of the future.

MASTER PLANNING

The systems concept can be implemented by means of design activity at the various planning levels throughout the organization. Referring to Figure 32, a master planning council engages in high-level design activity and establishes guidelines for the entire organization. Within that framework design activity is carried on by the resource-allocation planning group in order to put together combinations of manpower and facilities to form a working system organized to accomplish given objectives. The system so designed may be one of several integral parts of the total operation. Within either facilitating systems or major project systems, additional design activity—systems review—is necessary to maintain working systems on a current basis.

The master planning council must have a definite approach to developing premises which serve as the basis for systems design. Meaningful information must be translated from environmental data on such questions as economic activity, political developments, and social trends. It is important that top management develop clear-cut systems of such information flow as will provide inputs for planning and decision making. In most companies such systems are left to chance or, at best, periodic review.

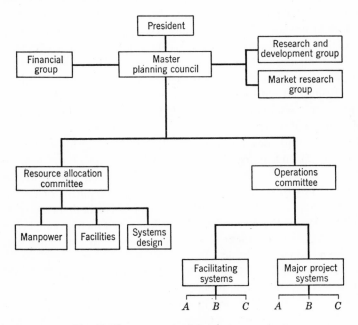

Fig. 32. The systems model: top management.

Another part of the environment that must be monitored continually is the competitive situation. Industry intelligence, or other similar approaches, should be set up to provide more meaningful data than are readily available from industry sources. Again, this system of data collection and screening must be established explicitly to complement other sources, thus augmenting top management's information-decision system.

Another aspect of this system is internal feedback. In order to establish broad guidelines for future activity and to make specific decisions on new projects or programs, top management must be apprised of skills and resources available.

Long-range Planning

Much of the activity of the master planning council can be described under the heading long-range planning. This activity provides the premises which underlie decisions concerning new ventures or new approaches to old ventures. The more progressive, dynamic companies have recognized the necessity of long-range planning. To stand still or do nothing in this era of accelerating technology and dynamic growth would mean a backward step and eventual oblivion.

As shown in Figure 32, the inputs for long-range planning on the part of the master planning council include research and development, market research, and finance. Companies must continually search for ways to expand existing markets and for new markets which can be tapped. The more successful companies often are cognizant of developing customer needs almost as soon as are the customers themselves. The market-research function can be carried out in a number of ways, including the use of consulting services, periodic studies of many types, or continuing activity on the part of an internal staff.

Research and development activities must dovetail closely with market-research endeavors. Depending on the nature of the firm and its industry, some basic or pure research may be carried out. However, the bulk of the effort is ordinarily devoted to the development of existing, or at least prototype, products in order to make them both marketable and producible. Again, the research and development function can be carried out by an internal staff, or it can be delegated to an external institution, possibly on a cooperative basis.

Market research and research and development activities can be geared to services as well as products. For example, continual research is necessary in order to understand the evolving consumer market for services such as banking, insurance, and recreation. Research and development could be devoted to either the service or the process involved in its dispensation.

Attention must also be focused on financial aspects in order to determine the feasibility of various plans for either new projects or alterations in existing activities. While top management must be farsighted and dynamic in their outlook, they must be realistic enough to consider the financial implications of long-range planning.

Product Missions

A useful approach to outlining the role of the master planning council in systems design is the product-missions concept. Rather than concentrate on the particular product, whether it be a piece of hardware or a service, it is often more beneficial to consider the role of such a product in a larger system. For example, automobile manufacturers should be cognizant of the role of their product in a larger system—vehicular transportation. Even this system, including automobiles, trucks, buses, highway networks, the petroleum industry, service stations, and others, is a part of a still larger system—the over-all transportation system, including water, rail, and air systems. The automobile manufacturer ought to recognize possible missions for his product. It might be transportation; it might be prestige; or it might be various combinations of the two. In any case, it is important to define exactly what mission is to be accomplished in order to design products to fit the need.

In recent years, several petroleum companies have advertised their recognition of a changing product mission. Instead of emphasizing the production of gasoline, these companies have described themselves as producers of energy. In this way they have broadened the scope of their mission and have included a number of things other than gasoline. This broader scope will allow such companies to maintain a position in a dynamic environment because of their ability to adjust to changing markets and breakthroughs in research. For example, in perceiving its role as a producer of energy rather than gasoline for automobile consumption, a company could maintain an active interest in the evolution of the automobile as a means of transportation and in research and development on sources of power. A company with such an outlook would be able to take advantage of the development of atomic-powered automobiles, adjusting its niche in the market as changes occurred.

This function of perception of need is of vital concern to the master planning council. It must continually appraise the future potential for the corporate system as a whole and be cognizant of where its output fits into larger systems. The ultimate utilization of products or services must be understood. For producers of component parts or semifinished goods, the manufacturer should be aware of the use of the components and the ultimate end-product mission. Even raw-material producers can benefit from this broad-gauged view and thereby be prepared to adjust to a dynamic environment.

By being cognizant of product missions and the role of the company's product or products in such missions, the master planning council can establish broad guidelines for systems design. Understanding the over-all system, which may involve several industries and multiple channels of distribution, provides premises for deciding on new ventures or adaptations of existing programs. Once the desirability and feasibility of projects or programs have been established, the matter is referred to the resource-allocation planning group for more specific action.

RESOURCE ALLOCATION

Systems design is a clearly defined function or activity under the heading resource-allocation planning. In other words, the systems-design function is set up specifically to develop integrated arrangements of facilities, manpower, and information flow in order to accomplish given objectives. This function involves providing the elements necessary for mission accomplishment. It may include the acquisition of new facilities and/or manpower or reallocation of those elements that have reverted back to the over-all system because of the "phrasing out" of a major project system. The system to be designed may be quite elaborate, or it may be fairly routine, depending on corporate experience in the planned area of endeavor. Several examples will help to explain the process of implementation.

A Missile System

A company in the aerospace industry might decide to pursue actively the acquisition of contracts for an advanced missile system. Questions of facilities would need to be considered; existing buildings might be available, or entirely new housing might be required. Similarly, equipment for research and development and prototype construction might exist in present company stocks, or all or part of the needed equipment might have to be purchased. Working relationships would have to be established with raw-material and subcomponent suppliers in orders to integrate the development of the entire missile system.

Similarly, the work force necessary to man the new system might be available internally, or it might be necessary to obtain all or part outside. The third basic element in any system, information, also would be defined explicitly in order to develop interrelationships among the key components of the system.

The systems design would take into account the relationship of the company with the customer (the military), with major subsystem suppliers, with component suppliers, and with raw-material sources. Physical facilities would be designed, a plant layout would be set forth explicitly, and organizational relationships would be established among the people involved in the project. Flow concepts could be introduced by the use of network analysis which would identify the critical points over a period of time and relate the accomplishment of various tasks to the over-all system. The decision points within the man-machine system could be identified, and the necessary data-processing system could be designed to provide meaningful information at such points. The result would be a systems design establishing a number of subsystems making up a total project system, which in turn might be one of a number for the business organization as a whole. The design would recognize the basic elements of material, energy, and information which are part of every system and would tie these elements together in meaningful relationships on the basis of flow concepts, particularly the information-decision system.

Other Project Systems

The introduction of compact automobiles by the United States manufacturers represents another example of a project system. In such cases manufacturers had to design a system which was significantly different from existing systems. This decision by top management represented more than a mere model change: objectives were set forth; facilities were acquired and adjusted; manpower was realigned; and advertising and promotion were directed toward a "new" market.

The entertainment industry provides good examples of project systems. For a movie production company, each new film represents a new project to which resources must be allocated. Existing facilities might be appropriate, or new sets or locations might be required. People must be acquired for both acting roles and all the behind-the-scenes activity. Publicity and distribution must be arranged. These tasks may be relatively routine, yet variations may be desirable. The entertainment industry in general—movies, television, radio, and the theater—provides good examples of the application of the systems concept.

Another example of the need for systems design in the allocation of resources would be the decision of a large casualty-insurance company to enter the life-insurance field. Again, the basic elements must be assembled in the form of facilities and manpower. Decisions must be reached with regard to a distribution system (advertising, promotion, and salesmen). The system must be designed to achieved its own mission, yet it must also fit into the existing corporate system in order to complement the casualty and/or accident and health business.

These examples illustrate the need for systems design in terms of resource allocation once a decision is reached by top management to embark upon a particular project or program. The decision by top management is made on the basis of external environmental conditions in relation to top management's perception of existing or readily obtainable skills and resources. The systems-design function must implement this decision by specifically aligning the available resources into a meaningful and integrated system for objective accomplishment.

However, the systems created at this level are not static; they too must evolve over time as the project progresses through its life cycle. This life cycle might be a few months, as in the case of some movie-making projects, or it might involve many years, as in the case of a missile program which runs from preliminary research and development efforts through operational status and eventual obsolescence. During the course of its life cycle the project system itself must be evaluated and adjusted continually; this is the function of systems review.

SYSTEMS REVIEW

As indicated in Figure 33, a systems-review function is an integral part of each project system. The system as a whole should be reviewed

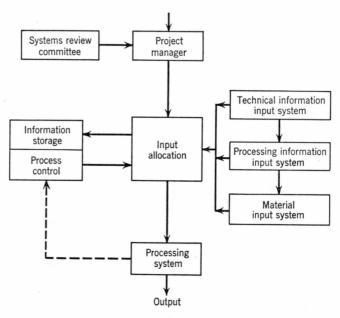

Fig. 33. An operating-system model.

periodically by means of a thoroughgoing analysis and synthesis of the system and its components. The system should be broken down into its individual subsystems, and each of these should be evaluated in terms of the likelihood of continuing efficiency. Adjustments can be made on the basis of the results of such analysis. Then a process of synthesis must take place in order to restructure an integrated whole.

Why is it that subsystems and/or project systems must be reviewed and adjusted continually? One obvious reason was mentioned above; system requirements change over a period of time, and hence the system must be redesigned in the light of evolutionary trends. Static systems design goes out of date almost immediately. In fact, the battle cry of some systems analysts and designers is, "If it works, it must be obsolete!" As a particular project progresses through its life cycle, the product mission may change, as may other environmental or competitive conditions. Organizational adjustments may be required, or technological advancements may allow improvements in the handling of either material or information flow.

Some systems are built around individuals within an organization. If identification of decision points is based on strong or dominant personalities, the information-decision system may be disrupted completely whenever key-personnel changes are made. Hence systems must be redesigned in order to accommodate the changes in managerial personnel.

The original allocation of resources may have been temporary in the sense of availability of necessary elements either internally or externally. Makeshift systems have a way of perpetuating themselves regardless of inefficiencies. It is important to reappraise the situation often enough to make sure that such temporary arrangements are revised when conditions allow.

Another typical problem is the tendency toward empire building, the accumulation of more than enough material, manpower, and facilities to accomplish given objectives. The project manager must resist the tendency toward bigness for the sake of prestige or status. A semidetached, hopefully objective systems-review group can help nurture such a point of view.

Continuing attention must be devoted to systems review and the implementation of proposed changes. Follow-up is necessary because of the seemingly inherent resistance to change on the part of people involved in the system. Unless such resistance can be overcome, poor systems may be prolonged. Once the atmosphere is established for continual analysis and review, implementation of change becomes progressively easier.

So far, we have talked primarily about the management's responsibility for systems design and the design activities appropriate at various levels. While it is important to establish this general conceptual framework for the systems-design function, it is also important to spend some time on the question of how this function should be carried out. Therefore the next section discusses in somewhat more detail a useful approach to systems design.

THE SYSTEMS APPROACH IN DESIGN

Previous sections have concentrated on designing new systems to implement top-management decisions. This section emphasizes the useful approaches to analyzing and redesigning existing systems. Although the emphasis is on existing systems, the tools and techniques described often can be applied when developing a system for the first time.

Problem Orientation

An important concept in systems analysis and design is th on the problem. Using the scientific method (or general appr lem solving) involves defining the problem initially in term jectives of the over-all system and its various subsystems. Eve specific system under analysis may be a minor subpart, it is the analyst to be cognizant of the composite system and the ship between it and its parts. Changes and adjustments in a subsystem could be disruptive unless the impact on interrelationships is considered.

Once a problem has been defined and placed in proper perspective with regard to an over-all system, various techniques of analysis can be employed. A list of the more familiar tools and techniques would include the following:

1. Space and layout analysis
2. Work simplification
3. Analysis of records, forms, and reports
4. Methods and procedures analysis
5. Organization studies
6. Analysis of communication channels

Since these specific techniques are all treated in considerable detail in other works, we shall not do so here. It is important for analysts to keep in mind the necessity of focusing on the problem rather than on the tools and techniques of analysis. Sometimes attention on the part of researchers or analysts is devoted to the improvement of a specific tool or technique regardless of its applicability to a particular problem. In such cases, "the tail begins to wag to dog," thus hampering the analysis.

Flow Charting

An important element in most all the tools and techniques indicated above is flow charting. The use of symbols and directional arrows allows the systems analyst to develop a graphic representation of the system under study. The use of such techniques may be as elaborate as deemed necessary. Simple skeletal charts describing the flow of material or information may be used as a first approximation. The symbols may be expanded to include many variations, and the actual operations to be performed may be written in the various blocks. In this way a complete description is obtained of the entire process of either material or information flow. The flow charts themselves might include photographs or other models of either documents, material, or equipment in order to portray the system for management.

Models

For either material or information flow, scale models of the layout of facilities may be utilized to model the system and point up any problems of physical distances. Visualizing such physical aspects is obviously important for plant layout of production processes, but it can also be a key element in designing information systems.

In any case, whether physical models are developed or not, the use of flow charts provides a model of the system under study. This approach allows the consideration of alternative systems designs before the actual implementation and possible disruption of existing arrangements. Once the problem has been defined and objectives established in order to assure proper perspective, a systems analyst can consider improvements. If the system can be modeled in terms of flow charts, tracing material, and/or information flow, then alternative approaches can be tested in the abstract. While the use of such models does not ensure that the proposed system will work in practice, it certainly provides more information than is available through trial-and-error efforts on the system itself. Once a better approach has been developed, it can be applied in real life.

The Basic Elements

Material, energy, and information flow must be considered in the systems approach to analysis and design. As pointed out previously, each can be developed as a flow process itself. On the other hand, they are all basic elements of any given system or subsystem. The approach to analysis and design may highlight one or another of these elements but must consider all of them.

For example, material flow could be traced by means of a process flow chart. A space and layout study could be made to determine optimal arrangement of facilities and equipment in light of the flow of raw material through the system. The layout must also consider the human element in the man-machine system in order to integrate all factors involved. Organization charts can be developed on a systems basis rather than in the traditional functional hierarchical manner. The organization, as structured around the flow of material and information between decision points, would cut across traditional, functionally specialized department boundaries. This would allow focusing the attention of the personnel involved on subsystem and total-system objectives rather than on departmental objectives and goals.

While a great deal of attention has been devoted over the years to problems of layout, materials handling, and organization (the arrangement of materials and energy), current attention under the general title of systems analysis and design has been focused primarily on the flow of information. Even the term systems engineering, which connotes the development of useful physical systems, has taken on a new meaning in recent years—the development of information systems. Much of the effort in this area has centered around the purchase and installation of high-speed, electronic-data-processing equipment and its use in implementing information-decision systems. While the impact of computers has fostered much effort in this area, our discussion will not necessarily involve the use of large-scale, electronic-data-processing equipment. The same principles of systems analysis and design apply regardless of the scale and sophistication of central-data-processing equipment.

Information-decision Systems

A number of approaches are available for analyzing and redesigning information systems. As mentioned above, one approach is concentration on equipment improvement, with attendant systems changes geared to machine requirements. While it may foster improvements, there is often the danger of converting existing systems to more elaborate equipment without really making any basic changes.

Another approach is that of attempting to develop as much data as possible for use in the system. Voluminous data of many types might be collected and stored in case they were needed at some point in time. It is easy to see that massive amounts of useless data might result.

A third approach is oriented to decision making. This approach minimizes the development of useless information because only data likely to be meaningful in decision making at various points are collected. Stoller and Van Horn describe this approach as follows:

> In essence, the approach consists of (1) defining the operating and planning decisions that are required to manage the organization, (2) exploring the types of policies available for making each decision, (3) determining the data requirements implied by each decision policy, and (4) developing preferred processing techniques for the desired data set. The decision orientation approach is appropriate for making long-term improvements in an information system.[2]

This approach emphasizes the problem involved rather than techniques of analysis. The objective is not optimization of data-processing systems; rather, the objective is development of better information-decision systems for management. Concentration on the decisions required in a business

---

[2] David S. Stoller and Richard L. Van Horn, *Design of a Management Information System,* The Rand Corporation, Santa Monica, Calif., P-1362, Nov. 22, 1958, p. 2.

operation points up the necessity of organizing on a project-system basis.

This concentration on orientation toward decision points in the organization can be maintained throughout the entire process of systems analysis and design. Many specific techniques might be developed for approaching the problem. Malcolm summarizes the steps involved, succinctly, as follows:

1. Establish criteria for management information needs.
    a. Lay out the current information, decision, display, and report practices, in graphical flow form.
2. Make preliminary design.
    a. Develop a preliminary statement of system requirements; i.e., specify reporting frequencies, types and routings of reports, types of equipments, display, etc.
    b. Determine what can be automated or programmed and what should be left as currently performed.
3. Evaluate preliminary design.
    a. Determine hardware cost, training implications.
    b. Assess the nature of the improvement to be gained.
4. Develop revised model of the proposed system.
    a. Test the design via the systems analysis approach or by experimental approach involving simulation or gaming, obtaining thereby the participation of the ultimate users.
5. Develop system specifications.
6. Install, de-bug, modify, extend the system.[3]

This outline of steps involved in the systems approach provides an inclusive framework. Some aspects involve more elaborate procedures than may be necessary for analysis and redesign of subsystems. On the other hand, this entire set of steps can be carried out in any case, whether a subsystem or a composite whole is involved.

By establishing criteria for management information needs, the decision system can be set forth explicitly. This approach has been emphasized repeatedly in this volume. A picture of the current information flow can be obtained by use of graphic flow charts. This key technique in systems analysis and design helps in visualizing the interrelationships among activities involved in the operation.

Preliminary designs spell out in rough form the requirements of the system under study. Considerable detail must be included, such as the

---

[3] Donald G. Malcolm, "Exploring the Military Analogy: Real-time Management Control," in Donald G. Malcolm, Alan J. Rowe, and Lorimer F. McConnell (eds.), *Management Control Systems,* John Wiley & Sons, Inc., New York, 1960, pp. 203–204.

timing of information needs, alternative routings, and types of equipment that might be utilized in implementing the system. At this stage benefits ordinarily will accrue whether or not new, more elaborate equipment is installed. The process of systems analysis is beneficial regardless of the equipment decisions involved.

The preliminary design should be evaluated in terms of the cost of required hardware for data collection and processing. Consideration must also be given to the training of operating personnel and managements. All the possible ramifications of the redesigned system must be considered; possible detrimental aspects must be balanced against the improvement likely to accrue from the suggested changes.

The desirability of using a model of the proposed system cannot be overemphasized. As mentioned previously, the new approach or approaches (given several alternatives) can be tested via simulation in order to assess the impact of revisions. It might be possible to simulate a complete man-machine subsystem on the basis of an information-decision system which includes the actual operators involved. Such an approach would allow the evaluation of a systems design without running the risk of undue disruption of the existing operation. The simulation of a large-scale decision system composed of various subsystems would tax the ingenuity of systems analysts. On the other hand, the amount of detail necessary in designing a system to the point of simulation fosters deeper understanding. Regardless of the feasibility of "running" the simulated system, the process of analysis can be extremely beneficial.

In order to install the revised system or to adjust the existing system in some manner, it is necessary to specify the changes explicitly. Haphazard or loose instructions with regard to implementation often negate excellent work on the part of the analyst-designer. He must be able to specify the required changes and communicate them to the organization in a manner that enhances acceptance, at least initially.

Upon installation, the system must be debugged and modified in order to fit the situation. Revised systems do not resemble interchangeable parts. The approach is more like watchmaking, where individual parts often must be filed and fitted in order to complement the other parts of the system. This process is vital and requires great skill. Once installed, debugged, and modified, the subsystem under study has become a part of the total system. The analyst can then look toward other aspects of the over-all system, possibly those systems which are interconnected with the one most recently under scrutiny. Moreover, the systems-review function requires periodic checking of all the systems in order to ensure that they maintain their complementary nature and are integrated toward efficient accomplishment of the objectives and goals of the system as a whole.

CONSTRAINTS ON THE DESIGN FUNCTION

In order to place the systems-design function in proper perspective it is important to consider the various constraints on this activity. Policy decisions on the part of the master planning council not only provide guidelines for systems design at lower levels, they also provide boundaries. If top management does not embrace the systems concept as a managerial philosophy, systems design, as set forth in this chapter, cannot be implemented. The proper atmosphere must be created at all levels in order for this approach to be utilized.

Other limiting factors include the amounts and kinds of facilities available as well as the work force and its skill mix. Elaborate and sophisticated systems designs might be forthcoming which could not be implemented because of lack of facilities and/or manpower. However, we suggest that the systems-design group start with designs for systems that are needed rather than those which obviously can be implemented. The organization will progress if it is forced to strain toward goals and objectives. If the design proves too much of a "cloud nine" approach, the system can always be scaled back to meet existing resources.

The resource-allocation council places constraints on the system-review function in terms of policy decisions with regard to allocation of the resources between major project systems and facilitating systems. It may be that systems analysts within major project systems have designed optimal arrangements for their own operation without regard to other project systems. The resource-allocation planning group may decide that certain facilitating systems common to several or all project systems should be set up to serve the entire group. Thus policy decisions throughout the total system provide constraints within which systems designers must operate.

Along with policy decisions and equipment and facility limitations, another constraint which must be taken into consideration by systems designers is people. The remark "It would be a great system if it weren't for the people involved" is appropriate here. Problems of resistance to change or of out-and-out antagonism are evident throughout the literature describing impacts of automation and electronic data processing. Similar reaction is often evident when designing information-decision systems which call for realignment of people and equipment according to the systems concept. The problems are evident; the solutions are not so evident. Because this is such a critical issue we shall devote the following chapter to the subject.

SUMMARY

Systems design is the key activity in implementing the systems concept. This function provides an over-all framework by establishing subsystems, larger systems, and a composite, integrated whole. Within this framework and within the philosophical setting of the systems concept, other tools and techniques of management science can be employed, e.g., linear programming, queuing theory, network analysis, and work simplification.

Systems design considers three basic elements in every system: material, energy, and information. In addition, each of these elements can be structured on the basis of flow concepts as systems in and of themselves. The flow concept facilitates the consideration of systems of systems by emphasizing the interconnections between subparts.

In terms of the suggested organization for implementing the systems concept, the master planning council utilizes a top-management information-decision system to facilitate long-range planning. On the basis of inputs from research and development, market research, and finance, it establishes the programs or projects upon which the organization will devote its time. The master planning council must consider project missions and be able to perceive the need for products or services. It is charged with the responsibility for recognition of the niche which the company occupies in a larger system or systems. In this way, top management establishes broad guidelines and parameters for the systems-design function.

Given policy decision on which projects or programs are to be undertaken, the resource-allocation planning group must design systems which can accomplish the objectives established. The design effort, at this level, involves putting together systems of manpower and facilities and coordinating such systems on the basis of information-decision systems. This group must decide on the appropriate facilities and manpower for the major project systems and must allocate appropriate resources to facilitating systems. The important task at this level is optimal allocation of resources among project systems and facilitating systems. All these subsystems must complement each other and must be integrated into the total corporate system.

Within project systems a review function must be established. At this level systems analysts must continually appraise the appropriateness of the major project system and its various subsystems as the program moves through its life cycle. Analysis and synthesis must be carried out to ensure up-to-date approaches at all times.

The scientific method and problem orientation underlie the systems approach. Model building, at least in terms of process and information flow charts, is a vital element in the systems-design procedure. While material and energy flows are important, as are tools and techniques for analyzing plant layout, materials handling, and organization, attention should be focused on information as the *sine qua non* of systems design. Formal and informal communication systems must be identified. Decision orientation helps identify the information flow appropriate for management purposes. The systems design must be cognizant of information requirements at decision points and desired output at various places in the system. The problem, rather than tools and techniques of analysis, should be the focal point in implementing the systems concept.

It is important to recognize constraints on the systems-design function. Policy decisions at various levels in the organization represent constraints on systems analysts at lower levels. Also, the facilities and equipment available, as well as the work force and its skill mix, represent limitations. The impact of systems design and change on people is critical—a point important enough to be deferred to a later chapter.

We cannot overemphasize the fact that, first and foremost, the systems concept is a frame of mind. Management must be receptive to this approach and develop a philosophy in which planning, organizing, controlling, and communication are accomplished in terms of subsystems integrated into a composite whole. Once there is acceptance of the systems concept and the feasibility of organizing on the basis of a master planning council, a resource-allocation planning group, and an operations planning group (with facilitating and project systems reporting to it), the systems-design function can be carried out in a progressive atmosphere. The atmosphere created is all-important; it fosters creativity and innovation on the part of systems designers.

Chapter Fourteen
PEOPLE AND SYSTEMS

Throughout Part Three, Implementation, discussion centered around the mechanistic aspects of systems applications. We should not forget that our primary consideration in this book is with the business organization as a social system; we are dealing with man-made systems. Therefore this chapter is devoted to a discussion of the human aspects of the systems concept. Certainly a society which places high value upon individual rights and freedoms and is geared primarily to the satisfaction of basic individual needs must give adequate recognition to the impact of the systems concept upon people. The material on people and systems will be concerned with the following six areas:

The Human Need for Systematic Relationships
The Need for Systems Change
Human Resistance to Change
How People Resist Change
Impact of the Systems Concept
Meeting the Human and Social Problems

Application of the systems-management concept has a major impact upon participants at all levels of the organization—the blue-collar worker, foreman, white-collar worker, and even middle and upper management. If the concept of systems management outlined in the foregoing chapters is to be applied for greater efficiency and broad social benefit, then recog-

278

nition must be given to the needs, motivations, and aspirations of all these groups.

THE HUMAN NEED FOR SYSTEMATIC RELATIONSHIPS

In discussing the impact of the systems concept on people it should not be assumed that people generally resist systems. Much of man's conscious activities are geared to creating system out of chaos. Man does not resist systemization of his behavioral patterns per se. Rather, the normal human being seeks satisfactory systems of personal and interpersonal relationships which guide his activities. Everyone has been taught or has developed habit patterns which provide a basis for systemizing many of his activities. Each human being has, in effect, developed his own unique system for relating a number of diverse activities within a broad operational whole—life's activities. Without systemization, behavior would be random, nongoal-oriented, and unpredictable. Certainly the complex modern industrial society demands more systemized human behavior than older, less structured societies.

Nor should the discussion be confined to talking about the systems by which each individual relates himself to his physical environment. Many of man's actions and much of his behavior are dependent upon his interpersonal relationship. As Sherif and Sherif have written, "Many motives of man are products of social interaction and exposure to sociocultural products. These motives of social origin (sociogenic motives) are revealed in our preferences, in the favorable or unfavorable stand we take toward groups and social issues—in brief in what constitutes our social attitudes." [1]

Thus man is a product of his own motives and aspirations, which are modified extensively by sociocultural factors. Every individual must develop systems of satisfactory relationships with other members of his society. The concept that "no man is an island" merely means that man is a social creature and—different from any other form of life—takes most of his norms and standards of conduct from other members of his society. Everyone must have a system of relationships which sets a pattern for his life.

Much has been written of the human consequences of the sociocultural changes brought on by advancing technology. One of the earliest and most pessimistic of these research findings was made at the turn of the century by the sociologist Émile Durkheim.[2] In his investigations he found that rapid industrialization brought on by the industrial revolution had broken down the *solidaire* within social groups. Old family and community relationships were destroyed, and the individual was unable to replace these

---

[1] Muzafer Sherif and Carolyn W. Sherif, *An Outline of Social Psychology,* Harper & Brothers, New York, 1956, p. 366.

[2] Émile Durkheim, *Le Suicide,* Librarie Felix Alcan, Paris, 1930.

with new satisfactory social interactions. In our own country, Mayo says, "This is a clear statement of the issue the civilized world is facing now, a rapid industrial, mechanical, physiochemical advance, so rapid that it has been destructive of all the historic social and personal relationships." [3]

The problem, then, is not one of requiring man to change his total pattern of living and to adapt for the first time to the systematic organization of his behavior. Rather, the problem is primarily one of requiring man to change from old systems of work and interpersonal relationships to a *new and different systems environment*.

But it should not be inferred that there is just one major sociocultural system to which each individual member belongs. Everyone of us has a number of "interpersonal systems" which have differing objectives, perform different functions, occupy a different place and role in our lives. Behavioral scientists call this the identification of the individual with the various groups with which he comes into contact. It is useful to classify individual identification with various types of systems or human groups. It would be impossible to do this for all man's activities. In this respect everyone is unique; no two people have the same set of group identifications or systems of interpersonal relationships. We are concerned primarily with the business organization and can classify this identification with major social systems as follows:

Identification with systems external to the organization (e.g., family groups, professional associations, community groups, educational groups). These systems of interpersonal relationships are unique to the individual and are largely determined by him rather than by the formal business organization. However, man's systems of interpersonal relationships cannot be separated into neat categories. Most certainly man's participation and identification with such groups as the church or educational institutions can have a profound effect upon his other organizational relationships.

Identification with the organization. Identification with the formal organization is one of the strongest systems of interpersonal relationships for most individuals. Ask a man what he is, and he will often respond, I work for General Electric, or IBM, or for the University of Washington. This apparent dominant need to identify and to maintain satisfactory relationships with the formal organization system is an important characteristic of our industrial society.

Identification with functional groups. Even within the complex organization, identification is most frequently made within subgroups. For ex-

[3] Elton Mayo, *The Social Problems of an Industrial Civilization,* Harvard University, Graduate School of Business Administration, Boston, 1945, p. 8.

ample, I work for the sales department, or I work in accounting, or I am in the College of Business Administration. Identification with these functional groups provides a more refined system of relationships for the individual in his work environment.

Identification with informal groups. All of us recognize the importance of informal interpersonal relationships and how these affect the formal-organizational requirements. With whom do we go to lunch? Who shares our coffee break? These are ramifications of the informal social system which is apparent within every formal organization. To be sure, the formal structure sets the broad structure and pattern within which these informal relationships occur, but the individual has a great deal of latitude in his participation in informal groups.

Many forces are geared to maintaining the system of relationships in the formal organization. For example, the organization structure which places each individual in a hierarchial relationship and specifies his functions and relationships to other people is one of the vital elements in the system. This structure establishes a common set of expectations as to individual performance. The organization establishes the goals to which the interpersonal systems are directed. Broad policies help establish the system of relationships, as well as the more detailed standard operating procedures and methods. Over all, the organization is a *system* which directly and specifically defines interpersonal relationships for every member.

We have traced some of the interpersonal relationships which tend to systemize individual behavior. It is not inherent within man to resist the systemization of his activities. Rather, it is just the opposite; man seeks to establish, in his social and interpersonal relationships, satisfactory and rewarding systems of behavior. What then is the major problem in terms of systems and people? The major problem is not one of total resistance to systemization; it is one of adherence to systems which are already in existence. The crucial problem, then, is one of adaptability of the individual and group to change from one type of systematic relationship to another.

A common characteristic in a rapidly advancing society is to make these systems of interpersonal relationships more formal. While many of these systems have been implicit in the past, they are becoming more explicit. This is one of the major precepts of our systems-management concept: systematic interpersonal relationships are necessary for accomplishing group objectives. Before looking at some of the basic factors which cause man to resist change in his system of relationships, it will be helpful to review briefly some of the reasons why our society has demanded greater change in these systems.

THE NEED FOR SYSTEMS CHANGE

Management in a modern industrial society requires the systematic and coordinated integration of many common elements, both human and physical. Scientific and technological advancements have progressed at an accelerating rate and have fostered wholesale changes. It has been necessary to adopt new managerial, organizational, and human relationships in order to meet the requirements of the new technology. The twentieth century has seen enormous advancement in science and technology, affecting everyone. In earlier times, increasing scientific knowledge was rarely, or at best slowly, translated into useful forces for the material betterment of man. Since 1850, however, the time between discovery and utilization of scientific knowledge has been decreasing. Science has become a pervasive force in modern society, having widespread influence over all man's activities.

Scientific and technological achievements have had an obvious impact upon business organizations; indeed, they have been the primary institutions for translating these achievements into goods and services, fundamental indicators of the standard of living. Every industry has seen advancements, not only in its products, but also in the means of production. Hardly a facet of man's existence or his social organizations has escaped influence by the all-pervasive effects of advancing science and technology.

The United States provided fertile ground for the exploitation of advancing technology and the changing social structure stemming from the industrial revolution. Our society was favorably inclined toward adaptation and change, a situation infrequently found in other, more restricted cultures. Expansion of science and technology is reflected in the substantial increase in funds spent for research. In fiscal year 1947, research and development expenditures totaled $2.1 billion; by fiscal year 1960, they had risen to over $12 billion.

These efforts are an indication of the importance attached to advancement in science and technology. But science and technology cannot stand alone; they are part of the complex environment of the twentieth century, and must be integrated into man's over-all effort toward a better society. Even though increasing emphasis has been given to science and technology, we must recognize that society without a broad background of human talents would be ill prepared for the future. Even though it were to allocate all its resources to scientific pursuits and to train the best brains in this direction, the problems of integrating the advancing knowledge into the framework of a complex society would be tremendous.

Importance of technological change and advancement within our society can be appreciated. One of the key elements stemming from the modern industrial society is *change.* It is no longer possible to maintain the *status quo.* We are in a dynamic society; the challenge of change is both a threat and an opportunity. We have evolved a new attitude toward change, one of welcome, of expectation and acceptance, as part of our cultural growth. This has not always been the case. As Drucker suggests, "Throughout most of history change was considered catastrophe, and immutability the goal of organized human efforts. All social institutions of man for thousands of years had as their first purpose to prevent, or at least to slow down, the onrush of change." [4] By contrast, in our modern society, change has become "the accepted pattern of life."

With advancing technology and the growing emphasis given to increased understanding of the environment, our society and established social organizations will undergo dramatic changes in the future. There is no alternative but to adapt to change. We can no longer rely upon structured systems of interference to ward off the problems of social change which will influence us. The primary question from the viewpoint of systems management in the business organization is to provide a means whereby change can be accomplished with a maximum of benefit to the organization and to the participants and a minimum of penalty to any individual or group. This is the challenge to people of the systems concept. Before looking at some of the ways in which the change from one system to a new and different type of system can be accomplished with the most advantages and least disadvantages in terms of human relationships, we shall investigate some of the forces which tend to create rigidity or resistance to change.

HUMAN RESISTANCE TO CHANGE

To say that man resists change per se would be an oversimplification of the problem. Certainly, in most activities people welcome and even demand change. Consumers are continually looking for new means and products for expressing their desires for change. Witness the ever-increasing tendency to give formerly standardized products higher style and fashion differentiation. Thus, in many areas, man seems to welcome change. Why, then, is there resistance to technological change within the business organization? Generally, we can make a distinction between these two types of change. The consumers of products have some degree of control over acceptance or rejection of change, whereas, within the organization, technological changes occur which are beyond influence or control of the individual. We tend to resist changes in our interpersonal and job relations because our sense of security and the way in which we have been accus-

[4] Peter F. Drucker, *Landmarks of Tomorrow,* Harper & Brothers, New York, 1959, p. 21.

tomed to doing things are threatened. People frequently resist changes by indifference or outright opposition and rebellion, because most changes result in a disturbance of the interpersonal equilibrium within the environment in which the individual and social group operates. It is generally not the technological change that is resisted; resistance is generated primarily because of changing sociological relations and because economic well-being may be threatened. In a case study of administering change, Ronken and Lawrence concluded:

> So the problems of "technological change" proved to be the everyday problems of people in an organization, who, like the rest of us, were trying to get along as best they could in the world as they saw it. The increased tempo of change accentuated these problems, and their result was the kind of behavior—"uncooperative attitudes," project delays, and even restriction of output—which has led to the cliché that "people resist change." Looked at in this broader perspective, the story shows unequivocally that the effects of technological change were not confined to technical materials but were critical largely through their effect on interpersonal relationships.
>
> At each stage the introduction of technological change forced readjustments in the social system. Again and again individuals on the projects found that they had to deal with other individuals who were either new to them or stood in a new relationship to them. That these changes in relationships were the major variable in the introduction of the new product emerged as the most insistent uniformity.[5]

Frequently, management is unaware of the impact of technological change. It looks primarily at the changes in the physical setup and in the physiological requirement for the individuals on the job. For example, it will require new time-and-motion studies, new job specifications, and other manifestations of the physical change in the work. However, even more important are changes in social equilibrium. Generally, any change will alter the informal or formal social hierarchical relationships which exist between people operating in groups. For some people status may be increased, while for others their positions will often be apparently diminished. As Roethlisberger points out, "Any move on the part of the company may alter the existing social equilibrium to which the employee has grown accustomed and by means of which his status is defined. Immediately this disruption will be expressed in sentiments of resistance to the real or imagined alterations in the social equilibrium." [6]

This section has suggested that social as well as technological changes

[5] Harriet O. Ronken and Paul R. Lawrence, *Administering Changes,* Harvard University, Graduate School of Business, Boston, 1952, p. 292.

[6] F. J. Roethlisberger, *Management and Morale,* Harvard University Press, Cambridge, Mass., 1941, pp. 61–62.

are important in understanding resistances. What are some of the more specific reasons for resistance to change?

Economic Security

Undoubtedly, the most obvious causes—also the most readily and generally acknowledged—of resistances to change are those which threaten the economic security of the worker. Any major threat to job security, any possibility that a change might adversely alter the income of the worker, will generally be met by immediate, intense, and determined resistance. Everyone is generally unimpressed by arguments about what is good for them or the country in the long run. They want assurance of economic security and a job for tomorrow, next month, and next year. One of the primary aims of economic activity is to provide the means of obtaining food, clothing, and shelter, that is, to satisfy basic physiological needs. Anything which threatens our ability to meet these needs for ourselves and our families will obviously evoke a major reaction. While it is true that most instances of technological change have a salutary impact upon the welfare of the company and the nation as a whole, it is unrealistic to expect that any individual would be willing to sacrifice his own needs and requirements to this greater benefit. He simply will not do so, and it is not natural to expect it of him. He will resist the kind of change which threatens to lower his economic well-being with all the means at his disposal, even though to the outsider his reactions may appear entirely irrational.

However, there generally is a tendency to overrate the importance or impact of economic factors as cause for resistance to change. In reality, much of the resistance, rather than being based upon economic issues or causes, is generated by sociological factors.

Job Status

In a handicraft society, where the craftsman began and completed all phases of his operation, he gained social and egotistic-need satisfaction directly from the products he created.[7] The products were his own work and could be identified as his contribution. However, mass-production techniques changed the social order of work, and workmen no longer could feel any particular pride of accomplishment. Workers still gained personal satisfaction from doing a good job, but their accomplishments could not be identified and recognized by others.

Today, workers and managers tend to use other means to symbolize

[7] Mason Haire, *Psychology in Management,* McGraw-Hill Book Company, Inc., New York, 1956, p. 62.

their status. Pride of accomplishment is secondary to pride in the job or position they hold. The job symbols include such things as the size of their desk, their parking area, the color of their employee's badge, the number of subordinates they supervise, and many other factors. These symbols of status cannot be eliminated or changed without threatening the things for which they stand.

The application of the systems concept through automation, automatic data processing, and management science will often upset these symbols and features of job status. It becomes harder and harder for the individual to identify himself with the job once the job becomes less understandable and influenced by his activities.

Uncertainty

"The new way is always strange, threatening, and laden with uncertainties—even if it is an improvement over the old." [8] A change will create a new situation, and there is conjecturing about the standards of performance and social contact which will be acceptable in the new environment. Anyone with work experience knows the uncertainty that is felt almost instantaneously when change is rumored. Even if a change is explained and complete information is given, the individual is not always certain how he will be affected by the change (nor does he always completely trust what he is told). The employee may like his present job and work group; a change might involve many unknown variables. It is common for an employee to worry about seemingly insignificant details, e.g., will the new job change my lunch hour? Will I have to park my car on the other side of the plant? Will my payday be the same?

Some people like to go to new places, make new friends, and do new things. However, the typical person feels uncertain and insecure when there are drastic changes in his familiar environment, unless there are incentives sufficient to offset this uncertainty.

Increased Complexities

People generally resist and fight any change which makes things more difficult or disagreeable. A period of adjustment is required. It is prudent for management to remember that the old job has become familiar; the worker has developed certain tricks of the trade and can probably perform quite satisfactorily without concerted and full-time attention. He feels a sense of security and confidence in knowing that he is proficient and capable in his job. Any change requires relearning and therefore greater concentration and uncertainty.

[8] George Strauss and Leonard R. Sayles, *Personnel: The Human Problems of Management,* Prentice-Hall, Inc., Englewood Cliffs, N.J., 1960, p. 266.

Changed Group Relations

To a major extent, satisfactory group and social relationships have replaced the void left when satisfaction of craftsmanship was destroyed by methods of specialization and mass production. Within most business organizations, social groups form in order to meet man's needs for satisfactory social relationships. Often management is cognizant of the necessity for this in the satisfaction of the workers and provides such things as the coffee break, cafeteria or other eating facilities, recreational areas, bowling teams, and a whole host of activities related to the need for and motivation of satisfactory social relationships. Quite often, as a result of the introduction of change, these group and social relationships suffer most severely. People who have worked together and associated closely on the job and have come to understand and value their social interaction are often separated. Perhaps it is no longer possible to go for coffee or to have lunch at the same time, or to participate in numerous other activities. Yet the impact of the change in the social relationships is often one that is kept below the surface. It is quite difficult, and even embarrassing, for a worker to explain his resistance in terms of the fact that he no longer is able to work closely with Joe and the other fellows and is now placed in a group of strangers. He is more likely to explain his resistance in terms of some technical factor, such as his inability to keep up with the pace of the job or complaints about tools or materials.

Disruption of Superior-Subordinate Relationships

Change from one system of operation or production to another often requires adjustments and changes in supervisory-subordinate relationships. Even though there is no direct change in a worker's superior, there are often indirect changes in the relationship. For example, during the process of change-over the superior may have to exercise more detailed control over the operations or output of the worker. He may be forced to centralize certain decisions in his hands and take them away from the employee. The change-over may also require the preoccupation of the supervisor with technical matters to the extent that he has little time for displaying his previous personal interest in the worker. Change in these relationships can be a major factor contributing to resistance, yet it is also frequently below the surface.

Union Attitudes

The union has certain institutional needs which must be met if it is to retain its function of leadership for the worker: first, it must represent the workers and be their official spokesman; second, it must work to improve the status of its members; and finally, it must maintain its membership and bargaining position. When management does not consider a change in terms of the needs of the union, the union will often resist the change, and this resistance will reflect throughout the entire union membership.

Thus we see that the primary forces leading to resistance to change are not necessarily technological forces, but rather the pressures on the individual to adjust to new and different social and group relationships. Social psychologists have taken this view of change. Sherif and Sherif, in discussing the impact of change, suggest, "The effects of technology are always upon individuals interacting with other individuals in group settings with particular organizations, concepts, values, and social norms." [9]

HOW PEOPLE RESIST CHANGE

Resistance to change can take many forms. The most obvious manifestation of a resistance to change is by complete disassociation of the worker from the job—he quits. This obviously is a major display of resistance and is in a way the easiest to deal with. For the most part employees do not take this alternative, at least not immediately. Frequently they have limited opportunities for change in employment and desire to maintain a continuing relationship with the organization. If an employee stays with the organization, a negative reaction can take many forms, ranging from open opposition, rebellion, and even destruction, to apathy and indifference.

The outward manifestations of resistance to change may take many forms which have a direct bearing upon the efficiency of the operation, such as decreased quality or quantity of production, increased absenteeism, tardiness, grievances, and strikes. Unfortunately, it is often difficult to trace these concrete results of the resistance back to the original change and to the original cause. Frequently, people do not display resistance in a direct fashion, but their behavior will show its influence in a variety of ways. Nor, in discussing the problem, is it always easy for the superior to determine what really is wrong. People will often disguise their real concern over the impact of change by trying to appear to be rationally motivated in the best interest of the company. It is especially difficult to deal with those who have rationalized their resistance in terms of the organizational benefits. This is one of the chief forms of resistance to change on the white-collar and managerial level. Individuals in this category will often resist change in their work environment by rationalizing that this will have a direct and adverse effect upon their performance and consequently organizational effectiveness will deteriorate.

Because of the many ways of displaying resistance to change and the

[9] Sherif and Sherif, *op. cit.*, p. 687.

great difficulty of correcting resistance and moving back into a new, effective equilibrium, it is highly desirable for management to make every effort possible to effectuate the change properly and to facilitate adjustments to it. Giving adequate consideration to the problems of change, both technical and social, prior to the change is much more satisfactory than simply making the change and waiting for the chips to fall. Before we look at some of the ways in which management can ease the transition and make the kinds of changes which are necessary in transition to a systems concept, it will be helpful to look at the areas in which the systems approach will have its greatest impact.

IMPACT OF THE SYSTEMS CONCEPT

Where will the application of the systems concept have its impact upon the business firm in the future? Perhaps the two most dramatic impact areas of the systems concept will be in the continuation of the trend toward automation of production operations and the further development of the trend toward automatic information-decision systems. Information-decision systems require the application of computers, data-processing equipment, and other techniques in a systematic way to help in planning, organizing, and controlling the business functions. Both automation and information-decision systems are adaptations of the systems concept and will have an impact upon people.

Automation and People

Since the beginning of the industrial revolution, with its substitution of mechanical power for human power, there has been an ever-increasing trend toward mechanization. In the early phases of the industrial revolution, this had a traumatic effect upon people. Their life-long skills were lost; unemployment was rampant; there was a wholesale displacement of workers; and women and children who could operate machines as effectively and at a much lower cost than men were utilized. From these early stages of industrialization rapid advances have been made in minimizing the impact of mechanization on employees. Basically, we have come to recognize the importance of sharing the benefits of technological improvements, but also of sharing some of the social costs involved. The economy has developed important social innovations, such as unemployment compensation, protection for the employee through legislation, collective-bargaining contracts, and efforts by business organizations to retrain and reorient their workers to new technologies.

In some ways automation can be thought of as a further extension of the trend toward mechanization which has been going on over the past few centuries. However, it is even more dramatic and brings into focus a number of new problems. Just what is automation? John Diebold, the author of one of the earliest books on automation, defines it as "a new word denoting both automatic operation and the process of making things automatic. In the latter sense it includes several areas of industrial activity such as products and process redesign, the theory of communication and control, and the design of machinery." [10]

From this definition, automation is thought of primarily as a mechanical process in which the entire system of machines regulate or control their own operations within prescribed limits. The introduction of such machines creates a dramatic and violent change—man is replaced by machines. This is obviously the kind of change which meets greatest resistance from people, and yet it is also the kind of change which is vitally necessary for our economy in order to increase the general welfare.

Automation is a well-known example of the application of the systems concept. Automation is not just further mechanization—the replacement of human power with mechanical power. It is an over-all system which integrates all the operations of the business firm—product research and development, manufacturing processes, distribution methods, and other facilitating activities—into an operational man-machine system. This broad concept of automation was described by Hurni: "The true roots of automation lie not in the mechanical feasibility of replacing hand operations but in the logic of an over-all system of operation. And this logic, in turn, is grounded not in manufacturing alone, but in marketing and engineering design as well." [11] Under this systems concept, automation has an impact upon the entire business organization, all the way from the initial design of the product to final distribution.

Automated equipment is practical only if it displaces labor, reduces per-unit labor cost, or makes possible some desirable results that could not be accomplished in any other way. The fact that machines will replace workers must be accepted; the vital question is whether or not the workers who have been replaced will be unemployed. Wiener is very pessimistic about the future impact of automation:

> Let us remember that the automatic machine, whatever we think of any feelings it may or may not have, is the precise economic equivalent of slave labor. Any labor which competes with slave labor must accept the economic conditions of slave labor. It is perfectly clear that this will produce an unemployment situation, in comparison with which the present recession and even the depression of the thirties will seem a pleasant joke. This de-

[10] John Diebold, *Automation: The Advent of the Automatic Factory,* D. Van Nostrand Company, Inc., Princeton, N.J., 1952, p. ix.

[11] Melvin L. Hurni, "Decision Making in the Age of Automation," *Harvard Business Review,* September–October, 1955, p. 53.

pression will ruin many industries—possibly even the industries which have taken advantage of the new potentialities.[12]

Certainly this is a most pessimistic view and is not shared by most businessmen or even labor leaders. It is pointed out that in the future productivity must increase tremendously if the growth in our standard of living and national income is to be continued.

Over the long run, technological change in the past has led to increasing rather than decreasing employment. We foresee this same trend in the future, as a result of automation. With a continuation of the growth in population, a rising standard of living, increasing expenditures for education, recreation, retirement, and so forth, and increasing competition on the international scene, our nation will need to expand productivity greatly in the next several decades.[13] Automation and advancing technology are the answers for this expansion. No matter how necessary this advancing automation is for our future well-being, however, there will be many short-run results which adversely affect a proportion of individuals.

There is some evidence, both over the long run and in the short run, that in some areas automation and increased mechanization have created major problems for certain groups of employees. In particular, in the coal-mining industry, which has increasingly mechanized over the past twenty years, the problems of technological unemployment are severe. Again, with increased automation in the automotive industry, the level of unemployment in the Detroit area has been substantially higher than in the nation as a whole. This technological unemployment seems to be a direct result of increased automation in the automotive plants.[14]

Often the impact of automation is to change substantially the nature and type of work. James Cross, President of the Bakers Union, said, "We have 170,000 members in the union as against 113,000 in 1946, but I doubt if 16,000 of them are bakers. . . . But the machines, while eliminating bakers, require great numbers of men to assemble the packaging

[12] Norbert Wiener, *The Human Use of Human Beings,* Houghton Mifflin Company, Boston, 1950, p. 189.

[13] *Automation and Technological Change, Hearings before the Subcommittee on Economic Stabilization of the Joint Committee on the Economic Report,* 84th Cong., 1st Sess., 1955, p. 182.

[14] The findings of the Congressional Committee on Automation and Technological Change indicated that the past shifts to automation and the accelerating pace of technology took place in a background of relatively high employment in a generally prosperous economy, most of the post–World War II period. Under these conditions, dislocation and adjustment tend to be less painful. The Committee pointed out, however, that any significant recession in levels of employment might create new problems, as it magnified the difficulty of adjustment. *Ibid.,* pp. 262–279.

materials, store and move the product. We've exchanged bakers for bakery workers." [15]

Frequently, under automation, certain groups of employees bear the brunt of the dislocation. Although unemployment can affect all classes of workers, some employees and groups appear to be more susceptible. Young person under twenty-five, Negro workers, manual or blue-collar workers, workers attached to construction, mining, and manufacturing, and, notably, workers with little or no education are affected most by unemployment.[16]

One of the most disputed questions about the application of the systems concept through automation is whether or not it will increase or decrease the skill level of workers. On the one hand, it is argued that with the advent of automatic equipment, fewer workers will be needed to feed the machines or to carry on the dull routine jobs and that it will be possible to place more workers in jobs that offer a greater amount of self-satisfaction. Evidence supporting this idea is taken from the past trends which show that the percentage of skilled and semiskilled workers in the total labor force have increased greatly over the past thirty years, whereas the proportion of unskilled workers has declined dramatically. This argument suggests that the whole range of skills from the worker level all the way to the designer of the automatic equipment will be generally upgraded.

There are others who feel that automation will downgrade the skill requirements of the work force. Bright, after an intensive study of a number of firms that had adopted automated operations, stated:

> The significant argument arising out of this study is that it is not true that automaticity—automation, advanced mechanization, or whatever we call it—*inevitably* means lack of opportunity for the unskilled worker and/or tremendous retraining problems. On the contrary, automation often reduces the contribution by the individual at the machine. Automated machinery requires less *operator* skill, or at least not any more skill, *after certain levels of mechanization are passed.* It appears as though the average worker can more quickly and easily master new and different jobs where highly automatic machinery provides the skill, effort, and control required. Furthermore, some "key" skilled jobs, currently requiring long experience and training, are reduced to easily learned machine-tending jobs.[17]

It appears impossible to determine from the present viewpoint whether or not automation will increase the skill-level requirements. It is

[15] "Automation: What the Unions Will Demand," *Fortune,* May, 1955, p. 59.

[16] U.S. Bureau of Census, "Educational Attainment of Workers, March, 1957," *Current Population Reports,* series P-50, no. 78, p. 8.

[17] James R. Bright, *Automation and Management,* Harvard University, Graduate School of Business Administration, Boston, 1958, pp. 176–177.

quite likely that the changes will not be simple but will be complex, in some companies skill requirements being enhanced, and in other companies, degraded. Generalization as to the total impact, from the present viewpoint, is difficult and perhaps foolhardy.

We can, however, suggest a number of other changes. With automation, the output per man-hour will increase and wage increases will probably result. Furthermore, there will be a continuation of the trend of the past century toward the reduction of hours of work per week, and automation will make this feasible without a reduction in over-all productivity. Furthermore, the benefit of automation to labor through better working conditions is significant. Generally, plants will be cleaner, less congested, and safer places to work.

Automatic technology, a systems concept, has major implications for our society. First, for man as a consumer, it will offer greatly increased productivity and output, hence a rising standard of living. For man as a producer, there are some difficulties. In this process of change, some individual workers will inevitably suffer losses as a result of displacement, whereas others will benefit as a result of upgrading.

There is a need for adequate measures to ease the hardships on displaced individuals, to train workers with new skills, and to adjust conflicting interest in the enterprise. These are likely to be important issues during the transition to automation. Labor, management, and government agencies responsible for education, vocational training, employment services, unemployment insurance, apprenticeship, wages and hours, and industrial relations are likely to be increasingly concerned with the problems created by advancing technology and automation.[18]

Automatic Information-decision Systems

The automation of manufacturing processes is a natural continuation and extension of the industrial revolution. There is an increasing trend toward the substitution of mechanical devices and equipment to replace man's physical activities in the factory. Automation also means some replacement of the decision-making and mental activities of man in the factory. However, it is not just in the factory that the systems concept is being implemented by means of new equipment and techniques. The clerical jobs and even the front office are feeling the impact of the new technology. Whereas mechanical operations have undergone a continual

[18] For a more complete discussion of the possible impacts of automation see U.S. Department of Labor, "Impact of Automation," *Bulletin* 1287, and Richard A. Johnson, *Employees—Automation—Management,* University of Washington, Bureau of Business Research, Seattle, 1961.

transition toward more mechanization, the traditional white-collar and managerial functions have remained to a major extent humanized. Although there were typewriters, dictating equipment, and other mechanical aids to these functions, much of the actual work depended directly upon human skills and applications. There has been a continual increase in the proportion of people in the white-collar and managerial classes, whereas people engaged in actual direct production—factory workers, and also farmers—have actually declined. But certainly on the horizon, and some would suggest moving rapidly, are the same kinds of technical developments that led to automation in the factory and that promise an even more dramatic revolution in large-scale clerical operations. For this revolution in clerical and managerial functions, we have utilized the concept *automatic information-decision systems*. Basically, this concept covers two primary areas of activity:

1. The use of automatic-data-processing equipment for the collection, processing, and comparison of information
2. The application of computers to aid directly in the managerial decison-making processes

The most apparent impact is in the first phase, that of the use of electronic-data-processing equipment for processing vast quantities of information. However, the second phase, the application of computers to decision making, may have the greatest impact in the future.

It should be emphasized that computers and data-processing equipment alone do not provide for an integrated systems concept. They merely provide a potentiality for integration which was nonexistent prior to their availability. As Postley says:

> Computers do not integrate systems functions, although they often provide the *means* to integrate operations when integration is a desirable objective. The use of large-scale computers need not bear at all on the decision as to which management system should be employed, although it may make *feasible* either centralized system management or dispersed system management. And in any management system, the proper use of digital computers as a tool can *allow* that system which may be required to achieve the system objectives to function at the greater level of complexity and volume.[19]

This viewpoint emphasizes that computers are not synonymous with systems. Rather, the computer provides the electronic and mechanical

---

[19] John A. Postley, *Computers and People*, McGraw-Hill Book Company, Inc., New York, 1960, p. 11.

equipment which can be utilized to implement the general systems concept because of its ability to process information.

Automatic data processing has had and will have a substantial impact upon clerical and white-collar workers. With the growing complexities of business operation and increases in size, many organizations have found the problem of record keeping and storage overwhelming, and clerical costs have increased disproportionately to total operating costs. In many ways, the process of replacement of clerical workers with data-processing equipment is similar to that involved in the replacement of the worker in the factory. The problems of resistance to change on the part of the white-collar workers will be equal to, or perhaps even greater than, that involved with the blue-collar worker.

Of even greater importance may be the impact that automatic information-decision systems have upon management itself. The integrative effects of this concept, with its emphasis upon systemization and development of rules and procedures and the increase in volume and accuracy of information circulation, can have a profound impact upon management decision making. It is quite probable that many of the routine programmed decision-making functions of lower- and middle-level management will be "mechanized." Programming of decision making in such areas as production and inventory control has already been accomplished in numerous organizations. In many ways this increased programming of the decision-making processes within the organization is characteristic of the trend established in the early history of the industrial revolution. Scientific management was geared primarily to programming decisions for the worker; that is, the worker was told exactly what to do and how to do it and was given specific directions and control over his efforts. Since that time there has been a gradual extension of these programmed activities toward higher levels of operation.

Simon has suggested that new data-processing technology has already been utilized to help in making programmed decisions—decisions which are repetitive and routine and have continuity. He suggests that for programmed decision making, (1) the electronic computer has brought a higher level of automation to routine, programmed decision making and data processing which were formerly done by clerks; (2) important strides have been made toward programming decision making which was formerly regarded as judgmental—primarily in the areas of manufacturing and inventory; (3) the computer has made possible the use of previously unavailable mathematical techniques for the programming of many types of decisions; and (4) companies are now combining mathematical techniques of decision making with the data-processing capabilities which are made possible by the business computer. Simon foresees, "The automated factory of the future will operate on the basis of programmed decisions produced in the automated office beside it." [20]

Even much further in the future is the possibility of using analytical techniques and computers for the processes of nonprogrammed decision making. By nonprogrammed decision making, we mean those decisions which are new and unstructured and do not have a set pattern for handling. It is this type of problem which is of most importance for middle and higher levels of management. Generally, problems requiring nonprogrammed decision making have not been applicable to computer and data-processing techniques. A number of people have suggested that through a greater understanding of the human decision-making processes for nonprogrammed decisions we can learn and transform these processes into computer programs. Theoretically, with heuristic programming, management could acquire the capacity to automate nonprogrammed decision making.

Although it is apparent that many of these projected changes are some distance away in the future, we can already see how data processing, the computer, and management science have made a major impact upon clerical operations and programmed managerial decision making, particularly at the lower and intermediate levels of management. These changes will have a rather dramatic impact upon the white-collar and management worker. In many ways they will bring changes to this group which are typical of those affecting the blue-collar worker in the early stages of industrialization. Decision making will most likely be more centralized, and work will be more routine and specified by the programming. The problems of motivation and identification of the white-collar worker and lower-level management with the organization will most likely become more difficult. Of great importance is the recognition that the white-collar worker and management, because of their position with the organization, generally have more effective means for resisting changes which affect them adversely. Numerous studies have suggested that the white-collar workers have been even more resistant to technological change than have the blue-collar workers. Furthermore, the new techniques place great demands upon management. Major changes usually increase the skill requirements of the supervisors in many areas: technical, administrative, and human relations. [21]

[20] Herbert A. Simon, *The New Science of Management Decisions,* Harper and Brothers, New York, 1960, p. 20.

[21] For a very good case study of the impact of the introduction of electronic-data-processing equipment and the changing managerial requirements as a result of this introduction, see Floyd C. Mann and Lawrence K. Williams, "Observations on the Dynamics of a Change to Electronic Data-processing Equipment," *Administrative Science Quarterly,* September, 1960, pp. 217–256.

With the dynamic changes which the applications of the systems concept—automation, electronic computers, integrated data processing, and management science—will bring, business management must be prepared to deal with resistances and problems of human adjustment to these changes. How effective management is in handling the human problems of adjusting to these new systems will have an important bearing on how effective these systems are in meeting their output potential and will also have an impact upon the social and individual well-being of people in business organizations.

MEETING THE HUMAN AND SOCIAL PROBLEMS

The manager who has been successful in administering people can foresee that the disruptions and traumas resulting from the rapid application of systems techniques are potential sources of difficulty both for the individual and for the organization. What can be done to minimize the impact? Primarily, this is a question of providing an atmosphere of confidence and mutual understanding between superior and subordinate. There are three primary ways in which management can help minimize employee resistance to change: (1) by appealing to the employees to cooperate with the organization in order to combat an outside force, (2) by applying pressures on the employees to cooperate, or (3) by reducing the basic forces which cause employee resistance to change.

The first approach was used during World War II and, to a lesser extent, during the Korean War. Sometimes it is used if a company is at a competitive disadvantage in the market, e.g., a small automobile manufacturer competing with the "big three." This method will work when management can convince the employees of the seriousness of the threat; however, the basic problem will return as soon as the outside threat is removed.

The second approach is an autocratic expression of management's right to make decisions and the employees' responsibility to accept this authority without reservation. The employee either will cooperate or will be fired. This approach, while apparently effective at times, has many dangers. Resistance to change can be manifested in so many ways—sabotage, absenteeism, and lowering production—that it is impossible for management to exert sufficient control over all these ramifications.

The third approach is generally the only constructive method of dealing with resistance to change, that is, to reduce the basic forces which cause resistance. It is this approach that is here discussed in more detail.

The Right Frame of Reference

Whether management is able to reduce resistance depends, first of all, on its attitude. The attitude of management must be one of genuine concern for the workers affected by the change, and this concern must be accompanied by an acceptance of the responsibility for the welfare of the workers who are affected. T. J. Watson, Jr., President of the International Business Machines Corporation, has stated that "an employee who has invested a share of his work life in a company's business and who performed competently in his job is entitled to every consideration we can give him should he find himself affected by technological advance." [22] IBM considers it a company responsibility to find new ways to use workers afflicted by technological unemployment.

Furthermore, management must be vigorous; it must furnish the kind of energetic leadership the employees of the company will respect and follow. A program of change that does not have management's wholehearted approval and support is doomed, and a program that is unsuccessful because of improper planning or administration becomes an obstacle to further change without resistance.

Planning the Change

A change should be based upon a careful study of all the factors in the situation, a logical and thorough program. The first test of any proposed change is to make sure the change is consistent with the objectives and policies of the company. A company should not decide to automate a portion of its operation merely because its management has been impressed by an advertising program or a newspaper announcement. Many companies have installed electronic computers without making a complete analysis beforehand only to be disappointed with the results. Companies can become fascinated by computers and other space-age gadgets which do not really increase efficiency but only upset a reasonably smooth and efficient operation. Prior to making any basic change in the systems, a complete analysis should be made of all factors. Certainly an analysis should include the economics of the change. It is advisable to consider any change in terms of outlay of capital and the meaning of this investment to the long-range growth and development of the company.

Every analysis must include the human factor. What will the change mean to the workers? Is the change compatible with the company's objectives? Are people available to plan the program of change? Is there a resource of people capable of accepting the new assignment of work? If not, is it possible to add qualified personnel from outside sources?

[22] "Automation's Impact," *Wall Street Journal,* Dec. 1, 1959, p. 1.

Administering the Plan

Effective administration is not possible without a feasible and logical plan. On the other hand, the best of plans will fail without successful administration. There are several factors that must not be overlooked in the effort to reduce resistance to change.

1. *Effective communications.* If anxiety and fear are to be overcome, it is necessary to develop an effective method of communication. People will not accept a change unless they can understand it; therefore they should be informed of the change that management intends to introduce, why the change is necessary, and what the change will mean to them. Every effort should be made to inform the workers of a contemplated change before erroneous information reaches them via the rumor mill. Furthermore, workers should be told both sides of the story. If the change will eliminate current grievances or discomforts, these points should be emphasized; however, if the change will cause some disadvantages to the workers, these disadvantages should also be reported and discussed.

2. *Timing the change.* It takes time to make a change in a large organization, and it is important to let the workers know the schedule of change. This serves several purposes. First, it informs the workers exactly when their part in the change will take place. Second, it points out the scope of the project in terms of the research and planning to be done, i.e., a well-thought-out project and not a change for the sake of change. Finally, a schedule serves as a time standard for those people planning the change. A proposed change may be "sold" on the basis of a trial period or test in actual practice. The objection to a tentative change is that it prolongs the unrest and allows those people opposed to the change an opportunity to sabotage it.

3. *Participation.* Another means used to gain acceptance to change is to have the workers participate in planning and administering the change. Advantages of this approach are that (1) the employees know the work situation and contribute many valuable suggestions; (2) the employees can express their viewpoints and establish a basis to aid communication; (3) the employees will work hard to introduce a new plan if they have been involved in its inception; (4) participation serves as an excellent program of indoctrination and education for the people who will operate the new plan.

4. *Training.* The first time a worker is exposed to a new, automated piece of equipment or an electronic computer, he is often aghast at the complexity of the situation. However, the same person, with proper instruction, can be talking the language of the computer in a relatively short period

of time. There are two important points to the process of training. First, the worker must be informed by management that they have confidence in him and that he will be given ample time and adequate training to master the new skill. Second, the training must be administered by competent and understanding people capable of motivating the worker to learn. The chance to receive additional training should be announced as a real opportunity for those workers who have qualified for this program.

5. *Changes of compensation.* Although we have come to recognize that economic incentives are not the only forces in gaining effective participation in the business organization, we should not completely discount the opportunities to use money as incentives to accept change. Generally speaking, automation, or the advent of automation and integrated data processing, will allow management to increase the compensation of those workers who are retained on the job because of the greatly increased output.

These points suggest a few ways in which management can reduce resistance to change and make the introduction of a new system successful while still maintaining effective organizational cooperation. However, it should be remembered that, in a business, people's reaction to a new situation is often based upon the conditioning they have undergone in the past; that is, an organization which has treated its employees fairly, which has a sound reputation for a regard for human and group rights, and whose employees are well aware of this will generally be able to make even the most dramatic kinds of changes successfully. The organization which has not had a favorable past employee-management relationship will generally find that even the most insignificant changes will meet great resistance.

It is necessary that management persist in using persuasion and influence on its workers for the acceptance of change, rather than attempt to bring to bear sheer power and authority. Along this line, we suggest that management will find it increasingly important to deal effectively with the human element in the organization if for no other object than to get effective participation and acceptance of change. We do not hold the view that management's job under the systems concept will become depersonalized or dehumanized; rather, management's function of dealing with the people within the organizational structure will become increasingly important. Furthermore, as the more routine, programmed management decision making is taken over through the newer techniques, management will have more time to spend on those nonprogrammed activities which are traditionally part of our social and human relationships.

SUMMARY

People do not resist systems per se. Rather, the normal human being seeks satisfactory systems of personal and interpersonal relationships which guide his activities. The problem arising from the use of systems concepts is not one of requiring man to change his total pattern of living and to adapt for the first time to the systematic organization of his behavior. Rather, the problem is primarily one of requiring man to change from old systems of work and interpersonal relationships to a new and different systems environment.

A dynamic society must expect and even welcome change; it is through change that better material and social welfare is achieved. Generally, it is not technological change which is resisted; resistance develops primarily because of changing sociological relations and because economic well-being is threatened. Resistance to change can take many forms, ranging from quitting, open opposition, and rebellion to apathy and indifference. Frequently, people do not manifest their resistance in a direct fashion, but it may influence their behavior in a variety of ways.

Two of the most dramatic areas of the impact of the systems concept upon people will be in the continuation of the trend toward automation of production operations and the further development of automatic information-decision systems. Automation is the best-known example of the application of the systems concept and will have its major impact upon factory operations. Automatic information-decision systems will cause a revolution in clerical and managerial functions. It will have two important phases: first, the use of electronic-data-processing equipment for processing vast quantities of information, and second, the application of computers to decision making. The first will affect the clerical worker, and the second, lower and middle management.

The successful administrator can foresee that the disruption and trauma resulting from the rapid application of systems techniques are potential sources of difficulty for both the individual and the organization. Because of the many ways of displaying resistance to change and the great difficulty of correcting resistance and moving back into a new, effective equilibrium, it is highly desirable for management to make every effort possible to effectuate the change properly and to facilitate adjustments to it. Giving adequate consideration to the problem of change, both technical and social, prior to its implementation is essential to long-run success.

It is management's function to determine some of the basic reasons for resistance to change and to meet these problems effectively. Increasingly,

American business has come to recognize that the changes resulting from automation, integrated data processing, and computers can be met by retraining, relocation, and readjustment of employees displaced by these innovations.

Over all, we are not pessimistic and do not think that the implementation of the systems concept will have major adverse effects upon individuals or society. Rather, we view the implementation of this concept as offering greater material rewards and providing more opportunities for gratifying personal and interpersonal relationships.

We now move forward into a new era in the handling of systems; an era in which man will base his understanding of control on the archetypal viable system of cerebral behavior, as he has already learned to base his knowledge of power on the archetypal energy system of hydrogen-helium fusion. I believe the outcome may be just as far-reaching and much more constructive. Let us hope that we can play our own parts with sufficient insight and sensitivity that we do not annihilate the very equilibria we seek to reinforce.

> S. Beer, *Below the Twilight Arch:*
> *A Mythology of Systems*

Part Four
THE FUTURE
Introduction

We have set forth the theoretical framework for a general systems theory and outlined its usefulness to the business organization in Part One. In Parts Two and Three, applications of the systems concept were presented, followed by ideas and techniques for implementation. In Part Four, we discuss the future.

The association of systems theory with management functions is a relatively new concept which has not had much theoretical or practical exploration. Because of widely diverse application of systems theory, it is difficult to discern a definite pattern of utilization based on past experience. So it will be in the future. We anticipate that business organizations will utilize *systems theory and concepts* more and more to integrate their operations. They really have no choice; they must if they are to survive in a dynamic environment and meet the growing demands which are being placed upon them.

Past experience with the systems concept provides a limited basis for evaluating future trends. Nevertheless, in Chapter 15 we shall "crystal-ball," using past experience and judgment to point up some of the most important applications, innovations, and problems arising from the utilization of the systems concept.

Chapter Fifteen
SYSTEMS MANAGEMENT IN THE FUTURE

A fundamental concept of this book is that business organizations are dynamic man-machine systems. We have developed a theoretical framework for applying systems concepts to planning, organizing, controlling, and communication—the primary management functions—and have illustrated various applications and techniques for the implementation of the systems concept. This chapter looks to the future. We shall investigate some of the possible applications of the systems concept and their effects upon management. Future sociocultural impacts of the systems concept will be explored also. The following topics will be discussed:

The Present Forecasts the Future
Future of the Systems Concept and Management
Patterns of Centralization-Decentralization
Management Selection and Training
Changing Job Satisfactions
Sociocultural Impacts of Systems Concept
Epilogue

THE PRESENT FORECASTS THE FUTURE

The systems concept views a business firm as an integrated whole, where each system, subsystem, and supporting subsystem is associated with the total operation. Its structure, therefore, is created by hundreds of systems arranged in hierarchical order. The output of the smallest system becomes input of the next level of systems, which in turn furnishes input for higher levels. A system was defined as "an array of components designed to accomplish a particular objective according to plan." There are three significant points in this definition: (1) there must be a design or an established arrangement of materials, energy, and information; (2) there must be a purpose or objective which the system is designed to accomplish; and (3) inputs of materials, energy, and information must be allocated according to plan.

Many examples of the application of the systems concept to business have been given. Weapon-system management, rhochrematics, automation, numerical control, and automatic-data-processing systems are examples of the application of this concept. Many techniques have been utilized in the implementation of this concept such as systems design, management science, and network analysis. In the future, all these applications and techniques for implementing the systems concept will have significant impacts upon the business firm.

There will be no drastic revolution in management functions or the business organization in order to encompass the systems concept. Rather, the adaptation of the systems concept to the business organizations has been and will continue to be an evolutionary process. Many of the examples cited throughout this book indicate that rudimentary applications of the systems concept occurred early in industrial history. Increasingly, managements have become more sophisticated in the use of this concept. This is the book's fundamental thesis: business organizations will utilize systems theory and concepts more and more to integrate their operations. They have no real choice if they are to survive in a dynamic environment and meet growing demands. Forrester has challenged management to move from rule-of-thumb processes to a systems approach.

> Management has been practiced, so far, as a skilled "art," lacking a foundation on a "science" of *integrated* underlying principles. The science of industrial systems is now rapidly evolving and should provide to management of the future a basis similar to that which physics provides to engineering. This does not imply "automatic management" but the reverse —a new managerial opportunity and challenge. The demands on the manager will become greater rather than less. In addition to experience, judgment and intuition, the manager will need a professional understanding of the dynamics of business growth and fluctuation. Adequate theory and technical methods now exist for "designing" more successful organizations. Lacking is the counterpart of an "applied science" and "practical engineering" for interpreting theory into results. As theory and methods are

extended and the gap between them and practicing management is closed, we can expect management and management education to take on the characteristics of a profession wherein skilled art is superimposed on a foundation structure of basic principles of economic growth and corporate evolution.[1]

If management is to make the transition from an art to a science successfully, it must take a "scientific" view of the enterprise—the view of the organization as a system of interrelated and interfunctioning parts. The systems concept is vital to effective application of scientific approaches in the business organization.

The dynamic changes affecting business in the future will result from a number of causal factors, such as general economic growth, advancing technology, and changing managerial concepts. The primary cause of these changes will not be the application of the systems concept alone. More likely, a combination of a number of forces, of which the systems application is a part, will create the evolutionary process.

There is a necessity for improving the managerial processes and effectiveness of business organizations. Business cannot depend upon the intuition of a few natural-born geniuses to operate economic enterprises effectively, but must establish principles and concepts of a discipline which can be taught and learned by future managers. As Drucker says:

> We know that these are urgent needs. In fact, the future of the free enterprise system may depend on our ability to make major managerial and entrepreneurial decisions more rationally, and to make more people capable of making and of understanding such decisions.[2]

It is difficult to make exact predictions as to the future applications and implications of the systems concept. The impact will be substantial and will be nearly universal. Analysis of past experience and evaluation of current trends point to some of the most important future applications, innovations, and problems arising from the use of the systems concept. We shall look first at the way in which the systems concept will affect the business organization internally. Then we shall evaluate some of the broader impacts which the systems concept will have upon our total society.

FUTURE OF THE SYSTEMS CONCEPT AND MANAGEMENT

Within the past fifteen years, with the accelerated application of this concept, there have been dramatic changes. Automation, by increasing

[1] Jay W. Forrester, *Management and Management Science,* MIT, School of Industrial Management, Memorandum D-48, June 1, 1959, p. 1.

[2] Peter F. Drucker, "Potentials of Management Science," *Harvard Business Review,* January–February, 1959, p. 148.

productivity and decreasing labor input, has had a significant impact upon many industries. Automatic-data-processing installations in the office have fostered wholesale changes in the white-collar sphere. Nor are the service industries free from the application of the systems concept. For example, a number of banks have established an automatic system for the processing of customer needs which replaces the teller's cage. This system, called the Bankograph, speeds up the transactions with customers and performs the functions more accurately and thoroughly than could be done by the individual teller. When this subsystem is tied into the over-all system, which includes the behind-the-scenes data-processing system performing operations such as check sorting and bookkeeping, there is a complete application of the systems concept to a service industry.[3] This example would seem to bear out Simon's statement that "the business organization in 1985 will be a highly automated man-machine system, and the nature of management will surely be conditioned by the character of the system being managed." [4]

When these dramatic changes occur we shall see many physical manifestations of change. However, of even greater importance will be the changing cultural and value systems within the business organization as it adapts to the systems concept. As Anshen says:

> Within the corporation, between the corporation and its national environment, and vis-à-vis the world around us, tomorrow's managers will face new challenges, new problems, and vast new opportunities. At each level, we see a world of dynamic change. At each level the manager must cope increasingly with new demands placed upon him and on his corporation by the diverse groups in his organization and in the society which provides his environment.[5]

In the discussion to follow on the impact of the systems concept, we shall discuss some of the more important effects on the managerial functions.

Impact on Planning Function

Under the systems concept, planning occurs at three different levels: (1) master planning for the establishment of goals, objectives, and broad policies, (2) resource-allocation planning for the project and facilitating systems, and (3) operations planning for each of the project systems. A substantial part of planning involves discovering and defining problem areas and then obtaining the necessary information prior to making the

[3] *The Wall Street Journal,* Feb. 7, 1962, p. 13.

[4] Herbert A. Simon, "The Corporation: Will It Be Managed by Machines?" in Melvin Anshen and George L. Bach (eds.), *Management and Corporation 1985,* McGraw-Hill Book Company, Inc., New York, 1960, p. 18.

[5] Melvin Anshen, "Management and Change," in *ibid.,* p. 238.

final decision. The extent to which the input or variables can be quantified determines how well structured or routine the problem is. Generally, there are significant differences in the ability to structure or quantify the planning process at these three levels.

Master planning, which includes establishment of broad goals, objectives, and policies, is usually unstructured. Many of the variables are unknown or uncertain. It is difficult to quantify them and to program the problems for automatic solutions via computers. Imagination and creative thinking are required. It is an innovative process and requires a relatively unstructured frame of reference which is typical of human processes. Although important strides have been made in heuristic programming of computers, there are major limitations on how far computers can assume the functions of decision making for ill-structured, nonroutine, managerial decision making. Even though it may be technically feasible to program a computer to make these decisions, it will still be a considerable time before it will be economically feasible to do so. The rate of substitution of the computer for the human mental process would depend upon the relative economic advantages, including supply and demand factors, of the computer versus the human decision process. The situation was summarized neatly in the remark of an airline pilot who, when asked if he worried about being replaced by electronic guidance systems, replied, "No. Where can you get a nonlinear servo-mechanism which reproduces itself for $1000 a month?" [6]

The systems concept at this level provides a rational process by which the manager can think in terms of the total system and the integration of subsystems activities toward the accomplishment of goals and objectives, including the organization's niche in the larger competitive and environmental systems.

The next level of planning, establishing the project and facilitating systems, also would be initiated by the master planning council but would be carried out by the resource-allocation and operating councils. In this planning it will be possible to quantify much of the informational input and to utilize automatic-data-processing and decision systems. Nonquantifiable information inputs also have to be considered.

The third level of planning, day-to-day operations within each system, is the one which most easily could be programmed for automatic decision systems. A few examples of typical problems calling for managerial decisions are:

1. Scheduling of over-all operations
2. Scheduling of work loads on machines

[6] Herbet A. Simon, "Supplementary Comments," in George P. Schultz and Thomas L. Whistler (eds.), *Management Organization and the Computer*, Free Press, Glencoe, Ill., 1960, p. 63.

3. Allocation of personnel to various functions
4. Inventory planning and control
5. Material and information flows

These are the types of managerial decisions which typically are made at the lower or middle management levels. Management science and the computer have had their greatest success in programming such decisions. Their greatest impact in the near future will continue to be at the lower management decision-making level. Even here, however, we do not expect a complete take-over of the managerial decision making by the computer. There are many types of decisions which can be made more economically and effectively by man than by a programmed computer. The orbital trips by the astronauts have shown that man can function in a strange environment. Recognition that he can make decisions and perform effectively in space has changed ideas about the relative role of man and machine. On the basis of man's successful experience in space, future, more elaborate ventures call for a much greater role for man and his decision-making abilities.

In the future, the planning and innovating functions will be taken over more and more by top management with the support of programmers and systems experts. The newer technologies of automation and data-processing systems require a heavy investment which commits an organization to a large capital outlay and heavy fixed expenditures for long periods of time. There will be more emphasis on future environmental factors such as political and economic influences. Planning will become more systematic and will require the coordination of the efforts of many specialists. The implementation of long-range plans will introduce new rigidities into business systems. Therefore forecasting techniques will have to be improved.

Formal long-range planning will have a centralizing effect. Department or division personnel will still need to participate in the planning process by providing informational inputs. Centralization of planning is evident in the increased use of central staffs such as operations-research teams, market-research groups, product-development staffs, and long-range planning councils.

Generally, increased mechanization of routine planning will allow management to spend more time on unstructured, nonprogrammed decision making. The application of the systems concept to planning will mean more effective planning at the lower operating levels and also will provide more time for planning at upper managerial levels. Through the utilization of the systems concept, management will be relieved of much of the minute, diversionary informational inputs which clog the planning process.

Impact on Organizing Function

Adapting the business organization to the systems concept places emphasis on the integration of all activities for the accomplishment of over-all objectives, but also recognizes the importance of efficient sub-system performance. In the organizing function, the manager should understand that the business is not a number of isolated parts, but is a system; he must have knowledge of the relationship between the parts and be aware of their potential interactions. The business manager will have to bring these individual, often diverse, functions into an *integrated, organized system,* with all the parts working toward the common organizational goal. With increasing specialization, size, and complexities, the demands for application of the systems concept to the organizing function have increased rapidly over the past few decades and will be of even greater importance in the future.

Under the systems concept, the future business will be organized on three major levels. The first level is the master planning council, which is aided by financial, research and development, and market-research groups. The next level would have a resource-allocation council which would provide the facilities and manpower for the various systems. Operations would be broken down into two types: (1) the facilitating systems, which would produce a function or service rather than a finished product, and (2) the major project systems, which would be the operating systems and would provide for total integrated activity related to a particular product or service. Each operating system would be structured to direct its own inputs, control its own operations, and revise its own systems design as required.

One of the most important impacts of the systems concept in organizing would be to reduce the reliance upon traditional functional specialization and vertical hierarchy. The application of the systems concept requires the integration of effort relating to the performance of a particular operation on a horizontal basis. All activities relating to the accomplishment of a particular task must be planned, organized, and integrated together. This requires the breakdown of traditional organizational relationships wherein each function was performed separately. It was shown in Chapter 7, Weapon-system Management, for example, that application of this concept to complex weapon systems required the integration of all functions necessary for mission accomplishment. In order to meet the program requirements effectively, it was necessary to establish integrating offices or agencies within the military which would cut through the traditional functional organization structure of the military. The Navy's Special

Project Office for the Polaris program and the Air Force Systems Command are examples of these integrated agencies.

The need for application of the systems concept in organizing is not limited to the military. Jasinski points out the need for rethinking about organizational relationships under conditions of rapid technological change as follows:

> Traditional business organization runs on a vertical line, relying almost solely on superior-subordinate relationships. Orders and instructions go down the line; reports and requests go up the line. But technology, including both integrated data processing and integrated machine production, has developed on what might be called a horizontal plane; that is, the machine cuts across superior-subordinate relationships, affecting the jobs of people in different areas, departments, and work groups. Superimposing a strictly vertical organization structure on a technology which emphasizes horizontal and diagonal relationships can and does cause obvious difficulties.[7]

This problem of integrating functional activities toward the accomplishment of a program or project has been faced most typically by the advanced-technology industries where complex products are designed, developed, and manufactured to meet predetermined performance specifications. It is composed of the newer and expanding fields such as electronics, nucleonics, astronautics, avionics, and cyrogenics. These industries are being organized on a project or program basis, where the program manager's function is to create a product or system of advanced-technology hardware. Gaddis defines a project as follows:

> A project is an organization unit dedicated to the attainment of a goal —generally the successful completion of a developmental product on time, within budget, and in conformance with predetermined performance specifications.[8]

We anticipate that the project or program type of organization, integrated around particular objectives to be accomplished, will be one of the fundamental bases of organizing in the future. This will cause significant changes in organizational structures and relationships. For example, the traditional line-staff relationships which have evolved in most companies will no longer suffice. The line-staff concept tends to emphasize the performance of functional specialization by the staff, with the line providing the integration. As specialization increases, it becomes increasingly difficult for the

[7] Frank J. Jasinski, "Adapting Organization to New Technology," *Harvard Business Review,* January–February, 1959, p. 80.

[8] Paul O. Gaddis, "The Project Manager," *Harvard Business Review,* May–June, 1959, p. 89.

line to perform this integrative function. We anticipate that the program team concept will replace the line-staff as an organizational basis.[9]

The systems basis of organizing has the advantage of creating concrete and definite management authority and responsibility relationships for the performance of tasks. This is one of the great defects of the line-staff relationship: it is difficult to determine who is responsible for what. The systems basis of organizing, combined with better communication and information-flow processes, makes it possible to have more effective control within the organization over managerial performance.

Impact on the Control Function

Managerial control will be improved as a result of the application of the systems concept. There will be a better basis for determining authority and responsibility for performance of the various operations. This will minimize the problem of control which exists today: the inability to determine responsibility for deviation from the plan. Under the systems concept there will be improvements in the application of automatic data processing, management science, and other techniques of control and measurement. Not only will management know, through the feedback system, that the planned objective is not being met, it will also be able to determine what forces are causing deviation from the plan. Great improvement in the control function also will occur because of the advancements in communication networks and systems of information flow.

The systems concept also fosters a fundamental change in the control process. For the majority of business operations control has not been automatic. It has required active evaluation and appraisal by the next level of management in order to be effective. In the future, a substantial part of the control process, particularly for the more routine programmed activities, will be accomplished through the cybernetic mechanism, the automatic feedback of corrective information into the system when there is a deviation from the original plan or objective. The cybernetic concept of control will relieve the business manager of many of the problems of routine checking which exist in the business organization today. This will not necessarily displace management; rather, it will allow executives to spend more time on longer-range planning and on control over those activities which cannot be adapted to the cybernetic model. More effective planning and

---

[9] Gerald G. Fisch, in "Line-Staff Is Obsolete," *Harvard Business Review,* September–October, 1961, states that the line-staff organizational basis is unsatisfactory in today's complex industries. He suggests that this concept be replaced by the *functional-teamwork* concept. His functional-teamwork concept tends toward our systems concept, providing for the integration of all functions on a systematic basis in the accomplishment of goals and objectives.

organizing, using the systems concept, provides the key ingredients for more efficient control. Another vital element in the control process is an effective communications network for securing timely and useful information.

Impact on Communications

The several managerial functions of planning, organization, and control are inexorably interwoven by communications. Since a system, by definition, requires interrelationships among parts to constitute a composite whole, a communication system is necessary to provide information throughout the various subsystems. The term *information-decision system* is used to emphasize the fact that information developed should be required in the light of the decisions to be made throughout the organization. Drucker points out the importance of the information-decision system as follows:

> The new organization, whether an army or a business, is above all an information and decision system. Information, ideas, questions, flow from the outside environment as well as from people within. They not only have to be perceived and transmitted; the relevant has to be separated from the merely interesting. Then somebody has to make a decision which in turn has to flow back to the places where it can become effective action. Information and decision systems are around us everywhere; every living being is one, and so is every machine. But the organization is probably the most complex.[10]

As a result of growing organizational complexities, rapid technological advances, and a rapidly changing environment, many business organizations have faced difficulties in maintaining a flow of up-to-date information for decision making. Generally speaking, companies are not organized for optimal communication or information flow. Other forces, such as the desire to maintain a hierarchical form and the demands for specialization, have been dominant in the organizing process. The systems concept applied to communication and information processes requires that the organization give consideration to all sources of information which are important for decision making and control. This would include at least three information subsystems:

1. Environmental
2. Competitive
3. Internal

[10] Peter Drucker, *Landmarks of Tomorrow,* Harper & Brothers, New York, 1959, p. 92.

In the future, business organizations will recognize the need for effective processes for the accumulation, storage, and evaluation of information from these various subsystems. As Daniel points out:

> It is important in every case for management to *formalize* and *regularize* the collection, transmission, processing, and presentation of planning information; the data are too vital to be ignored or taken care of by an occasional "special study." It is no accident that many of the most successful companies in this country are characterized by well-developed planning information systems.[11]

A number of changes will improve the communication and information system of the future. Application of the systems concept to planning will provide more definite and precise long-range plans which can serve as the informational input for more detailed planning at lower operational levels. Also, the change in organizational relationships resulting from the application of the systems concept will provide a more clear-cut communications network. In current organizations, information often is lost in the channels of communication, or, in order to ensure that it reaches the right decision point or destination, great redundancy is introduced. With more clear-cut organizational relationships it will be possible to improve the information-decision system. Effective control will enable a business organization to minimize the accumulation, storage, and tabulation of irrelevant, erroneous, and inappropriate data. The ability to reduce static and increase meaningful informational input will be one of the contributions of the systems concept.

In recent years many new tools have been developed which provide more useful information for managerial planning and control. For example, the evolution of automatic-data-processing systems, the development of management science, and the opportunities to test effectiveness through simulation provide invaluable means for creating better information-decision systems in the future. Already the technology for improving information systems has advanced further than our conceptual ideas on how it can be put to use. As Evans and Hague state:

> But, oddly enough, the rapid advance of technology, the abundance of new computers and new techniques, and the tremendous changes in the capacity and potential of new computers, all have been so intriguing that planning for their use has lagged. Nor has it helped matters that computers have become so complex that the very job of selecting one over another has been made difficult, especially in the face of an implied threat of 24-hour obsolescence. As a result, the ability of the average company to utilize the

---

[11] D. Ronald Daniel, "Management Information Crisis," *Harvard Business Review,* September–October, 1961, p. 117.

new computers and techniques falls far short of the potential the computer has to process the information necessary to operate the system.[12]

This conceptual lag behind technological advances is transitional. Some of the more progressive companies devote more and more attention to the problems of developing an effective communication network and information-decision system.

PATTERNS OF CENTRALIZATION-DECENTRALIZATION

The prevailing tendency in American business for the past thirty years has been in the direction of decentralization of managerial decision making. In order to grow and to diversify into wider product lines, management saw the necessity of delegating authority and responsibility to lower operating levels. One of the major reasons for this decentralization was to ensure that the information and action were closely related.

It is currently argued by some that the application of the systems concept, automatic data processing, and more effective information-decision systems creates a growing trend toward recentralization of managerial decision making. Shultz and Whisler say:

> Our argument is that use of the high-speed computer and associated techniques, "information technology," will be a force for centralization of decision making, along with an expanded staff at the top levels and fewer jobs, with more highly programmed content, at lower levels in the management hierarchy.[13]

It is their view that top management has generally been forced into patterns of decentralization because of the lack of adequate information and control over lower operating levels. With better information, it is argued that it will be possible for management to recentralize decision making. Speed and flexibility will be feasible despite large size, and top management will not need to depend upon subordinates for judgmental and experience inputs. Ida Russakoff Hoos, in a two-year study of nineteen organizations in the San Francisco Bay area that had introduced electronic data processing, found that these innovations led to recentralization. She concluded:

> Analysis of the experience of San Francisco Bay Area firms reveals that EDP stimulates two distinct types of recentralization. One type relates to the integration of specific functions and affects primarily the internal organization of the company. The other involves regrouping of entire units of the operation and causes sweeping changes of external structure as

---

[12] Marshall K. Evans and Lou R. Hague, "Master Plan for Information Systems," *Harvard Business Review*, January–February, 1962, pp. 92–93.

[13] George P. Shultz and Thomas L. Whistler (eds.), *Management Organization and the Computer*, Free Press, Glencoe, Ill., 1960, p. 28.

well. Both types lead to shrinking of job opportunities, downgrading, and so on.[14]

On the other hand, the decentralized model is much more than a mechanistic impersonal process. Its primary purpose has been to develop creativeness and adaptiveness on the part of management at lower organizational levels and to provide a basis for growth and training of executive personnel. It has also been a means of relating the individual to the organization, increasing both the individual's morale and organizational productivity through participative processes. For a firm that is dedicated to the concept of decentralization, the improvements in the information-decision system can strengthen the decentralization process. Burlingame supports this argument by saying:

> Counter to many arguments, the anticipated advances in information technology, in my opinion, can *strengthen* decentralization in those businesses that have adopted it and will encourage *more* management to experiment and to operate in accordance with the decentralization philosophy.[15]

This viewpoint certainly has merit. The information-decision system will allow more accurate information flow in all directions, including top down, bottom up, and horizontally. With a more efficient communication system, the lower-level managers can be provided with adequate information to make more effective decisions. Furthermore, it is recognized that decentralization will not be effective unless there are adequate controls to ensure that the decisions do not deviate too far from top-management desires. A well-defined information-decision system will provide for improvements in the control mechanism and will allow top management to assign authority and responsibility for decision making to lower operating levels.

Furthermore, under the systems concept, top management will be primarily responsible for the establishment of broad goals and objectives of the organization and for the allocation of resources to the individual project systems. The directors of these facilitating or project systems will have a substantial degree of autonomy in their individual operations. They will receive inputs of goals and parameters from the master planning council. They will be provided with full information, which will allow them to make decisions for the effective, profitable operation of their individual facilitating or project system. Thus it is likely that the systems concept will provide a basis for more effective and efficient decentralization

[14] Ida Russakoff Hoos, "When the Computer Takes Over the Office," *Harvard Business Review,* July–August, 1960, p. 106.

[15] John F. Burlingame, "Information Technology and Decentralization," *Harvard Business Review,* November–December, 1961, p. 124.

of decisions down to the project level. To be sure, there will be some inputs which must be determined at a higher organizational level, particularly those inputs which may create conflict in the operation of a given project system with other project systems. At these points of interaction, the decision making will have to be accomplished at the next management level. However, a wide latitude for decision making would remain within the project system.

MANAGEMENT SELECTION AND TRAINING

As a result of the application of the systems concept, dramatic changes may take place in the selection and training of executives. First, and perhaps most important, will be the change in the way the executive conceptualizes his function. As Simon points out:

> I suppose that managers will be called on, as automation proceeds, for more of what might be described as "systems thinking." They will need, to work effectively, to understand their organizations as large and complex dynamic systems involving various sorts of man-machine and machine-machine interactions. For this reason, persons trained in fields like servomechanism engineering or mathematical economics, accustomed to dynamic systems of these kinds, and possessing conceptual tools for understanding them, may have some advantage, at least initially, in operating in the new world. Since no coherent science of complex systems exists today, universities and engineering schools are understandably perplexed as to what kinds of training will prepare their present students for this world.[16]

Top management will have to deal with longer-range planning and will have to have a better perception of how the business system interacts with the competitive and environmental systems. Training for this broad perspective and conceptualizing skills will provide a vital challenge for the business organization and for the university. Training for the programmers and specialists in application of the various techniques of implementing the systems concept—mathematical models, flow charting, and computer technology—will not be nearly as difficult as training for top management. These specialists can be trained without having the broad perspective and experience of top management. However, this very specialization presents problems for management development. Staff people will have skills to deal with specialized problems. At the same time, they will not have the broad conceptual skills and wisdom necessary for the top-management positions. How will the business organization train its future top executives? It is likely that it will come to rely less upon internal training for top-

[16] Herbet A. Simon, "The Corporation: Will It Be Managed by Machines?" in Melvin Anshen and George L. Bach (eds.), *Management and Corporations 1985,* McGraw-Hill Book Company, Inc., New York, 1960, p. 52.

management positions and more upon external training sources, such as universities and other training institutions which are geared to provide the broader viewpoint.

Even the lower supervisory levels will be affected by applications of the systems concept. In a study of the effects of a change-over to electronic-data-processing equipment in a light and power company, Mann and Williams reported that the pressures of converting from the old system to the new demanded a substantial change on the part of supervisors. It was necessary for them to develop a much broader view of the entire system. Mann and Williams said:

> As the organization moved farther into the conversion period, the duties of first-line supervisors became more involved and increasing demands were made of this level. The change-over provided a thorough test of their abilities as well as those of higher management. When change is gradual, supervisors, like employees, become thoroughly familiar with that part of the total work process for which they are immediately responsible. With such a drastic change it was necessary for supervisors to develop a much broader view of the system.[17]

All levels of management will feel the impact of the application of the systems concept. This will not mean a downgrading of management skills. It will be more difficult to operate in an environment where the manager is required to have the broad approach and to give consideration to the total system operation. Even the lower-level management will have to recognize the interaction between performance in their subsystems and in other subsystems throughout the organization.

Changing Occupational Levels

As a result of the application of the systems concept, changes will occur in the occupational requirements of the business. Automation will eliminate those routine activities which can be performed most effectively by machine. The trend in the reduction of direct factory workers in proportion to total employees will continue. They will be replaced by specialists. The business firm of the future will have a growing proportion of people with technical and engineering skills. Even such areas as plant maintenance will require personnel with a high level of skill and qualification.

The introduction of a number of specialists with an orientation toward the performance of their specialized skills may create major problems for

[17] Floyd C. Mann, and Lawrence K. Williams, "Observations on Dynamics of a Change to Electronic Data-processing Equipment," *Administrative Science Quarterly*, September, 1960, p. 230.

the top management. Merging the interest of these very diversified groups with organizational objectives may be one of the motivational problems of the future. Thompson has pointed out the conflict in the modern organization between the technical specialist and general management as follows:

> The combination in modern bureaucracy of technological specialization and the older institution of hierarchy has produced an organizationally determined pattern of conflict in modern organization caused ultimately by the growing gap between authority and perceptions of technical needs, these two elements of organization being largely now in the hands of two separate sets of officials.[18]

CHANGING JOB SATISFACTIONS

Adapting to the systems concept will undoubtedly have significant organizational impacts and will greatly affect job satisfaction for various employees. The relationships will be particularly upsetting during the transition period. With the acceleration of formalization within the organization, work becomes more rationalized and rules and regulations are substituted for individual decision making. With the programming of decision making inherent in the application of the systems concept, there will be changes in the level and status of the various employees and managers within the organization. Under the systems concept many of the functional specialists may find that their operations have been subsumed in a project approach. Mann and Williams found that:

> In this study the elimination of these status positions and the further restrictions of the areas of employee decision making was a severe blow to men in these status positions. Employees of long service were stripped of many of their responsibilities at a time when the right and ability to make such decisions was the principal reward of the job.[19]

If the prognostication that many of middle management's functions can be programmed holds true, then there will be a severe decline in work satisfaction. Michael suggests:

> Middle management is the group in the society with the most intensive emotional drive for success and status. Their family and social life is molded by these needs, as the endless literature on life in suburbia and exurbia demonstrate. They stand to be deeply disturbed by the threat and fact of their replacement by machines. One wonders what the threat will do to the ambitions of those who will be students and who, as followers of

[18] Victor A. Thompson, "Hierarchy, Specialization, and Organizational Conflict," *Administrative Science Quarterly,* March, 1961, p. 485.

[19] Mann and Williams, *op. cit.,* p. 251.

one of the pervasive American dreams, will have aspired to the role of middle management "on the way up." [20]

We do not think that such dire predictions will come true. While a good part of structured decision making may be reduced under the application of the systems concept, there will be a substantial need for middle management to think in a broader systems context. While their routine activities may be structured, they will operate their subsystems with a degree of autonomy, and will be required to integrate their activities with the other subsystems in the organization. Furthermore, while their functions of dealing with the mechanistic aspects of the operation may be reduced, they will be required to concentrate increasingly on the human problems.

It is quite likely that the role of middle management will tend to become even more unstructured than today. There will be no decline in the opportunities for job satisfaction and status on the part of the middle and higher levels of management. However, it is true that for the worker and first-line supervisor, whose functions are apt to be highly structured, the opportunities for job satisfaction and status may be diminished. As a result of the application of the systems concept, there will be increase in productivity with decrease in working hours. The worker may have to substitute increased leisure time for job status and satisfaction. In the future the worker's life will be less oriented toward his work activities and more toward his activities external to the busines organization.

These, then, are just a few of the possible impacts of the systems concept upon the business organization in the future. Our society has just begun to perceive the dynamics of the application of this concept. It is likely that many more dramatic changes will occur. These changes will not happen immediately, nor at any one stage in time. Rather, they will occur over an extended period of time, with some companies and industries affected more rapidly than others. In addition to the consequences of the application of the systems concept to the business firm itself, there will be significant effects upon the total society.

SOCIOCULTURAL IMPACTS OF SYSTEMS CONCEPT

Since the industrial revolution large-scale business enterprises have been a tremendous force in shaping the environment. They have been the primary vehicle for increasing the standard of living and have provided a major outlet for ingenuity and creativity. With the application of the systems concept through such things as automation, automatic data processing, and information-decision systems, there will be important changes in the

[20] Donald N. Michael, *Cybernation: The Silent Conquest*, The Center for the Study of Democratic Institutions, Santa Barbara, Calif., 1962, p. 19.

role of the business enterprise in its environment and in the satisfactions it can provide participants.

The impact of the systems concept upon our society will take many forms. The future effects of automation and automatic information-decision systems upon levels of employment, skill requirements, and types of occupations have been discussed. We also looked at the problems of human resistance to change and of retraining workers displaced by these applications. These certainly will present major social issues, which will have to be met by effective cooperation of business, local, and state governmental agencies and the Federal government.

The systems concept will be one of the dynamic forces in the future leading to increased productivity and greater abundance. We are already showing signs of trouble adjusting to abundance. As scarcity is banished or partially eliminated in a society, the old system of beliefs may become outmoded. These "concepts of the conventional wisdom," as Galbraith calls them, do not recognize the dynamic changes that have required new conceptual foundations of thought.[21] In a society that has made rapid advancements, where a small proportion of the population is engaged in the direct production of goods and where the basic necessities and requirements have been met for the great majority, the concepts based upon scarcity are not satisfactory. Ferry points out some of the major problems resulting from continuing rapid advancements in technology and productivity as follows:

> The United States is advancing rapidly into a national economy in which there will not be enough jobs of the conventional kind to go around. The acceleration of technology is responsible. A social and political crisis will be the result. Substitutes for such presently accepted goals as full employment will have to be found. Fresh definitions of the conceptions of work, leisure, abundance, and scarcity are needed. Economic theories adequate to an industrial revolution are not good enough for the conditions of the scientific revolution.[22]

One of the results of the broad impact of the systems concept, the increasing productivity and abundance, will lead to the reproportioning of the national effort. With greater productivity and abundance a smaller proportion of national effort will be geared to the production of physical goods. A greater part of the resources will be directed toward increased services and other social benefits. There will be greater resources allocated to education, medical research, urban redevelopment, recreational facilities, and travel and leisure activities.

[21] John Kenneth Galbraith, *The Affluent Society,* Houghton Mifflin Company, Boston, 1958, pp. 7–20.

[22] W. H. Ferry, "Caught on the Horn of Plenty," *Bulletin of the Center for the Study of Democratic Institutions,* Santa Barbara, Calif., January, 1962, p. 1.

Increasing productivity will lead to a further decline in the number of hours of work. Shorter working hours will be an alternative to technological unemployment. The new leisure will have important effects upon many of our activities, although some of these effects are not clearly discernible. Denney suggests:

> One of the results of this gradual change in the nature of work and the work week is that leisure begins to turn up in unexpected times and places where it is hard to recognize as leisure and, therefore, is hard for individuals and society to deal with in any but improvised, arbitrary and stereotyped ways.[23]

Thus leisure can be seen in the time for coffee breaks or socializing in the office or factory. Opportunities for attending conventions, conferences, or to work on special projects are other examples of increasing organizational leisure. There will also be the more direct and obvious results such as increased vacation periods, shorter work days, and fewer days worked per week. In these cases, the leisure-time activities will take place external to the business firm. However, it is possible that the business firm will find itself taking some responsibilities for workers' off-the-job leisure activities through a continuation of the trend toward company-sponsored athletic, recreational, social, and other activities.

But the impact of the increasing leisure will certainly not be limited to the business firm. Even though business is the prime cause of the increased leisure time, other agencies will be important in filling man's activities. These outside agencies, including education institutions, churches, governments, and many other formal and informal groups, will become more important to man's leisure activities. As his work life becomes a smaller part of his total life, he will seek fulfillment of his needs for status, satisfactory social relationships, and self-realization outside his work life. Leisure will have a more important role in man's self-fulfillment.

The Conflict of Cultures

Throughout this book we have emphasized the importance and dynamic nature of the changes in our society. Certaintly, the systems concept and its application will be one of the most dynamic forces creating innovations within the business organization. Furthermore, these forces will not be isolated, but will have an effect upon society as a whole. The very roots and structure of our social system will be subject to innovation and change. As Anshen has suggested:

[23] Reuel Denny, "The Leisure Society," *Harvard Business Review,* May–June, 1959, p. 47.

Whenever we look in the years ahead we see dynamic evolution. This unceasing challenge to the *status quo* will test the survival capacity of our institutions. Within a corporation, a new technology of decision making is beginning to raise critical questions about adaptation in the organizational structure and in the functions of managers. It poses equally critical questions about the effect on human beings of a new order of man-machine relationships. Outside the corporation new economic and social requirements will appear on both the national and world scene. How creatively management and corporations respond to these demands will determine the character of our future business institutions. More importantly, it will determine the performance of our society and the durability of a civilization built on economic freedom and political democracy.[24]

Business management has contributed importantly toward material betterment. The systems concept will augment this trend. Yet this will not be enough. As Drucker points out:

> And yet—as in our philosophical systems and our social and political institutions—our ideas, our methods, our preoccupations, our rhetoric, are still those of an earlier age which is fast becoming obsolete. In respect to the human situation we are also on a voyage of transition. We are still trying to steer by the old landmarks, even though we already sail new, uncharted seas.[25]

The material changes in man's culture through advancing technology will continue to have important effects upon man. The question which both Drucker and Anshen are asking is whether or not man's nonmaterial culture—his system of beliefs, systems of communications, and modes of conduct—will be able to remain in equilibrium. Will the so-called cultural lag—the discrepancy between material and nonmaterial cultures—grow greater? The conflict of these two cultures, the material and the nonmaterial, will remain basic to human society. The satisfactory resolution of this conflict will remain one of the key problems for human society in the future.

EPILOGUE

In discussing various approaches to the study of management, Koontz states:

> From the orderly analysis of management at the shop-room level by Frederick Taylor and the reflective distillation of experience from the general management point of view by Henri Fayol, we now see these and other early beginnings overgrown and entangled by a jungle of approaches and approaches to management theory.

[24] Anshen and Bach, *op. cit.*, pp. 199–200.
[25] Drucker, *Landmarks of Tomorrow*, p. 257.

There are the behavioralists, born of the Hawthorne experiments and the awakened interest in human relations during the 1930's and 1940's, who see management as a complex of interpersonal relationships and the basis of management theory the tentative tenets of the new and undeveloped science of psychology. There are also those who see management theory as simply a manifestation of the institutional and cultural aspects of sociology. Still others, observing that the central core of management is decision-making, branch in all directions from this core to encompass everything in organization life. Then, there are mathematicians who think of management primarily as an exercise in logical relationships expressed in symbols and the omnipresent and ever revered model. But the entanglement of growth reaches its ultimate when the study of management is regarded as a study of one of a number of systems and subsystems, with an understandable tendency for the researcher to be dissatisfied until he has encompassed the entire physical and cultural universe as a management system.[26]

We plead guilty as charged, for we have shown how the management process can be applied to the business organization as a system. We also suggest that recognition should be given to systems of systems, leading ultimately to the entire physiocultural universe. This latter aspect was portrayed in the prologue to Part Two:

> All philosophers find
> Some favorite system to their mind
> In every point to make it fit
> Will force all nature to submit.

The point that must be emphasized is that the systems concept is primarily a "way of thinking," a mental frame of reference which can be utilized by management in performing its traditional primary functions of planning, organizing, and controlling operations. These activities have been and will continue to be fundamental functions in the management process. The systems concept provides a new framework for carrying out and integrating these activities.

However, the systems concept does not provide a ten-step algorithm, the application of which ensures success. It is not a clearly defined bundle of techniques and is not limited in application to particular industries or functional departments. It is not only automation of the factory or automatic data processing in the office. Rather, it is a broad frame of reference which views the organization as a total system and seeks to achieve the objectives of that system by clearly understanding and relating subsystem performance to the whole. In the future, the systems concept as a "way of

[26] Harold Koontz, "The Management Theory Jungle," *Journal of the Academy of Management,* December, 1961, pp. 174–175.

thinking" will become more and more pervasive in the managerial process.

So far the primary reasons for the emergence and application of the systems concept have been the advancing technologies and increasing industrial complexities within our society. These forces will continue, possibly accelerating in the future. The systems concept will allow more effective adaptation to changing scientific and technological environments.

Rapid changes over the past two decades have forced managers to reevaluate their ideas regarding the role of the business organization as a system within society as a whole. And so it will be in the future. One of the fundamental theses of this book has been that the business organization as a system must be considered as a subsystem of a larger environmental system. Even industry or interindustry systems must be recognized as subelements of the economic system. And the economic system should be regarded as a part of society in general.

Within business organizations the application of the systems concept will foster significant changes in the managerial process of planning, organizing, and controlling. The systems concept, hopefully, can provide a means of "getting out of the rut."

> For men are prone to go it blind
> Along the calf-path of the mind,
> And work away from sun to sun
> To do what other men have done.

One of the major changes within business organizations will be the breakdown of traditional functional specialization geared to optimizing performance of particular departments. There will be growing use of organizational structures designed around projects and information-decision systems. The systems concept calls for integration, into a separate organizational system, of activities related to particular projects or programs. This approach currently is being implemented in some of the more advanced technology industries. The business organization can no longer be thought of as a functional division of activities such as sales, finance, production, and personnel. Its breakdown into separate functional areas has been an artificial organizational device, necessary in light of existing conditions. Management-science techniques, computer simulation approaches, and information-decision systems are just a few of the tools which will make it possible for management to visualize the firm as a total system. This would not have been possible two decades ago; it is currently becoming feasible for some companies and will become a primary basis for organizing in the future.

The application of the systems concept to the business organization should not be viewed as a dehumanizing force. Rather, its application will provide greater opportunities for human expression and self-fulfillment. Concerted application of the systems concept will continue the trend whereby man has been able to create known and systematic relationships out of the seeming chaos of his natural environment. A careful scrutiny, on the other hand, reveals the generally systematic relationships in nature. This would seem to suggest the need to recognize natural man-machine systems arranged to accomplish specific goals and objectives. The systems concept, as applied in the business organization, will release man's physical and mental processes from the more difficult and mundane activities in order that he may direct his efforts toward higher-level, creative, and rewarding tasks.

The writers against religion, whilst
they oppose every system, are wisely
careful never to set up any of their own.

Edmund Burke, *A Vindication of
National Society*

BIBLIOGRAPHY

Ackoff, Russell L. (ed.): *Progress in Operations Research,* John Wiley & Sons, Inc., New York, 1961.

Air Force Ballistic Missile Management, H.R. 324, 87th Cong., 1st Sess., 1961.

Alberts, Warren E.: "Report of the Eighth AIIE National Conference on the System Simulation Symposium," *Journal of Industrial Engineering,* November–December, 1957, pp. 366–369.

Allison, Harry: "Framework for Marketing Strategy," *California Management Review,* Fall, 1961, pp. 74–95.

American Management Association: *Establishing an Integrated Data-processing System,* Special Report 11, New York, 1956.

————: *Systems Planning and Control,* Special Report 12, New York, 1956.

Anshen, Melvin: "The Manager and the Black Box," *Harvard Business Review,* November–December, 1960, pp. 85–92.

———— and George L. Bach (eds.): *Management and Corporations 1985,* McGraw-Hill Book Company, Inc., New York, 1960.

Argyris, Chris: *Personality and Organization,* Harper & Brothers, New York, 1957.

————: *Understanding Organizational Behavior,* The Dorsey Press, Inc., Homewood, Ill., 1960.

Arrow, Kenneth J.: "Decision Theory and Operations Research," *Operations Research,* December, 1957, pp. 764–765.

Ashburn, Anderson: "Detroit Automation," *Annals of the American Academy of Political and Social Science,* March, 1962, pp. 21–28.

Ashby, W. Ross: *An Introduction to Cybernetics,* John Wiley & Sons, Inc., New York, 1956.

Authorizing Establishment of Bureau of Naval Weapons, Report from the Senate Committee on Armed Services, 86th Cong., 1st Sess., 1959.

Automation and Technological Change, Hearings before the Subcommittee on Economic Stabilization of the Joint Committee on the Economic Report, 84th Cong., 1st Sess., 1955.

Avots, Ivars: "The Management Side of PERT," *California Management Review,* Winter, 1962, pp. 16–27.

Babcock, C. Morton: "A Dynamic Theory of Communication," *Journal of Communications,* May, 1952, pp. 64–68.

Balderston, F. E.: "Communication Networks in Intermediate Markets," *Management Science,* January, 1958, pp. 154–171.

Barish, Norman N.: *Systems Analysis for Effective Administration,* Funk & Wagnalls Company, New York, 1951.

Becker, Esther R., and Eugene F. Murphy: *The Office in Transition,* Harper & Brothers, New York, 1957.

Beer, Stafford: *Cybernetics and Management,* John Wiley & Sons, Inc., New York, 1959.

Bekker, John A.: "Automation: Its Impact on Management," *Advanced Management,* December, 1959, pp. 20–24.

Bell, William D.: *A Management Guide to Electronic Computers,* McGraw-Hill Book Company, Inc., New York, 1957.

Bellman, Richard: *Dynamic Programming,* Princeton University Press, Princeton, N.J., 1957.

Bennis, Warren G.: "Leadership Theory and Administrative Behavior," *Administrative Science Quarterly,* December, 1959, pp. 259–301.

———, Kenneth D. Benne, and Robert Chin (eds.): *The Planning of Change,* Holt, Rinehart and Winston, Inc., New York, 1961.

Bentley, W. H.: "Management Aspects of Numerical Control," *Automation,* October, 1960, pp. 64–70.

Blau, Peter: *Bureaucracy in Modern Society,* Random House, Inc., New York, 1956.

Boulding, Kenneth E.: "General Systems Theory: The Skeleton of Science," *Management Science,* April, 1956, pp. 197–208.

——— and W. Allen Spivey: *Linear Programming and the Theory of the Firm,* The Macmillan Company, New York, 1960.

Bowman, Edward H., and Robert B. Fetter: *Analysis for Production Management,* Richard D. Irwin, Inc., Homewood, Ill., 1957.

——— and ———: *Analyses of Industrial Operations,* Richard D. Irwin, Inc., Homewood, Ill., 1959.

Brewer, Stanley H.: *Rhochrematics: A Scientific Approach to the Material Flows,* University of Washington, Bureau of Business Research, Seattle, 1960.

Brewer, Stanley H., and James Rosenzweig: "Rhochrematics and Organizational Adjustments," *California Management Review,* Spring, 1961, pp. 52–71.

Bright, James R.: *Automation and Management,* Harvard University, Graduate School of Business Administration, Boston, 1958.

———: "Does Automation Raise Skill Requirements?" *Harvard Business Review,* July–August, 1958, pp. 85–98.

Bromfield, George: *Numerical Control for Machining Warped Surfaces,* MIT, Servomechanisms Laboratory, Engineering Report 14, D.I.C. 6873, Cambridge, Mass., 1956.

Bross, Irwin D. J.: *Design for Decision,* The Macmillan Company, New York, 1953.

Bruner, William G., Jr.: "Systems Design: A Broader Role of Industrial Engineering," *Journal of Industrial Engineering,* March–April, 1962, pp. 91–93.

Burlingame, John F.: "Information Technology and Decentralization," *Harvard Business Review,* November–December, 1961, pp. 121–126.

Caples, William G.: "Automation in Theory and Practice," *Business Topics,* Autumn, 1960, pp. 7–19.

Carasso, Max: "Total Systems," *Systems and Procedures,* November, 1959, pp. 22–27.

Chapin, Ned: *An Introduction to Automatic Computers,* D. Van Nostrand Company, Inc., Princeton, N.J., 1957.

Chapple, Eliot D., and Leonard R. Sayles: "The Man, the Job, and the Organization," *Personnel,* March–April, 1958, pp. 8–20.

———— and ————: *The Measurement of Management,* The Macmillan Company, New York, 1961.

Chase, Stuart: *The Proper Study of Mankind,* Harper & Brothers, New York, 1956.

Chernoff, Herman, and Lincoln E. Moses: *Elementary Decision Theory,* John Wiley & Sons, Inc., New York, 1959.

Churchman, C. West: *Prediction and Optimal Decision,* Prentice-Hall, Inc., Englewood Cliffs, N.J., 1961.

————, Russell L. Ackoff, and E. Leonard Arnoff: *Introduction to Operations Research,* John Wiley & Sons, Inc., New York, 1957.

Coch, Lester, and John R. P. French, Jr.: "Overcoming Resistance to Change," in Dorwin Cartwright and Alvin Zander (eds.), *Group Dynamics,* Row, Peterson & Company, Evanston, Ill., 1953 and 1960.

Conway, B., J. Gibbons, and D. E. Watts: *Business Experience with Electronic Computers,* Controllers Institute Research Foundation, Inc., New York, 1959.

Cooper, W. W.: "Some Implications of the Newer Analytic Approaches to Management," *California Management Review,* Fall, 1961, pp. 51–64.

Culbertson, James T.: "Automation: Its Evolution and Future Direction," *Computers and Automation,* November, 1960, pp. 14–18, and December, 1960, pp. 34–36.

Cyert, R. M., E. A. Feigenbaum, and J. G. March: "Models in a Behavioral Theory of the Firm," *Behavioral Science,* April, 1959, pp. 81–95.

Dahl, Robert A., Mason Haire, and Paul F. Lazarsfeld: *Social Science Research on Business: Product and Potential,* Columbia University Press, New York, 1959.

———— and Charles E. Lindblom: *Politics, Economics and Welfare,* Harper & Brothers, New York, 1953.

Dalton, Melville: *Men Who Manage,* John Wiley & Sons, Inc., New York, 1959.

Daniel, D. Ronald: "Management Information Crisis," *Harvard Business Review,* September–October, 1961, pp. 111–121.

Dennis, Jack B.: *Mathematical Programming and Electrical Networks,* MIT, The Technical Press, Cambridge, Mass., and John Wiley & Sons, Inc., New York, 1959.

Design, Development and Evaluation of a Numerically Controlled Milling Machine, MIT, Servomechanisms Laboratory, Final Report D.I.C. 6875, Cambridge, Mass., 1956.

Deutsch, Karl W.: "Mechanism, Teleology, and Mind," *Philosophy and Phenomenological Research,* December, 1951, pp. 185–222.

————: "On Communication Models in the Social Sciences," *Public Opinion Quarterly,* Fall, 1952, pp. 356–380.

Diebold, John: *Automation: The Advent of the Automatic Factory,* D. Van Nostrand Company, Inc., Princeton, N.J., 1952.

————: "Automation: The New Technology," *Harvard Business Review,* November–December, 1953, pp. 63–71.

————: "The Application of Information Technology," *Annals of the American Academy of Political and Social Science,* March, 1962, pp. 38–45.

Dorfman, Robert: "Operations Research," *American Economic Review,* September, 1960, pp. 575–623.

Dorfman, Robert, Paul A. Samuelson, and Robert M. Solow: *Linear Programming and Economic Analysis,* McGraw-Hill Book Company, Inc., New York, 1958.

Dorsey, John T.: "A Communication Model for Administration," *Administrative Science Quarterly,* December, 1957, pp. 307–324.

Drucker, Peter F.: *The Practice of Management,* Harper & Brothers, New York, 1954.

————: *America's Next Twenty Years,* Harper & Brothers, New York, 1955.

————: "Potentials of Management Science," *Harvard Business Review,* January–February, 1959, pp. 25–30, 146 ff.

————: "Long-range Planning, Challenge to Management Science," *Management Science,* April, 1959, pp. 238–249.

————: *Landmarks of Tomorrow,* Harper & Brothers, New York, 1959.

Eckman, Donald P. (ed.): *Systems: Research and Design,* John Wiley & Sons, Inc., New York, 1961.

Editors of *Scientific American: Automatic Control,* Simon and Schuster, Inc., New York, 1955.

Edwards, Ward: "The Theory of Decision Making," *Psychological Bulletin,* July, 1954, pp. 380–418.

Ernst, Martin L.: "Operations Research and the Large Strategic Problems," *Operations Research,* July–August, 1961, pp. 437–445.

Etzioni, Amitai: *Complex Organizations,* Holt, Rinehart and Winston, Inc., New York, 1961.

Evans, Marshall K., and Lou R. Hague: "Master Plan for Information Systems," *Harvard Business Review,* January–February, 1962, pp. 92–103.

Ewell, James M.: "The Total Systems Concept and How to Organize for It," *Computers and Automation,* September, 1961, pp. 9–13.

Fazar, Willard: "Progress Reporting in the Special Projects Office," *Navy Management Review,* April, 1959, pp. 1–7.

Ferguson, Robert O., and Lauren F. Sargent: *Linear Programming,* McGraw-Hill Book Company, Inc., New York, 1958.

Ferry, W. H.: "Caught on the Horn of Plenty," *Bulletin of the Center for the Study of Democratic Institutions,* Santa Barbara, Calif., January, 1962.

Fisch, Gerald G.: "Line-Staff Is Obsolete," *Harvard Business Review,* September–October, 1961, pp. 67–79.

Flagle, C. D., W. H. Huggins, and R. H. Roy (eds.): *Operations Research and Systems Engineering,* Johns Hopkins Press, Baltimore, 1960.

Flood, Merrill M.: "Operations Research and Automation Science," *Journal of Industrial Engineering,* July–August, 1958, pp. 239–242.

———: "System Engineering," *Management Technology,* Institute of Management Sciences, Monograph 1, pp. 21–35, January, 1960.

Forrester, Jay W.: "Industrial Dynamics," *Harvard Business Review,* July–August, 1958, pp. 37–66.

———: *Management and Management Science,* MIT, School of Industrial Management, Memorandum D-48, June, 1959.

———: *Industrial Dynamics,* MIT, The Technical Press, Cambridge, Mass., and John Wiley & Sons, Inc., New York, 1961.

Gaddis, Paul O.: "The Project Manager," *Harvard Business Review,* May–June, 1959, pp. 89–97.

Galbraith, John Kenneth: *The Affluent Society,* Houghton Mifflin Company, Boston, 1958.

Gallagher, James D.: *Management Information Systems and the Computer,* American Management Association, Inc., New York, 1961.

Gardner, Burleigh B., and David G. Moore: *Human Relations in Industry,* Richard D. Irwin, Inc., Homewood, Ill., 1955.

Garrott, P. B.: "Integrated Data Processing Brings Automation in Paperwork," *Automation,* December, 1954, pp. 31–39.

Garvin, Walter W.: *Introduction to Linear Programming,* McGraw-Hill Book Company, Inc., New York, 1960.

Goldman, Stanford: *Information Theory,* Prentice-Hall, Inc., Englewood Cliffs, N.J., 1953.

Goode, Harry H., and Robert E. Machol: *System Engineering,* McGraw-Hill Book Company, Inc., New York, 1957.

Gott, Rodney C.: "Integrating Product and Process," *Automation,* October, 1959, pp. 42–47.

Grabbe, Eugene M. (ed.): *Automation in Business and Industry,* John Wiley & Sons, Inc., New York, 1957.

Gregory, Robert H., and Thomas V. Atwater: *Economic Studies of Work Performed on a Numerically Controlled Milling Machine,* MIT, Servomechanisms Laboratory, Engineering Report 18, D.I.C. 6873, Cambridge, Mass., 1956.

——— and Richard L. Van Horn: *Automatic Data-processing Systems,* Wadsworth Publishing Company, Inc., San Francisco, 1960.

Haberstroh, Chadwick J.: "Controls as an Organizational Process," *Management Science,* January, 1960, pp. 165–171.

Haire, Mason: *Psychology in Management,* McGraw-Hill Book Company, Inc., New York, 1956.

——— (ed.): *Modern Organization Theory,* John Wiley & Sons, Inc., New York, 1959.

Hammerton, J. C.: "Automatic Machine Scheduling," *Computers and Automation,* May, 1961, pp. 17–22.

Harling, John: "Simulation Techniques in Operations Research: A Review," *Operations Research,* May–June, 1958, pp. 307–319.

Hayakawa, S. I.: *Language in Thought and Action,* Harcourt Brace and Company, Inc., New York, 1949.

Henderson, Lawrence J.: *Pareto's General Sociology,* Harvard University Press, Cambridge, Mass., 1935.

Heslen, Robert: "Choosing an Automatic Program for Numerical Control," *Control Engineering,* April, 1962, pp. 109–113.

Hickey, Albert E., Jr.: "The Systems Approach: Can Engineers Use the Scientific Method?" *IRE Transactions on Engineering Management,* June, 1960, pp. 72–80.

Hoos, Ida Russakoff: "When the Computer Takes Over the Office," *Harvard Business Review,* July–August, 1960, pp. 102–112.

Hopkins, L. Thomas: *Integration: Its Meaning and Application,* Appleton-Century-Crofts, Inc., New York, 1937.

Hopkins, Robert C.: "Possible Applications of Information Theory to Management Control," *IRE Transactions on Engineering Management,* March, 1961, pp. 40–48.

Hurni, Melvin L.: "Decision Making in the Age of Automation," *Harvard Business Review,* September–October, 1955, pp. 49–58.

"Impact of Automation," *U.S. Department of Labor Bulletin* 1287, 1960.

Jacobson, Howard Boone, and Joseph S. Roucek (eds.): *Automation and Society,* Philosophical Library, Inc., New York, 1959.

Jasinski, Frank J.: "Adapting Organization to New Technology," *Harvard Business Review,* January–February, 1959, pp. 79–86.

Jodka, John: "PERT: A Control Concept Using Computers," *Computers and Automation,* March, 1962, pp. 16–18.

Johnson, Ellis A.: "The Long-range Future of Operations Research," *Operations Research,* January–February, 1960, pp. 1–23.

Johnson, Richard A.: *Employees—Automation—Management,* University of Washington, Bureau of Business Research, Seattle, 1961.

————: "Rhochrematics: A System for Production and Marketing," *Advanced Management,* February, 1961, pp. 16–19.

Jones, Manley H.: *Executive Decision Making,* Richard D. Irwin, Inc., Homewood, Ill., 1957.

Kami, Michael J.: "Electronic Data Processing: Promise and Problems," *California Management Review,* Fall, 1958, pp. 74–80.

Kast, F. E., and Jim Rosenzweig: "Planning: Framework for an Integrated Decision System," *Washington Business Review,* April, 1960, pp. 31–42.

———— and ————: "Minimizing the Planning Gap," *Advanced Management,* October, 1960, pp. 20–23.

———— and ————: "A Survey of the Intra-company Impact of Weapon System Management," *IRE Transactions on Engineering Management,* March, 1962, pp. 37–40.

Kelley, James E., Jr.: "Critical-path Planning and Scheduling: Mathematical Basis," *Operations Research,* May–June, 1961, pp. 296–320.

Klass, Phillip J.: "PERT/PEP Management Tool Use Grows," *Aviation Week,* Nov. 28, 1960, pp. 85–91.

Kompass, E. J.: "Information Systems in Control Engineering," *Control Engineering,* January, 1961, pp. 103–106.

Koontz, Harold: "The Management Theory Jungle," *Journal of the Academy of Management,* December, 1961, pp. 174–188.

Kozmetsky, George, and Paul Kircher: *Electronic Computers and Management Control,* McGraw-Hill Book Company, Inc., New York, 1956.

Krick, Edward V.: *Methods Engineering,* John Wiley & Sons, Inc., New York, 1952.

Lach, E. L.: "The Total Systems Concept," *Systems and Procedures,* November, 1960, pp. 6–7.

Leavitt, Harold J.: *Managerial Psychology,* University of Chicago Press, Chicago, 1958.

——— and Thomas L. Whisler: "Management in the 1980's," *Harvard Business Review,* November–December, 1958, pp. 41–48.

Le Breton, Preston P., and Dale A. Henning: *Planning Theory,* Prentice-Hall, Inc., Englewood Cliffs, N.J., 1961.

Ledgerwood, Byron K. (ed.): *Control Engineering Manual,* McGraw-Hill Book Company, Inc., New York, 1957.

Lieberman, Irving J.: "A Mathematical Model for Integrated Business Systems," *Management Science,* July, 1956, pp. 327–336.

Likert, Rensis: *New Patterns of Management,* McGraw-Hill Book Company, Inc., New York, 1961.

Lindsey, Franklin E.: *New Techniques for Management Decision Making,* McGraw-Hill Book Company, Inc., New York, 1958.

Lipstreu, Otis: "Organizational Implications of Automation," *Journal of the Academy of Management,* August, 1960, pp. 119–124.

Litterer, Joseph A.: "The Simulation of Organizational Behavior," *Journal of the Academy of Management,* April, 1962, pp. 24–35.

Livingston, J. Sterling: "Decision Making in Weapons Development," *Harvard Business Review,* January–February, 1958, pp. 127–136.

———: "Weapon System Contracting," *Harvard Business Review,* July–August, 1959, pp. 83–92.

Luce, R. Duncan, and Howard Raiffa: *Games and Decisions,* John Wiley & Sons, Inc., New York, 1957.

MacMillan, R. H.: *Automation,* Cambridge University Press, London, 1956.

Magee, John F.: "The Logistics of Distribution," *Harvard Business Review,* July–August, 1960, pp. 89–101.

Malcolm, D. G.: "System Simulation: A Fundamental Tool for Industrial Engineering," *Journal of Industrial Engineering,* May–June, 1958, pp. 177–187.

———, and A. J. Rowe: "Computer-based Control Systems," *California Management Review,* Spring, 1961, pp. 4–15.

———, ———, and Lorimer F. McConnell (eds.): *Management Control Systems,* John Wiley & Sons, Inc., New York, 1960.

"Managing Progress through Operations Research," *3d Annual Conference Proceedings, Society for Advancement of Management,* 1958.

Mann, Floyd C., and Richard L. Hoffman: *Automation and the Worker,* Henry Holt and Company, Inc., New York, 1960.

———— and Lawrence K. Williams: "Observations on the Dynamics of a Change to Electronic Data-processing Equipment," *Administrative Science Quarterly,* September, 1960, pp. 217–256.

Mangell, Stanley: "PL: A New Concept in Complete Management Thinking," *Advanced Management,* August, 1960, pp. 6–11.

March, James G., and Herbert A. Simon: *Organization,* John Wiley & Sons, Inc., New York, 1958.

Martin, Elizabeth (ed.): *Top Management Decision Simulation: The AMA Approach,* American Management Association, Inc., New York, 1957.

Mason, Edward S. (ed.): *The Corporation in Modern Society,* Harvard University Press, Cambridge, Mass., 1959.

McGrath, Joseph D., Peter G. Nordlie, and W. S. Vaughn, Jr.: *A Systematic Framework for Comparison of System Research Methods,* Human Sciences Research, Inc., Arlington, Va., November, 1959.

McGregor, Douglas: *The Human Side of Enterprise,* McGraw-Hill Book Company, Inc., New York, 1960.

McGuire, W. J.: "Operations Research in Management Planning and Control," *Journal of Industrial Engineering,* July–August, 1959, pp. 308–312.

McKean, Roland N.: *Efficiency in Government through Systems Analysis,* John Wiley & Sons, Inc., New York, 1958.

McRainey, J. H., and L. D. Miller: "Numerical Control," *Automation,* August, 1960, pp. 70–100.

Melitz, Peter W.: "Impact of Electronic Data Processing on Managers," *Advanced Management,* April, 1961, pp. 4–6.

Michael, Donald N.: *Cybernation: The Silent Conquest,* The Center for the Study of Democratic Institutions, Santa Barbara, Calif., 1962.

Military Astronautics, Report of the Committee on Space and Astronautics, House of Representatives, H.R. 360, 87th Cong., 1st Sess., 1961.

Miller, David W., and Martin K. Starr: *Executive Decisions and Operations Research,* Prentice-Hall, Inc., Englewood Cliffs, N.J., 1960.

Miller, Robert W.: "How to Plan and Control with PERT," *Harvard Business Review,* March–April, 1962, pp. 93–104.

Mishkin, Eli, and Ludwig Braun, Jr.: *Adaptive Control Systems,* McGraw-Hill Book Company, Inc., New York, 1961.

Murphy, Gardner: "Toward a Field Theory of Communication," *Journal of Communication,* December, 1961, pp. 196–201.

Muschamp, G. M.: "Tomorrow's Integrated Office and Plants," *Automation,* May, 1961, pp. 46–51.

Neuschel, Richard F.: *Management by System,* McGraw-Hill Book Company, Inc., New York, 1960.

Newman, William H., and Charles E. Summer, Jr.: *The Process of Management,* Prentice-Hall, Inc., Englewood Cliffs, N. J., 1961.

Optner, Stanford L.: *Systems Analysis for Business Management,* Prentice-Hall, Inc., Englewood Cliffs, N.J., 1960.

Organization and Management of Missile Program, Eleventh Report of the Committee on Government Operations, H.R. 1121, 86th Cong. 1st Sess., 1959.

Osborn, Alex F.: *Applied Imagination,* Charles Scribner's Sons, New York, 1953.

Owens, Richard N.: *Management of Industrial Enterprises,* Richard D. Irwin, Inc., Homewood, Ill., 1957.

Parsons, Talcott: "Suggestions for a Sociological Approach to the Theory of Organizations," *Administrative Science Quarterly,* September, 1956, pp. 225–239.

PERT Familiarization Manual, Boeing Company, Aero-Space Division, Seattle, July, 1961.

PERT Summary Report, Phase 1, Department of the Navy, Bureau of Ordnance, Special Projects Office, 1958.

Pfiffner, John M., and Frank P. Sherwood: *Administrative Organization,* Prentice-Hall, Inc., Englewood Cliffs, N.J., 1960.

Polaris Management, Department of the Navy, Special Projects Office, 1961.

Postley, John A.: *Computers and People,* McGraw-Hill Book Company, Inc., New York, 1960.

Presthus, Robert V.: "Toward a Theory of Organizational Behavior," *Administrative Science Quarterly,* June, 1958, pp. 48–72.

Program Planning and Control System, Department of the Navy, Special Projects Office, 1960.

Ramo, Simon: "Weapon System Management," *California Management Review,* Fall, 1958, pp. 14–19.

Redfield, Charles E.: *Communication in Management,* University of Chicago Press, Chicago, 1958.

Reintjes, J. E.: "The Intellectual Foundations of Automation," *Annals of the American Academy of Political and Social Science,* March, 1962, pp. 1–9.

Research and Development in the Gross National Product, National Science Foundation, Washington, D.C., February, 1961.

Roman, Daniel D.: "The PERT System," *Journal of the Academy of Management,* April, 1962, pp. 57–65.

Ronken, Harriet O., and Paul R. Lawrence: *Administering Change,* Harvard University, Graduate School of Business, Boston, 1952.

Rose, T. G., and Donald E. Farr: *Higher Management Control,* McGraw-Hill Book Company, Inc., New York, 1957.

Rosenzweig, Jim: "The Weapon System Management and Electronic Data Processing," *Management Science,* January, 1960, pp. 149–164.

Rubenstein, Albert H., and Chadwick J. Haberstroh (eds.): *Some Theories of Organization,* The Dorsey Press, Inc., and Richard D. Irwin, Inc., Homewood, Ill., 1960.

Ruesch, Jurgen, and Gregory Bateson: *Communication,* W. W. Norton & Co., Inc., New York, 1951.

Salveson, Melvin E.: "Planning Business Progress," *Management Science,* April, 1959, pp. 217–237.

Samuel, Arthur L.: "Artificial Intelligence: A Frontier of Automation," *Annals of the American Academy of Political and Social Science.* March, 1962, pp. 10–20.

Sasieni, M., A. Yaspan, and L. Friedman: *Operations Research, Methods and Problems,* John Wiley & Sons, Inc., New York, 1959.

Sayer, J. S., J. E. Kelly, Jr., and Morgan R. Walker: "Critical Path Scheduling," *Factory,* July, 1960, pp. 74–77.

Schaller, Gilbert S.: *Engineering Manufacturing Methods,* McGraw-Hill Book Company, Inc., New York, 1959.

Schramm, Wilbur (ed.): *The Process and Effects of Mass Communication,* University of Illinois Press, Urbana, Ill., 1954.

Scott, William G.: "Organizational Theory: An Overview and an Appraisal," *Journal of the Academy of Management,* April, 1961, pp. 7–26.

————: *Human Relations in Management,* Richard D. Irwin, Inc., Homewood, Ill., 1962.

Shannon, Claude, and Warren Weaver: *The Mathematical Theory of Communication,* University of Illinois Press, Urbana, Ill., 1949.

Shenton, D. W., and H. Gleixner: "Automated Material Control," *Automation,* January, 1961, pp. 50–59.

Sherif, Muzafer, and Carolyn W. Sherif: *An Outline of Social Psychology,* Harper & Brothers, New York, 1956.

Shubik, Martin: "Simulation of Industry and Firm," *American Economic Review,* December, 1960, pp. 908–919.

Shultz, George P., and Thomas L. Whistler (eds.): *Management Organization and the Computer,* Free Press, Glencoe, Ill., 1960.

Shycon, Harvey N., and Richard B. Maffei, "Simulation: Tool for Better Distribution," *Harvard Business Review,* November–December, 1960, pp. 65–75.

Simon, Herbert A.: "Comments on the Theory of Organizations," *American Political Science Review,* December, 1952, pp. 1130–1139.

————: *Administrative Behavior,* The Macmillan Company, New York, 1959.

————: *The New Science of Management Decision,* Harper & Brothers, New York, 1960.

———— and Allen Newell: "Heuristic Problem Solving: The Next Advance in Operations Research," *Operations Research,* January–February, 1958, pp. 1–10.

Smiddy, Harold F., and Lionel Naum: "Evolution of a 'Science of Managing' in America," *Management Science,* October, 1954, pp. 1–31.

Snow, C. P.: *The Two Cultures and the Scientific Revolution,* Cambridge University Press, London, 1959.

Stockman, Lynn H. (ed.): *Advancing Marketing Efficiency,* American Marketing Association, Chicago, 1959.

Stout, Thomas M.: "Process Control: Past, Present, and Future," *Annals of the American Academy of Political and Social Science,* March, 1962, pp. 29–37.

Strauss, George, and Leonard R. Sayles: *Personnel: The Human Problems of Management,* Prentice-Hall, Inc., Englewood Cliffs, N.J., 1960.

Stoller, David S., and Richard L. Van Horn: *Design of a Management Information System,* Institute of Management Sciences, Monograph 1, January, 1960, pp. 86–91.

Tannenbaum, Robert: "Managerial Decision Making," *Journal of Business,* January, 1950, pp. 22–39.

"The Automatic Factories," *Fortune,* October, 1953, pp. 168–171.

Thompson, James D., and Frederick L. Bates: "Technology, Organization, and Administration," *Administrative Science Quarterly,* December, 1957, pp. 325–343.

Thompson, Victor A.: "Hierarchy, Specialization, and Organizational Conflict," *Administrative Science Quarterly,* March, 1961, pp. 485–521.

Tonge, Fred M.: "The Use of Heuristic Programming in Management Science," *Management Science,* April, 1961, pp. 231–237.

Vance, Stanley: *Industrial Administration,* McGraw-Hill Book Company, Inc., New York, 1959.

Van Deusen, Edmund L.: "Electronics Goes Modern," *Fortune,* June, 1955, pp. 132–148.

Vazsonyi, Andrew: *Scientific Programming in Business and Industry,* John Wiley & Sons, Inc., New York, 1958.

Villers, Raymond: *Dynamic Management in Industry,* McGraw-Hill Book Company, Inc., New York, 1960.

von Bertalanffy, Ludwig: "General System Theory: A New Approach to Unity of Science," *Human Biology,* December, 1951, pp. 303–361.

Voris, William: *Production Control,* Richard D. Irwin, Inc., Homewood, Ill., 1956.

Walker, Charles R.: *Toward the Automatic Factory,* Yale University Press, New Haven, Conn., 1957.

Warner, W. Lloyd, and J. O. Low: *The Social System of the Modern Factory,* Yale University Press, New Haven, Conn., 1947.

Wasserman, Paul, and Fred S. Silander: *Decision-making: An Annotated Bibliography,* Cornell University Press, Ithaca, N.Y., 1958.

Weapon System Management, Department of the Air Force, Air Force Pamphlet 25-2-1, 1959.

Weiner, Milton G.: "Observations on the Growth of Information-processing Centers," in Albert H. Rubenstein and Chadwick J. Haberstroh (eds.), *Some Theories of Organization,* The Dorsey Press, Inc., and Richard D. Irwin, Inc., Homewood, Ill., 1960.

Weinwurm, George F.: "Computer Management Control Systems through the Looking Glass," *Management Science,* July, 1961, pp. 411–419.

Whyte, William Foote: *Men at Work,* The Dorsey Press, Inc., and Richard D. Irwin, Inc., Homewood, Ill., 1961.

Whyte, W. H., Jr.: *The Organization Man,* Doubleday & Co., Inc., New York, 1956.

Wiener, Norbert: *The Human Use of Human Beings,* Houghton Mifflin Company, Boston, 1954.

Wilson, E. Bright, Jr.: *An Introduction to Scientific Research,* McGraw-Hill Book Company, Inc., New York, 1952.

Zaleznik, A., C. R. Christensen, and F. J. Roethlisberger: *The Motivation, Productivity, and Satisfaction of Workers,* Harvard University, Graduate School of Business, Boston, 1958.

INDEX